TEACHING OTHER VOICES

TEACHING OTHER VOICES
Women and Religion in Early Modern Europe

⁊

Edited by Margaret L. King

and

Albert Rabil Jr.

THE UNIVERSITY OF CHICAGO PRESS
Chicago & London

Margaret L. King and Albert Rabil Jr. edit the Other Voice in Early
Modern Europe series for the University of Chicago Press.

The University of Chicago Press, Chicago 60637
The University of Chicago Press, Ltd., London
© 2007 by The University of Chicago
All rights reserved. Published 2007
Printed in the United States of America

16 15 14 13 12 11 10 09 08 07   1 2 3 4 5

ISBN-13: 978-0-226-43632-6 (paper)
ISBN-10: 0-226-43632-2 (paper)

Library of Congress Cataloging-in-Publication Data

Teaching other voices : women and religion in early modern Europe / edited by
Margaret L. King and Albert Rabil, Jr.
    p.   cm.
  Includes bibliographical references and index.
  ISBN-13: 978-0-226-43632-6 (pbk. : alk. paper)
  ISBN-10: 0-226-43632-2 (pbk. : alk. paper) 1. Women and religion—History.
2. Women—Religious life.   I. King, Margaret L., 1947–   II. Rabil, Albert.
  BL458.T43 2007
  274'.05082–dc22
                                                    2006026922

The University of Chicago Press gratefully acknowledges the generous
support of James E. Rabil, in memory of Scottie W. Rabil, toward the
publication of this book.

⊗ The paper used in this publication meets the minimum requirements of
the American National Standard for Information Sciences—Permanence of
Paper for Printed Library Materials, ANSI Z39.48-1992.

CONTENTS

ACKNOWLEDGMENTS

We would like to thank, first, Randy Petilos, our editor at the University of Chicago Press, whose initial idea it was that we should publish a teaching volume to commemorate the tenth anniversary of the publication of the first volume in the series. This volume is the result of his suggestion.

We would also like to thank the editors of a number of volumes in the series and others who have taught these volumes for their contributions to this commemorative volume. Their names and a short vita may be found at the end of this volume.

We anticipate that we shall publish other teaching volumes based on the series as the number of texts in other genres grows large enough to warrant one. Our doing so will depend in part on whether this volume meets a need felt by teachers who offer courses that include one or more volumes from the series. We would very much appreciate the responses of those who read and make use of this volume.

Margaret L. King and Albert Rabil Jr.

WOMEN AND RELIGION IN
EARLY MODERN EUROPE:
THE HISTORICAL CONTEXT

Margaret L. King and Albert Rabil Jr.

From 1350 to 1750, women as well as men were actively involved in Europe's religious struggles and aspirations. This introduction provides an overview of the religious history of the era, placing the religious experience of women specifically in the context of that standard narrative.

Many people think of the European Middle Ages as deeply religious, and the following period—the "Renaissance" or the "Early Modern"—as increasingly secular. On the contrary, the four centuries from 1350 to 1750 are a period of intense religious experience and institutional transformation. Consider the religious history of the period in fifty-year segments.[1]

The period 1350–1400: As this period opens, the papacy is in its "Babylonian captivity" (1309–78). It has been removed from Rome to Avignon in Provence (modern France), a displacement signaling high tension between the papacy and secular politics throughout Europe. In 1378, the pope returns to Rome. His return, however, is followed by the "Great Schism" (1378–1415), when different sets of interest groups affiliate themselves with two different popes. Meanwhile, in the Low Countries and north Germany, a religious movement of laymen known as the *devotio moderna* ("new devotion") flourishes. It emphasizes personal responsibility in the pursuit of the religious

---

1. Among numerous overviews of the history of late-medieval Christianity and the Protestant and Catholic reformations, these recent titles are usefully consulted: John Bossy, *Christianity in the West, 1400–1700* (Oxford: Oxford University Press, 1988); Euan Cameron, *The European Reformation* (Oxford: Clarendon Press, 1991); Diarmaid MacCullough, *The Reformation: A History* (Harmondsworth: Penguin, 2004); Michael Mullett, *The Catholic Reformation* (London: Routledge, 1999); Bob Scribner, Roy Porter, and Mikulas Teich, eds., *The Reformation in National Context* (Cambridge: Cambridge University Press, 1994); James D. Tracy, *Europe's Reformations, 1450–1650* (Totowa: Rowman & Littlefield, 1999).

life. The spiritual guide attributed to Thomas à Kempis, *The Imitation of Christ*, is popular in this movement and elsewhere.

The period 1400–1450: The Great Schism is resolved by the Council of Constance, called for that purpose and to combat heresy. In addressing the matter of heresy, the Council condemns and executes Jan Hus (1369–1415), the Bohemian (Czech) religious reformer who had urged the reading of the Bible by the laity in vernacular translation and the right of laypersons to receive communion in "both kinds"—both bread and wine, the two elements that, according to Catholic doctrine, are transformed, respectively, into the body and blood of Christ during the sacrifice of the Mass. Upon the deposition of all three schismatic popes, the Council elects Martin V, who proceeds to Rome in 1417. The Constance gathering further marks the high point of conciliar theory, the set of arguments defending the case that papal power should be exercised in consultation with, or limited by, an assembly of delegates.

The period 1450–1500: In Rome, the papal authority is asserted in verbal communications as well as in an architectural and urbanistic program enhancing the figure of the pope and the iconic figure of Saint Peter, considered to have been the first in the papal succession. The popes establish the Vatican Library, approve a new drive to seek out and punish witchcraft, designate a meridian separating Portuguese and Spanish claims in the New World, and condemn the Florentine visionary and reformer, the Dominican friar Girolamo Savonarola (1452–98), who is executed in 1498. The Spanish Inquisition is launched, and all unconverted Jews and Muslims are expelled from Spain and Portugal in 1492 and 1497.

The period 1500–1550: At the height of their power, the Renaissance popes are faced with a rebellion against their authority, the legitimacy of the sacraments, and the validity of the veneration of saints, led by the German Augustinian friar Martin Luther (1483–1546). Luther himself had been preceded by a number of protoreformers, including the archhumanist Desiderius Erasmus (1466–1536), critic of empty ritual and abusive clerics and editor and translator of the original Greek New Testament. Many reformers join Luther's revolt, some launching independent reform traditions, as did the French scholar John Calvin (1509–64), who eventually becomes head of the Swiss Reformed Church at Geneva. In England, the king separates from the Catholic Church so that he may marry again and gain a male heir, bringing about in 1535 the martyrdom of the learned Thomas More (1478–1535), former lord chancellor of England. The term "Protestant" is used for the first time in 1529 by an alliance of reformed cities and principalities objecting to imperial attempts to dismantle the movement, and the Protestant Reformation is launched. The Scandinavian kingdoms, along with many of the German states, have established Lutheran churches. Both Protestants and Catholics persecute sectarian groups that also spring up in this period of religious change, among them principally the Anabaptists. The Spanish and Roman inquisitions staunch the tide of Protestantism in those regions. In Italy, the pope approves the formation of the Jesuit Order, dedicated to the service of the papacy and the expansion of Catholic Christianity. In Spain, the persecution of Jewish and Muslim converts continues.

The period 1550–1600: From Geneva, Reformed (Calvinist) Protestant churches spread in the Low Countries, Scotland, and France. In Geneva itself, Calvin asserts Protestant orthodoxy with the execution in 1553 of the Spanish physician and unitarian Michael Servetus (1511–53). England seesaws from Protestantism to Catholicism and back again, with a via media ("middle-of-the-way") Protestant Anglican church finally established— despite a minority Reformed, or Puritan, presence—in 1559. France is embroiled in religious warfare between Catholic and Protestant nobles and burghers, climaxing in the 1572 Massacre of Saint Bartholomew's Day, in which hundreds, perhaps thousands of Protestants are killed. The struggle finally concludes with the ascension of the Protestant-born king Henry IV, who subsequently converts to Catholicism but issues in 1598 the Treaty of Nantes assuring religious toleration to his former coreligionists.

In the German lands, the Peace of Augsburg of 1556 settles nearly thirty years of intermittent war. That treaty establishes the principle *cuius regio eius religio* ("whosesoever realm it is, shall determine its religion"), meaning that each state determines which religion shall be established within its borders. In the northern provinces of the Low Countries, a Protestant revolution against Spanish overlordship is launched. Intermittently from 1545 to 1563, a church Council meets at Trent (Italy) to reaffirm papal authority, the validity of the sacraments, and the veneration of saints and to reform Catholic institutions in the face of the Protestant challenge.

In 1600–1650: Competition among the German states is fueled further by religious antagonisms, leading to the outbreak of the Thirty Years' War (1618–48) that will involve not only the German lands but also the Swedes, the Danes, and the French. By its conclusion, with the Treaty of Westphalia in 1648, political rivalries have overtaken religious issues as matters of contention. Meanwhile, in England, parliamentary leaders begin a civil war against the monarchy that has religious as well as political origins. It culminates in the execution of King Charles I (r. 1625–49) in 1649 and the ascendancy for a time of Puritan and sectarian currents. The revolution of the Netherlands is concluded with the constitution in 1648 of the Dutch Republic, largely Protestant, but tolerating all religious confessions. In Poland and the Habsburg lands, the Jesuits lead a successful drive to re-Catholicize regions that had previously adopted Protestant confessions. Throughout Europe, confessional boundaries become firmer and established churches extend the ways in which they exert discipline over church members.

In 1650–1700: The Interregnum, during which England is ruled by the Puritan general Oliver Cromwell (1599–1658), ends in 1660, two years after the latter's death, with the Restoration of the Catholic king Charles II (r. 1660–85)—but not the restoration of Catholicism. Determined to prevent a lapse to Catholicism, Parliament intervenes in the reign of Charles's successor, his brother James II (1685–88), upon the birth of a Catholic male heir. James's Protestant daughter and her Protestant Dutch husband ascend to the throne. French king Louis XIV (r. 1643–1715) revokes the Edict of Nantes in 1685, removing royal protection from French Protestants, called Huguenots, who now seek refuge in the Netherlands, England, and the American colonies. At home, the heterodox Jansenist movement, while remaining under the Catholic umbrella, attracts many followers. Among European Jews, messianic movements arise, especially that attracting the followers of Sabbatai Zevi (1626–76).

The period 1700–1750: John Wesley (1703–91) leads a reform movement within the Anglican Church that will eventually be designated the separate Methodist denomination, characterized by a more impassioned form of Christian piety. Similarly, in the German Lutheran lands, Pietism spreads, an evangelical and intensely pious form of Lutheranism. Hasidism, a popular and emotion-laden movement within Judaism, spreads in central and eastern Europe. Further west, many Jews seek assimilation into secular, mainstream society.

This brief recapitulation includes no mention of women and indeed could not rightly do so. With a very few exceptions, women were not at the forefront of the institutions or movements that contribute to the mainstream narrative of religious institutions and belief in this period. But neither were they absent. Women participated fully and critically in the religious history of the age, although generally from positions far from institutional or state power. The record of that participation gives us an alternate history.[2]

---

2. Useful recent studies on women and religion in the early modern period include Daniel Bornstein and Roberto Rusconi, eds., *Women and Religion in Medieval and Renaissance Italy* (Chicago: University of Chicago Press, 1996); Patricia Crawford, *Women and Religion in England, 1500–1750*

The period 1350–1450: As in earlier centuries, women of mostly elite social origin are nuns resident in convents throughout Europe. They also participate in heretical movements and in the tolerated group of the Beguines (specific to the Low Countries and northern Germany), who form women-only communities outside the convent dedicated to spiritual reading and reflection and good works. In France, the hero of the Hundred Years' War, Joan of Arc (1412–31), who wages battles and helps secure the coronation of the king of France, is burned at the stake as a witch and heretic. The English anchoress, or hermit, Julian of Norwich (1342–1416), writes of her mystical experience. A generation later, Margery Kempe (d. ca. 1438), mother of fourteen children, embarks on her unique and original version of the religious life outside the cloister. In Italy, the phenomenon of the "holy woman," an uncloistered solitary living an ascetic life alone or within a household, comes to the fore. Among these, the most famous is Catherine of Siena (see below), who vigorously urged the pope, then in Avignon, to return to Rome. Many women are active in the "tertiary" orders (as was Catherine) attached to Franciscan and Dominican houses that engage in charitable work. Women also participate in lay confraternities whose purpose is repentance, praise of God, and charitable service.

The period 1450–1550: Elite women of the High Renaissance acquire serious educations and often write on religious themes, among them Lucrezia Tornabuoni and Marguerite de Navarre (see below). Reform movements in the early 1500s, followed by Protestant and Catholic Reformations, attract women participants. In Italy, several high-ranking women patronize reformers and themselves give voice to evangelical opinions that would later be considered heretical. In the German lands, wives of reformers and of princely patrons of the Reformation act and write as advocates of the new religion. Cloistered women are faced with the alternatives of leaving the convent and joining the Reformation or remaining loyal to the old church, and they

(London: Routledge, 1993); Craig Harline, *The Burdens of Sister Margaret: Private Lives in a Seventeenth-Century Convent* (New York: Doubleday, 1994); Richard Kieckhefer, *Unquiet Souls: Fourteenth-Century Saints and Their Religious Milieu* (Chicago: University of Chicago Press, 1984); Kate Lowe, *Nuns' Chronicles and Convent Culture in Renaissance and Counter-Reformation Italy* (Cambridge: Cambridge University Press, 2003); Phyllis Mack, *Visionary Women: Ecstatic Prophecy in Seventeenth-Century England* (Berkeley: University of California Press, 1992); Sherrin Marshall, *Women in Reformation and Counter-Reformation Europe: Public and Private Worlds* (Bloomington: Indiana University Press, 1989); Jo Ann Kay McNamara, *Sisters in Arms: Catholic Nuns through Two Millennia* (Cambridge, Mass.: Harvard University Press, 1996); Lyndal Roper, *The Holy Household: Women and Morals in Reformation Augsburg* (Oxford: Oxford University Press, 1989); Anne Jacobson Schutte, *Aspiring Saints: Pretense of Holiness, Inquisition, and Gender in the Republic of Venice, 1618–1750* (Baltimore: Johns Hopkins University Press, 2001).

leave reflections of this predicament in their works. Women participate in the radical sects that emerge alongside mainstream Lutheran and Calvinist reform movements, often speaking as "prophets" and accepting martyrdom.

The period 1550–1750: Following the Council of Trent, women's religious activity is strictly limited in the Catholic countries. The extraclaustral phenomenon of the "holy woman" is delegitimized, and even the charitable and educational activities of laywomen are placed under ecclesiastical surveillance. The same holds for private life, with the priest in the confessional serving as an agent of the church in enforcing the Catholic domestic ideal. Under intense scrutiny, female mysticism continues as a dimension of religious experience; in this era, Saint Teresa of Ávila is its most noted representative. In Protestant countries, where the cloister is no longer an option, bourgeois wives, widows, and noblewomen write devotional works. The radical sects, especially that of the Quakers, remain more open than mainstream Protestantism to women's activity as leaders or preachers. The Jansenist and Pietist revival movements in Catholicism and Protestantism, respectively, also attract female adherents.

The differential history of women's participation in religious life is striking in several ways. It has, to begin, longer arcs: we look at periods of a century or more at a time because of the greater continuities in women's religious activity.

Those continuities are tendencies not present in every figure, but in many of them; and they weave their way through the tapestry of women's religious expression. They include above all these four: first, the convent (or alternate type of informal female community) as a force that shapes women's lives; second, women's special pull toward inner vision and the mystical experience; third, the somatic expression of religious devotion, as participants in religious exercises and as agents of charitable service; finally, women's resistance to authority, seen in their evasion of limits on imagination and movement.

These tendencies are features of the religious experience of women in the period 1350–1750, as they were in the centuries from the sixth to the thirteenth. They will emerge as we look at the individuals examined in this book. The figures we highlight include a sampling of women writing about religion in the Western world during this era—some, not all—and all included here are Protestant or Catholic Christians. Omitted, because they are not yet represented in the Other Voice in Early Modern Europe series, are any exemplars of Jewish, Eastern Orthodox, or sectarian (Anabaptist, Quaker, and the like) female authorship.

ITALIAN HOLY WOMEN OF THE FOURTEENTH
AND FIFTEENTH CENTURIES

The first group of women authors encountered is presented in two volumes in the Other Voice series. The first is an anthology of works by various holy women, including, among several others, Catherine of Siena (1347–80), a famous and representative figure; Francesca of Rome (Romana; 1384–1440); and Angela Merici of Brescia (1474–1540). The second consists of two brief works by the little-known Bartolomea Riccoboni (1395–1436). Of these figures named, Catherine was a Dominican tertiary, active in Siena and elsewhere in northern Italy; Francesca was the wife of a prosperous Roman burgher; Merici was a Franciscan tertiary; and Bartolomea was a nun in a Venetian convent. Their diverse circumstances give a sense of the multiplicity of possibilities available to devout women in medieval and Renaissance Italy.[3]

And why was that? Because Italy in this period was a bustling center of commercial, political, and intellectual innovation. The northern half of the peninsula was home to some forty cities and many smaller towns and villages, aggregated in larger and smaller states of diverse political organization. Here a stratum of bankers and merchants engaged in profitable long-distance trade, and managers of textile industries, professionals including judges, notaries, physicians, and experts in canon and civil law, and highly skilled artisans dominated an urban society that was inexhaustibly inventive. This wealthy, urban society required and supported an intellectual elite, both lay and clerical, that not only produced essential documents for commerce and governments, but also engaged in creative thought.

This advanced urban society that many observers, incorrectly, have assumed was secular in fact gave women opportunities for religious expression and activity not found in the quieter, less populous, agricultural societies of some other parts of Europe, or an earlier era in Italy. (The Low Countries was the one other region that offered women similar opportunities.) In those more traditional settings, most of the women engaged in religious expression were nuns drawn from prominent families; in Italy, their origins and their destinies were both more varied.

---

3. The works discussed here are the Other Voice volumes (Chicago: University of Chicago Press) Sister Bartolomea Riccoboni, *Life and Death in a Venetian Convent: The Chronicle and Necrology of Corpus Domini, 1395–1436,* ed. and trans. Daniel Bornstein (2000); and *Women Religious in Late Medieval and Early Modern Italy: An Anthology,* ed. and trans. Lance Lazar (in press). The essays by Bornstein and Lazar in this volume discuss the teaching of these texts.

Bartolomea Riccoboni

The works of Bartolomea Riccoboni provide a unique opportunity to view women's conventual life close up. Literate in the vernacular and likely of middling, although not noble, origin, Riccoboni was a founding member of the convent of Corpus Domini ("the body of the Lord"). After twenty years of residence, she began her *Chronicle*, which records her memory of early events and direct observations of more recent ones. From the convent's early years, as well, she kept a *Necrology* briefly apostrophizing all the women who died. Together these documents describe daily conventual life: a round of worship at prescribed hours several times a day, solitary prayer, ascetic practice, including flagellation, the work of cleaning and nursing, the sharing of all possessions, including clothing, all punctuated by visits from male ecclesiastical visitors and the deaths of the sisters. The theme of the cloister is thus preeminent.

Striking, as well, are those themes of inner vision and corporeal allusion. The sisters frequently had visions: of angels and devils, of the heaven that awaited them as death approached. And they worshiped with their bodies. Their sufferings, both from self-inflicted pain and from the pains of illness and age, they saw regularly as creative acts conforming them to the suffering of Christ. Their denials of the flesh, required by the vows of poverty, chastity (chastity above all), and obedience, they embraced. Their experiences of worship, especially the taking of communion, were sensual.

The sisters of Corpus Domini would seem to be a docile lot, but they too, in a mode characteristic of female piety, resisted authority. It was a handful of women who insisted on founding a new convent, in a city that already had many, and enlisted support and funds from high-ranking men to enable them to do so. Not only was their institution-building an assertive act, but so too were the decisions made by many of the nuns, who consciously rejected marriage (or remarriage, in the case of several widows, some mere adolescents at the time) when they chose the conventual life. These were not women passively pursuing a religious vocation mapped out for them by the church, but women actively seeking deep, meaningful lives unfolded in female community.

The three women highlighted here of the sixteen included in the anthology on *Women Religious in Late Medieval and Early Modern Italy* did not enter convents (Francesca did so, but only at the end of her long career). Indeed, they represent the pattern juxtaposed to that of the conventual life: that of the *beate*, or "holy women," who lived within the world while observing the commitment and austerities of those who remained within the cloister.

This phenomenon peaked in Italy especially, but was known elsewhere in Europe, from the thirteenth through the sixteenth centuries, when it was cut short by the decisions of the Council of Trent. The careers of these "holy women" were inherently a protest against the limitations placed on women's religious expression. Thus even as they move outside the cloister, all three are exemplars of one of the main themes of women's religious experience: resistance.

Catherine of Siena

Catherine of Siena was the youngest of twenty-five children of a skilled Sienese artisan. Encouraged by visions, she yearned to commit herself to the religious life already in childhood and at age sixteen had become a Dominican tertiary. In that role, she engaged sacrificially in charitable work, serving the bodies of others even as she imposed harsh austerities on her own. She also became the charismatic leader of a circle of disciples of both men and women, whom she called her children as they called her their mother. She composed many devotional works and wrote public and private letters of great importance, including notably those by which she summoned Pope Gregory XI, then in Avignon, to return to his rightful place in Rome—as he soon did. Her works and letters describe her many mystical visions, often highly sensual in their details. In Catherine's career, the themes of "inner vision" and "corporeal metaphor" are both displayed.

Francesca Romana

So too in Francesca Romana's work were these themes prominent. Francesca was a married woman who yearned to give herself totally to God. Living in the flesh, she abused her body in order to rise above it and was comforted by visions. The mother of three children, yet with her husband's consent, she and her female companions devoted themselves to the sacrificial service of the poor and sick of Rome. Francesca determinedly pursued a life of religious austerity blessed by the gift of spiritual experience; eventually, as a widow of fifty-two, she gained the refuge of the convent.

Angela Merici

Angela Merici was the daughter of a Brescian professional. She was orphaned young and spurned the convent, but as a Franciscan tertiary, she sought to form a community of women who, while residing in their own households, met regularly for religious services. Her particular mission was the education of girls, for which goal she formed a new, noncloistered order guided by a rule: the Ursulines. In Merici's career, the themes of bodily abuse and spiritual experience are quieter, dominated by those of assertive institution building for women's welfare within the religious mission but outside of the normative conventual setting.

ELITE WOMEN OF THE HIGH RENAISSANCE

The burgeoning phenomenon of the "holy woman" coincided—some would say ironically—with the huge creativity of the Renaissance in Italy, seen especially in the visual arts and in the intellectual movement of humanism. During the peak Renaissance years (late fifteenth and early sixteenth centuries), some elite women sought to give expression to their religious experience and conviction through their writings. These women were not cloistered, but married or widowed; and they did not pursue a mission of charitable service. Rather, within their lofty social niches, equipped with excellent educations, they wrote, and in their writings they gave voice to a profound piety.[4]

The four principal women considered here and meeting this description are each represented by a volume of works in the Other Voice series. The first is Lucrezia Tornabuoni (1425–82), wife and mother of rulers of Florence, the first home of the Renaissance, and the author of religious poems of praise, or *laudi*, and versified *storie sacre*, or "sacred stories," about biblical figures. The second is Antonia Tanini Pulci (ca. 1452–1501), author of at least five religious plays, or *sacre rappresentazioni*; Tanini was married to poet Bernardo Pulci, who was, in turn, brother of poet Luigi Pulci, who was in Tornabuoni's literary circle and wrote for her the renowned chivalric epic *Morgante*. The third is Vittoria Colonna (1490–1547). A widowed noblewoman, patron of a covert evangelical religious movement, and a poet of the very highest rank, her love poems and spiritual works were marked by equal intensity. The fourth

---

4. The works discussed here are the Other Voice volumes (Chicago: University of Chicago Press) Lucrezia Tornabuoni de' Medici, *Sacred Narratives*, ed. and trans. Jane Tylus (2001); Antonia Pulci, ed. Elissa Weaver, trans. James Cook (rev. ed., 2007); Vittoria Colonna, *Sonnets for Michelangelo: A Bilingual Edition*, ed. and trans. Abigail Brundin (2005). Colonna is also represented in a second Other Voice volume, along with the two later women poets Chiara Matraini and Lucrezia Marinella, all authors of *Marian Writings*, works praising the Virgin Mary, ed. and trans. Susan Haskins (in press); Marguerite de Navarre, *Humanist and Writer*, ed. Rouben Cholakian, trans. Rouben Cholakian and Mary Skemp (in press). The essays by Brundin, Cholakian, Tylus, and Weaver in this volume discuss the teaching of these texts.

is Marguerite de Navarre (1492–1549), sister of the king of France Francis I (and grandmother of King Henry IV), a participant in a proto-Protestant coterie that was summarily silenced by her brother and author of stories, poems, and other works, variously secular, feminist, and devotional in nature.

Lucrezia Tornabuoni

Tornabuoni's translated sacred stories—all five of those extant—are about the female figures Susanna, Judith, and Esther and the male figures Tobias and John the Baptist (patron saint of Florence). Probably meant to be read aloud in small groups, these are simple verse retellings of biblical stories that instruct and engage—at a time when, although vernacular translations of the Bible circulated, only the Latin Vulgate was considered authoritative. Her narratives highlight the priority of marriage as a social institution, the importance of the mother-child bond, the vulnerability of young girls, and the need to provide them with dowry funds so that they may marry appropriately.

And so Tornabuoni's stories are not just biblical paraphrases, but biblical episodes hoisted into a contemporary context and used to provide moral counsel and encouragement to ordinary Florentines. In addition, they highlight the deeds of heroic women: Susanna, who remained chaste despite blandishments; Judith, who slew a tyrant; Esther, who convinced her husband to save her people. Within her message of religious counsel, there is a subtextual message about the validity also of female efforts in the service of the good.

Antonia Pulci

Whereas Tornabuoni's stories were directed only to a private audience, Pulci was a professional author who saw her own works go to press. They belong to the uniquely Florentine genre of *sacre rappresentazioni*, or "sacred portrayals," one-act dramatizations in verse of tales from the Bible, religious legend, and the lives of the saints. These religious plays were performed on holidays for the education and entertainment of the Florentine public, a group of generally high cultural tastes. Among the authors of *sacre rappresentazioni* who were contemporary with Pulci was Lorenzo de' Medici—another connection with Tornabuoni, who was the mother of that Florentine prince and poet.

Like Tornabuoni's sacred stories, Pulci's sacred plays highlight women's roles in religious narrative. The virgin martyr Domitilla goes bravely to her destiny; the chaste and patient wife Saint Guglielma humbles herself to serve others; the mother of Saint Francis encourages his saintly vocation; the widow of the biblical king Saul, horribly martyred, displays her courage and spirit. In Pulci's portrayals, women are seen to be capable of facing great dangers and accomplishing good.

Vittoria Colonna

If Pulci wrote for a broad and plebeian public, Colonna writes for herself and her circle—including none less than the great artist Michelangelo. She wrote sonnets in the Petrarchan mode, intensely emotional and tightly structured, on two themes: her love for her deceased warrior husband, whom she married at age nineteen and lost at age thirty-five and saw little of in between, and her love of God. As the years of her widowhood passed, she tended more to the spiritual sonnets.

Colonna's religious experience was deepened by her contacts, during the 1530s and 1540s, with two intellectual circles. The first was the circle that formed around the evangelical Juan de Valdés. Gathered here were the leaders of evangelical reform who later, when their views were found to be heretical, fled Italy for safe havens in northern and eastern Europe. The second was the Viterbo circle in which Colonna's close friend, the English reformer and cardinal Reginald Pole, was active. It was here that she became close also to Michelangelo, for whom in 1540 she prepared a small book of spiritual sonnets, published in the Other Voice series. (Colonna also addressed a small gift volume of sonnets to Marguerite de Navarre, with a prefatory letter, around the same time.)

Both of these circles sparkled in the uncertain period when reformist and even proto-Protestant ideas were circulating and the eventually repressive Catholic response had not yet crystallized. That was fortunate for Colonna; and it was fortunate for her as well that she died in 1547, before the Roman Inquisition cast its web wide in search of heresy. For Colonna's passionate religious verse, marked by the corporeal analogies long characteristic of female spirituality, is also marked by its acceptance of the *sola fide* doctrine (salvation "by faith alone") that Italian protoreform shared with Martin Luther.

Marguerite de Navarre

Marguerite de Navarre, like Colonna, engaged with evangelical circles in the years before the pendulum swung and repression silenced those she had once protected, including the evangelicals Guillaume Briçonnet, bishop of Meaux, and Lefèvre d'Étaples—and the irreverent novelist François Rabelais. Marguerite corresponded with Erasmus and Calvin as well—whose ideas would later be forbidden to Catholics. Marguerite herself engaged in extended personal devotions and, from 1523, composed religious poetry. Her verse work *Miroir de l'âme pecheresse* (Mirror of the Sinful Soul), like Colonna's spiritual sonnets, enunciates telltale evangelical doctrines. It was published in 1531 and republished in 1547 as the first of a volume of her *Marguerites* (Pearls), or collected poems. In 1544, the eleven-year-old Elizabeth Tudor, future Elizabeth I the Great of England, translated the *Miroir* into English.

This phase of Marguerite's religious experimentation came to a sudden end in 1535. Responding to the famous "affair of the placards" of 1534 (publicly posted anti-Catholic broadsides), her royal brother launched the vigorous persecution of evangelical or Protestant reformers, many of whom, including Calvin, fled the country. Marguerite was increasingly reclusive in her later years, during which she wrote the story collection entitled the *Heptameron*, published posthumously, whose main themes are feminist, yet within them there still thunders a strong evangelical undercurrent.

None of these four highborn women (Pulci, perhaps, of the burgher rather than noble stratum) was a consecrated nun or member of a third order or unofficial religious community. None was a recluse. Their social positions did not easily permit these vocations. But Tornabuoni's sacred stories, as well as Pulci's plays, resemble the kinds of devotional materials read by women with religious vocations. Based on scripture, they were presented in attractive vernacular verse and focused on female figures and women's issues—such as marriage and children. Colonna and Marguerite, in contrast, are writing for a literary audience, and in Colonna's case, very much a male one. Their religious verse is deeply interior, consonant with the interiority of traditional female spirituality. And it features descriptions of religious experience in corporeal terms, also familiar in that tradition.

All of these women were fiercely original in their religious authorship. Tornabuoni and Pulci were pioneers in highlighting issues of female experience within traditional genres specific to their Florentine context. Colonna and Marguerite were bolder still: engaging in high-level intellectual circles alongside major male thinkers; writing publicly and publishing their works; and above all, giving voice to evangelical themes of grace, faith, and redemption, whose riskiness was becoming clear once Luther launched his revolt. The women next to be considered were caught up in the turbulence of that revolt.

WOMEN AND THE REFORMATION

In courtly settings in Italy and France, Vittoria Colonna and Marguerite de Navarre lived on the periphery of the epochal events of the Protestant Reformation. The three women discussed here lived in the vortex. Yet, as women, their experience was, again, somehow peripheral. Since they were not male, they were not the makers of the Reformation. But they were battered by its violence; it impacted their lives, and their experience of faith was permeated with their experience of social disruption, as we see in their works published in the Other Voice series.[5] Two other figures—Olympia Morata (1526–55) and Gabrielle de Coignard (1550–86)—also experienced the tumult of the Reformation; their work, however, is more aptly considered in eventual volumes on Renaissance humanists and early modern women poets.

Marie Dentière

The first figure is the fiercely Protestant Marie Dentière (1495–1561), a former nun born into the nobility who became the wife, then widow, and wife again of two former priests turned leaders of the Swiss Reformation. Active with her husbands in Strasbourg and Geneva, her irrepressible and irritating presence is recorded by various reformers. A learned woman with a solid grasp of Protestant theology, she displays her abilities on three occasions: once as actor, and twice as author.

On the first occasion, in 1535, along with two male reformers, Dentière entered a Catholic convent in Geneva and in hectoring tones urged the nuns to leave the convent and marry. As recorded by one of the nuns who witnessed the verbal assault—Jeanne de Jussie, the fourth of our figures, about whom more below—Dentière pleaded with them saying, "Ah, poor creatures, if only you knew how good it was to be next to a handsome husband..." She then described her own abandonment of the convent, with happy and pious result.

On the second occasion, in 1539, Dentière addressed *A Very Useful Epistle* to Marguerite de Navarre (see above), with whom she had a personal relationship, responding to Marguerite's request for an explanation of the

---

5. The works discussed here are the Other Voice volumes (Chicago: University of Chicago Press): Marie Dentière, *Epistle to Marguerite de Navarre and Preface to a Sermon by John Calvin*, ed. and trans. Mary B. McKinley (2004); Jeanne de Jussie, *The Short Chronicle: A Poor Clare's Account of the Reformation of Geneva*, ed. and trans. Carrie F. Klaus (2006); Katharina Schütz Zell, *Church Mother: The Writings of a Protestant Reformer in Sixteenth-Century Germany*, ed. and trans. Elsie McKee (2006). The essays by McKee, Klaus, and McKinley in this volume discuss the teaching of these texts.

banishment from Geneva the previous year of the reformers John Calvin and Guillaume Farel. Dentière's letter includes a defense of women's ability to engage in the discussion of religious issues and an attack on her enemies, who had, as she saw it, betrayed the reform mission. In this extended letter, effectively a treatise, Dentière exhibits her considerable knowledge of scripture (as well as canon law) and matters of Protestant doctrine, affirming the principle of justification by faith alone and attacking the sacraments of Mass and penance.

On the third occasion, in 1561, more than twenty years later, when Calvin's domination of Geneva and the Reformed movement were well-established, Dentière's preface appeared in the published version of Calvin's *Sermon on the Modesty of Women in Their Dress*. Employing appropriate scriptural passages, Dentière affirms Calvin's instruction that women avoid finery and cosmetics as barriers to piety.

Jeanne de Jussie

The second figure is the Catholic Jeanne de Jussie (1503–61), the contemporary and almost the mirror image of Dentière—whom, indeed, she encountered face-to-face, as has been discussed in the section above, in 1535. The last child born to a family of modest means, she was probably one of the many women of this era who entered the convent as part of her family's economic strategy: inheritances to sons, marital and conventual dowries for daughters. But Jussie was fully accepting of this decision and contentedly pursued the vocation assigned her. Far from being tempted by Dentière's arguments, as discussed in the section above, she was appalled by them.

This we learn from her work, the *Short Chronicle*, in which as convent secretary she records the experiences of the Genevan sisters of Saint Clare who were forced by Protestant reformers to abandon their convent. In the end, Jussie and her companions fled on foot with what possessions they could carry and reestablished their community in an abandoned Augustinian monastery at Annecy; eventually, Jussie became their abbess. The conscious decision to remain as nuns when offered freedom from the convent and its vows of chastity shows that Jussie and her comrades, however they came to enter the convent, persisted willingly and conscientiously in the conventual life.

Katharina Schütz Zell

The third figure is the Protestant Katharina Schütz Zell (1498–1562), the wife and widow of one of the leading Protestant reformers who was the head of the Reformed Church at Strasbourg. Born to a family of artisan rank, Katharina Schütz married the former priest of Strasbourg Matthew Zell in 1524—very much in parallel to her contemporary Marie Dentière. Like Dentière, she was well educated, and she was as prepared as her counterpart was to be not only a wife, but a co-reformer with her husband. Composed over a career of thirty-four years, her works are more varied and numerous as well as more conceptually rich than those of the other women in this section. They show her understanding of reform theology and her shrewd grasp of the complex issues that emerged when a society completely changed its assumptions—as European society did with the advent of the Reformation.

One work in particular highlights Schütz Zell's position, and by implication, the altered role women played in Protestant society. In her spirited *Apologia for Matthew Zell*, in defiance of Catholic principles, she defended the right of priests to marry—and implicitly her own right to have married a priest. Not only were Schütz Zell's arguments provocative, at a time when reform was just beginning to take root in Strasbourg, but so too was her speaking out publicly. Prior to this generation, with the exception of a handful of saints and holy women and, more recently, royal or noblewomen, women were expected not to engage publicly in the discussion of ideas—and least of all, religious ones.

The one Catholic woman in this group, the nun Jussie, is reminiscent in some ways of Bartolomea Riccoboni, the Venetian nun with whom this study begins. Like Bartolomea, Jussie found the convent to be a very adequate world. If she was a deeply spiritual woman, that dimension is not apparent in the work that we now read. Jussie provides a precious account of how the Reformation erupted amid her life. Jussie's lengthy account is packed with incident as she depicts the eradication of a way of life, the violation of the quiet and protected zone of the convent that for nearly 1,000 years had been a refuge for devout women.

The Protestant authors—Dentière and Schütz Zell—are, in contrast, iconoclasts. Dentière wants to rip the Clarist sisters out of their convent; to engage the powerful Marguerite de Navarre in the Reformation mission; to defend the righteous reformers, as she sees them, Calvin and Farel; to employ her arsenal of historical and scriptural knowledge to defend her arguments. Similar themes are voiced by Schütz Zell, who engages in polemics with reform leaders and pioneers a role for women in reformed Protestant society.

In the works of these four women, there are only the merest echoes of the otherworldly visions and somatic effects experienced by the holy women discussed above. All are enmeshed in a world of events that buffet them about.

HOLY WOMEN IN THE AGE OF THE INQUISITION

Women inclined to the religious life in Catholic southern Europe also faced forces beyond their control. Here there was no Protestant challenge, as any evangelical tendencies had been suppressed in the early decades of the sixteenth century. Instead, devout women were subject to the scrutiny of male clerics: their priests and confessors if they lived in a domestic household; their ecclesiastical superiors if they were in religious orders; and in all walks of life, the Inquisition. In Spain, they confronted the uniquely repressive Spanish Inquisition, established to ensure religious conformity in a society just emerging from the centuries-long struggle of Reconquest, the reclamation of the Iberian Peninsula from Islam. In Italy, the Roman Inquisition and local, city-based inquisitorial boards exercised discipline over women who were suspected of pretensions to holiness.[6]

The Other Voice series includes the works of two sixteenth-century Spanish holy women who, in different ways, confronted inquisitorial demands. These are the *beata* (holy woman) Francisca de los Apóstoles (1539–after 1578) and the nun María de San José Salazar (1548–1603). (Not included in the series is the epochal Spanish Saint Teresa of Ávila, whose *Autobiography* and devotional works are published in multiple editions and widely available. Although a larger figure than those discussed here, Teresa's experience is consonant with theirs.) In addition, the Other Voice series includes the record of the inquisitorial proceedings against an Italian would-be saint, the Venetian self-styled holy woman Cecilia Ferrazzi (1609–84).

Francisca de los Apóstoles

What is known about Francisca de los Apóstoles is what can be gleaned from the records of her inquisitorial trial, which was conducted 1574–78. She and her sister had been active as devout women, attempting to build an informal community of devout women of the sort known, for instance, in Italy in the fourteenth and fifteenth centuries. It was not this activity, however, but her apocalyptic visions that brought her to the attention of the Inquisition. That organization, ever on the alert for lapsed *conversos* (those who had converted

6. The works discussed here are the Other Voice volumes (Chicago: University of Chicago Press) Francisca de los Apóstoles, *The Inquisition of Francisca: A Sixteenth-Century Visionary on Trial*, ed. and trans. Gillian T. W. Ahlgren (2005); María de San José Salazar, *Book for the Hour of Recreation*, ed. Alison Weber, trans. Amanda Powell (2002); Cecilia Ferrazzi, *Autobiography of an Aspiring Saint*, ed. and trans. Anne Jacobson Schutte (1996). The essays by Ahlgren, Horodowich, and Weber in this volume discuss the teaching of these texts.

to Christianity, sometimes opportunistically, from Judaism or Islam), also had its eyes out for women who falsely claimed to have had divine revelations.

This was the crime of "false sanctity," an accusation that led to the persecution of many devout women whose pursuit of the holy life would have aroused little comment, and perhaps great admiration, in other times or places. Francisca described her life and her visions in her trial and related documents. She was condemned as an *alumbrada* (someone who claims to have been "enlightened"), sentenced to appear in an auto-da-fé (public repentance and declaration of conformity to the church), publicly flogged, and exiled. She then disappeared from the historical record.

María de San José Salazar

A child of the nobility (although perhaps an illegitimate one), María de San José Salazar received an advanced education before, in 1571, she was placed in the convent endowed by her kinswoman and quickly rose to be abbess. Soon she became a disciple of Teresa of Ávila, participating in the mission of founding houses of the strictly reformed, or Discalced ("barefoot"), Carmelites that the latter had pioneered. Founded in Castile, the order extended south into Andalusia, where at age twenty-seven, in 1575, María became abbess of the new foundation at Seville. From here, she frequently corresponded with Teresa about the administration of the convent and spiritual matters. After Teresa died, María participated in the founding of a new convent in Lisbon, where she became abbess in 1585.

But María's path was not all smooth. On three occasions, she was accused of improprieties, silenced, and imprisoned. The first time, in 1578, she was restored to authority after a year of confinement. The second time, in 1593, she was confined incommunicado for nine months but subsequently reinstated. In 1603 she was once again silenced and exiled to a remote place of confinement; she died at the end of that final journey. Although the charges included personal matters, they stemmed from the ongoing clerical mistrust (directed also against Teresa herself) of women taking leadership roles in the church, even as strictly cloistered nuns. Unlike Francisca, she did not endure a trial before the Inquisition or the humiliation and pain of the auto-da-fé, but she too faced enormous barriers in pursuing her spiritual vocation.

María was the author of several works as well as letters and occasional pieces. The most important is her *Book for the Hour of Recreation*—referring to the hour of conversation permitted the Discalced nuns, one of two in a convent day. It is a dialogue between nuns ranging over a number of topics and illustrating, as María gives them words, the serious, sincere, and witty verbal exchanges between women committed to an austere and holy life. Two principal topics are a history of the Carmelite order and a concise biography of Teresa of Ávila. The *Book for the Hour of Recreation* bears testimony to the erudition and literary grace of María de San José Salazar.

In Italy, meanwhile, women could speak out publicly—at least for a time. The establishment of the Roman Inquisition in 1542 spelled the end of the evangelical reform movement, as over the next several years its leaders "fled or bled." Women who had supported that movement—including the high-ranking figures Vittoria Colonna (discussed above), Giulia Gonzaga, and Renée de France—died opportunely ahead of the Inquisition's reach or were silenced. The Italian press, however, remained vigorous into the last decades of the sixteenth century and displayed a particular liking for works by women. In that climate, women authors, including religious women, were able to publish at least into the early 1600s. The seventeenth century, however, became increasingly repressive of heterodox ideas and, indeed, any forms of transgression across strict post-Tridentine cultural barriers.

In this context, the Venetian woman Cecilia Ferrazzi was brought before religious inquisitors in 1664–65. The record of her trial, reminiscent of the inquisition of her Spanish predecessor Francisca de los Apóstoles, documents the case of a would-be holy woman who in an earlier era might have won popular approval as a charismatic visionary but who is now silenced by the Inquisition.

Cecilia Ferrazzi

Daughter of a prosperous Venetian artisan but orphaned at age twenty-one, Ferrazzi was unable, for lack of the required dowry, to enter a convent as had been planned. Instead she was placed *in salvo* ('in safekeeping'), under careful supervision, as all women must be, it was thought, if they were not to be sexually used and fall into prostitution. In 1648, when she was thirty-nine, Ferrazzi became herself a guardian of the chastity of young women entrusted to her care.

Denounced to the Inquisition, at the instruction of the inquisitors Ferrazzi dictated her autobiography to a scribe, intending to demonstrate her innocence. Instead, she provided more evidence that led to her condemnation for *pretesa santità* ('pretense of sanctity'). In 1665, she was condemned to seven years of imprisonment, plus assorted other penalties. In 1669, in consequence of interventions by different Venetian officials, she was released. She lived fifteen years more, without a trace.

Why was Ferrazzi condemned by the Inquisition? She presented herself to her interrogators, as to all those who knew her, as a holy woman: she had visions, she heard voices, she experienced ecstasies, she received the stigmata. Her dictated *Autobiography*, first published in 1990, is an un-self-conscious recitation of the subject's religious experiences, accompanied by bodily pains and periods of unconsciousness. In an earlier age, Ferrazzi might well have been believed; her career was not unlike that of the holy women of the past. In post-Tridentine Italy, however, which was inherently skeptical of female religious experience, she was an object to be controlled and silenced.

POST-REFORMATION CURRENTS IN FRANCE AND GERMANY: JANSENISTS AND PIETISTS (SEVENTEENTH–EIGHTEENTH CENTURIES)

For a century after the Reformation, boundaries between religious groups hardened in a process called "confessionalization." Soon mainstream ortho-doxies, Protestant and Catholic alike, touched off oppositional movements seeking renewal, joining those radical sects that had survived persecution. Women participated conspicuously in these revivalist trends, especially among the Quakers in England, the Pietists in Lutheran regions, and the Jansenists in the Netherlands and France.

Two figures are presented here from the Other Voice series who were adherents, respectively, of Jansenism and Pietism: the French noblewoman Jacqueline Pascal (1625–61) and the German noblewoman Johanna Eleonora Petersen, née von und zu Merlau (1644–1724). A third figure whose works are also published in the Other Voice series, Anna Maria van Schurman (1607–78), hailed as the "star of Utrecht," was similarly active in the Labadist movement, which was akin to Pietism. As her major contribution, arguably, is her work advocating female education, she is left for another volume.[7]

Jacqueline Pascal

The close-knit Pascal family, whose widower head-of-household person-ally educated his one son, the future philosopher Blaise Pascal, and two

---

7. The works discussed here are the Other Voice volumes (Chicago: University of Chicago Press) Jacqueline Pascal, *A Rule for Children and Other Writings*, ed. and trans. John J. Conley, SJ (2003); Johanna Eleonora Petersen, *The Life of Lady Johanna Eleonora Petersen, Written by Herself: Pietism and Women's Autobiography in Seventeenth-Century Germany*, ed. and trans. Barbara Becker-Cantarino (2005). The essays by Conley and Becker-Cantarino in this volume discuss the teaching of these texts.

daughters, all participated in the Jansenist reform movement centered in France at the convent of Port-Royal, twenty miles south of Paris. Jansenism was fully Catholic, continuing sacramental practices and devotions to the Virgin Mary and the saints that Protestants had jettisoned. It was also Augustinian, its characteristic feature, stressing the sinfulness of the human being and the impossibility of salvation without complete dependence on the grace of God. In addition, like earlier reform and heretical movements, it made available vernacular translations of the Bible and encouraged individual struggle in the journey of faith, thus diminishing the importance of the ecclesiastical hierarchy.

Defying her father and siblings, Jacqueline Pascal entered the convent of Port-Royal in 1652 and took final vows in 1653. She soon became the head of the convent school, a central mission of the Jansenist movement. But Jansenism threatened absolute monarchy as much as it threatened the mainstream Catholic Church, which had condemned the movement in 1653 and 1656. When Louis XIV took up personal power in 1661, his officials shut down Port-Royal, evicting the nuns, who were subjected to inquisitorial examination, and razed the convent—including the cemetery where Pascal was buried shortly after her own bout with the inquisitors.

Pascal died young—at age thirty-six—but her active career occasioned a variety of works that testify to her high intelligence and wide learning. These include her poetry (she published a book of verse when she was thirteen) and her correspondence; a meditation on the death of Jesus; a report to the abbess of Port-Royal of her road to the conventual life; a memoir of the abbess of Port-Royal; her *Rule* for the children of the convent school; and the record of her interrogation.

The meditation *On the Mystery of the Death of Our Lord Jesus Christ* is especially remarkable as a Jansenist text. Unlike the works of earlier mystics, many of them female, who dwelled on the bodily torments of the crucified Christ, Pascal draws on Pauline and Augustinian theology to elucidate the meaning of Jesus' sacrificial death. The *Rule for Children* in a different vein proclaims its Jansenist context. The children are required to observe a disciplined routine, modeled on the monastic regimen. At the same time, they are given extensive personal attention, requiring of the mentor a full and precise understanding of the heart and mind of each child.

Johanna Eleonora Petersen

The Life of Lady Johanna Eleonora Petersen . . . Written by Herself is similarly imbued with theological understandings, although these are, in contrast to Pascal's, clearly Protestant and, indeed, skewed toward the radical sectarian pole of

Protestant thought. Pietism encouraged the close reading of scripture and a zealous, personal faith commitment. It also tended toward chiliasm (the expectation of Jesus' reign on earth) and apocalypticism and expected with the eventual apocalypse the conversion and salvation of all.

These beliefs the young Johanna Eleonora von Merlau already embraced, along with the practice of regular pious devotion in a circle of women pledged to virginity, when she was urged by the Pietist leader to marry the pastor and theologian Johann Wilhelm Petersen. She did so, at the advanced age of thirty-six, joining in a marriage that was an active partnership in pastoral mission. In the course of that forty-four-year marriage, she published fourteen works, all devotional in character. The last was her *Life*, published in 1718. An early exemplar of the Pietist genre of spiritual autobiography, it recounts the events of her life in the frame of her conversion to and progress in the Pietist faith, which led her to marry outside of her class and to the pursuit of most uncommon undertakings for someone of her origin.

Both Pascal and Petersen, writing in the late early modern era on the eve of the Enlightenment, remind us in some ways of the holy women with whom this discussion began. They both sought female community for sustenance, Pascal in the convent. Their piety was inward, meditative, and tending toward the mystical. Although neither, coming from Augustinian and Lutheran traditions that would not have encouraged them, displays the somatic references found so frequently in earlier cases, each from a different heterodoxical vantage point resists ecclesiastical authority: Pascal, that of the Catholic church; Petersen, that of the Lutheran.

⁓

From the fourteenth century to the eighteenth, women engaged in the religious life, and in the development of our religious traditions, in ways that men did not. Just as they spoke with an "other voice" in these early modern centuries, they have left to the world their legacy of another kind of religious experience pursued with boldness and commitment. The works of the women noted here would constitute in themselves a course on Women and Religion. Individual works or clusters of related cases would greatly enrich courses in early modern history, women's studies, or any of the relevant European literatures. As they illumined those for whom they wrote, they can illumine our students today.

CHRONOLOGY

KEY EVENTS AND MALE FIGURES	FEMALE FIGURES
1450 Babylonian Captivity of the church (1309–78)[1] Great Schism (1378–1415)[1] Jan Hus (1369–1415)[2] Council of Constance (1415–17)[1]	Saint Bridget of Sweden (ca. 1303–73)[3] Saint Catherine of Siena (1347–80)[3] Bartolomea Riccoboni (1395–1436)[3] Saint Francesca of Rome (1384–1440)[3] Saint Catherine of Bologna (1413–1463)[3] Saint Catherine of Genoa (1447–1510)[3]
1450– 1550 Spanish Inquisition launched (1478–81)[1] Expulsion of Jews from Spain, Portugal (1492,1497)[1] Girolamo Savonarola (1452–98)[2] Saint Thomas More (1478–1535)[2] Desiderius Erasmus (1466–1536)[2] Jesuit order founded (1540)[1] Roman Inquisition founded (1542)[1] Council of Trent (1545–63)[1] Martin Luther (1483–1546)[2]	Lucrezia Tornabuoni (1425–82)[3] Antonia Pulci (ca. 1452–1501)[3] Saint Angela Merici (1474–1540)[3] Vittoria Colonna (1490–1547)[3] Marguerite de Navarre (1492–1549)[3]
1550– 1650 Council of Trent (1545–63) continues[1] Michael Servetus (1511–53)[2] Peace of Augsburg (1556)[1] Anglican Church established (1559)[1] John Calvin (1509–64)[2] Saint Bartholomew's Day Massacre (1572)[1]	Olympia Morata (1526–55)[2] Marie Dentière (1495–1561)[3] Jeanne de Jussie (1503–61)[3] Katarina Schütz Zell (1498–1562)[3] Francisca de los Apóstoles (1539–after 1578)[3]

23

Edict of Nantes (1598)[1]

Thirty Years' War (1618–48)[1]

Saint Teresa of Ávila (1515–82)[2]

Gabrielle de Coignard (1550–86)[2]

María de San José Salazar (1548–1603)[3]

Ana de San Bartolomé (1549–1626)[2]

Cecilia del Nacimiento (1570–1646)[2]

1650–
1750

Sabbatai Zevi (1626–76)[2]

Revocation of Edict of Nantes (1685)[1]

Glorious Revolution (1688)[1]

John Wesley (1703–91)[2]

Jacqueline Pascal (1625–61)[3]

Anna Maria van Schurman (1607–78)[2]

Cecilia Ferrazzi (1609–84)[3]

Colonna, Matraini, and Marinella,
   Marian Writings[1]

Sor Juana Inés de la Cruz (1648–1695)[2]

Johanna Eleonora Petersen (1644–1724)[3]

Figures are placed in chronological sequence according to date of death.

1. Indicates events.

2. Indicates contextual figures.

3. Indicates figures discussed in this volume.

COURSES AND MODULES

There are many possibilities for either one- or two-semester courses based on the volumes published in this series. Although all the volumes included here are religious texts, they lend themselves to a variety of approaches and so would "fit" into many courses whose focus is not only or not primarily religious in an institutional or theological sense. The texts also lend themselves to the creation of modules or units within a wide variety of courses. What follows are two course possibilities, each of which lends itself to manipulation in a number of ways, and a few suggested course modules. See the appendix for a wide array of possibilities for courses or modules suggested by the authors of the essays included in this volume.

COURSE 1

Follow the outline of the introductory essay in this volume, selecting sources from within each unit (this could be a one-semester or a one-year course).

1. Italian holy women in the fourteenth and fifteenth centuries
   a. Women's devotional writing anthology (and Lazar essay in this volume)
   b. Bartolomea Riccoboni (and Bornstein essay in this volume)
2. Elite women of the High Renaissance
   a. Lucrezia Tornabuoni (and Tylus essay in this volume)
   b. Antonia Pulci (and Weaver essay in this volume)
   c. Vittoria Colonna (and Brundin essay in this volume)
   d. Marguerite de Navarre (and Cholakian essay in this volume)
3. Women and the Reformation
   a. Marie Dentière (and McKinley essay in this volume)
   b. Jeanne de Jussie (and Klaus essay in this volume)

      c.   Katharina Schütz Zell (and McKee essay in this volume)

      d.   Olympia Morata

4.   Holy women in the age of the Inquisition

      a.   Francisca de los Apóstoles (and Ahlgren essay in this volume)

      b.   María de San José Salazar (and Weber essay in this volume)

      c.   Cecilia Ferrazzi (and Horodowich essay in this volume)

5.   Post-Reformation currents in France and Germany: Jansenists and Pietists (seventeenth–eighteenth centuries)

      a.   Gabrielle de Coignard (late sixteenth century)

      b.   Anna Maria van Schurman

      c.   Jacqueline Pascal (and Conley essay in this volume)

      d.   Johanna Eleonora Petersen (and Becker-Cantarino essay in this volume)

COURSE 2

Thirteen-week set of readings for a fourteen-week semester, grouped by chronology first, then theme. Regions are combined, suggesting the possibility of cross-cultural comparison. (Texts joined by "and" are meant to be read comparatively, in conjunction with one another.) The excerpts from each work total fifty to one hundred pages per week. A number of the units that make up this course could be used as modules in various kinds of courses.

An asterisk (*) denotes an essay in this volume of this writer or text.

1.   Bartolomea Riccoboni* (Venetian chronicle 1395–1436) and the letters of Saint Catherine of Siena (1347–80), either from *Women Religious in Late Medieval and Early Modern Italy** or from *The Letters of Catherine of Siena*, 2 vols, ed. Suzanne Noffke (Tempe, Ariz.: Medieval and Renaissance Studies and Texts, 2000)

2–3.   Lucrezia Tornabuoni* (1425–82), *Sacred Narratives*, and Antonia Pulci* (1452–1501), *Miracle and Mystery Plays, 1483–92*

4–5.   Vittoria Colonna* (1490–1547), *Sonnets for Michelangelo*, and Marguerite de Navarre* (1492–1549), *Religious Reformist*

6–7.   Marie Dentière* (1495–1561), *Epistle* and *Preface*, and Margaret Schütz Zell* (1498–1562), *Church Mother*, and Olympia Morata

(1526–55), *Complete Writings,* selected letters from Germany, 104–77, esp. nos. 28, 42, 63

8–9.   Jeanne de Jussie* (1503–61), *Short Chronicle,* and Arcangela Tarabotti (1604–52), *Paternal Tyranny*

10–11. Saint Teresa of Ávila (1515–82), *Life* (Penguin), and María de San José Salazar* (1548–1603), *Book for the Hour of Recreation,* and María Anna Agueda de San Ignacio (1695–1756) in *Untold Sisters*

12.   Francisca de los Apóstoles* (1539–after 1578) and Cecilia Ferrazzi* (trial 1664–65)

13.   Jacqueline Pascal* (1625–61), interrogation, and Johanna Eleonora Petersen* (1644–1724)

MODULES

The courses for which the modules below are set forth are specified in each case, but *all* of them would be appropriate for courses in literature or history of women writers or gender. Whenever items are separated by numbers, they represent discreet units. Whenever texts are joined by "and" they are meant to be studied comparatively.

Module 1

For a Renaissance course (literature or history), Italian focus. The aim is to highlight major figures (one class for each) and types of expression across two centuries—didactic verse, spiritual poetry, rhetorical defense, Inquisitional testimony.

1.   Lucrezia Tornabuoni, *Sacred Narratives,* or Antonia Pulci, *Miracle and Mystery Plays,* 1483–92
2.   Vittoria Colonna, *Sonnets for Michelangelo*
3.   Arcangela Tarabotti, *Paternal Tyranny*
4.   Cecilia Ferrazzi, *Autobiography*

Module 2

For a course in biography or autobiography, two to four weeks.

1.   Saint Teresa, *Life,* and María de San José Salazar, *Book for the Hour of Recreation* (see Weber essay), and Cecilia Ferrazzi, *Autobiography*

2.   Johanna Eleonora Petersen, *The Life*, and Anna Maria van
Schurman, *Eukleria*, chaps. 1–2 in *Whether a Christian Woman Should
Be Educated*

Module 3

For a literature course in theater/drama, two to four weeks.
1.   Lucrezia Tornabuoni, *Sacred Narratives*, and Antonia Pulci, *Miracle
and Mystery Plays, 1483–92* (see the Tylus and Weaver essays)

Module 4

For a Reformation course, focus on early history and/or theology, two to
four weeks.
1.   Vittoria Colonna, *Sonnets for Michelangelo*, and Marguerite de
Navarre, *Religious Reformist*
2.   Marie Dentière, *Epistle* and *Preface*, and Margaret Schütz Zell,
Church Mother (see McKinley and McKee essays), and (from
outside the Other Voice series) *The Examinations of Anne Askew*, ed.
Elaine Beilin (New York: Oxford University Press, 1991)

Module 5

For a history course that includes monasticism, one to two weeks.
1.   Bartolomea Riccoboni, *Life and Death in a Venetian Convent*, and
Jeanne de Jussie, *Short Chronicle*, and Arcangela Tarabotti, *Paternal
Tyranny*

Module 6

For a history course that includes the Inquisition, two to three weeks.
1.   Francisca de los Apóstoles and Cecilia Ferrazzi and Jacqueline
Pascal's interrogation
2.   The unit could be extended, or rather preceded, by the movement
that developed around Saint Teresa and that avoided the fates of
the (later) writers above: Saint Teresa, María de San José Salazar
(although the end of her life bears some comparison with those in
module 1 above), Ana de San Bartolomé (to be published in the
Other Voice series).

I

Italian Holy Women of the Fourteenth and Fifteenth Centuries

TEACHING WOMEN'S DEVOTION IN
MEDIEVAL AND EARLY MODERN ITALY[1]

Lance Gabriel Lazar

Religious symbols, beliefs, and traditions profoundly influenced the cultural contributions and achievements of early modern women across Europe. Thus, it is rewarding to consider women's religious formation and the devotional models set before them, which absorbed so much of their time and attention. My experience teaching devotional texts to undergraduates (using selections in various scattered translations) suggests that this material can contribute not only to historical surveys but also to courses in comparative literature, Italian literature, art history, and music history, owing to the important role women played in convents and pious associations as patrons and also as producers of literature, art, and music.[2] Still more importantly, the study of devotional texts opens up the religious experiences and practices that were at the core of women's identities in premodern Europe.

I shall divide my discussion into three sections. The first considers the kinds of questions that arise from the perspective of religious studies. The second addresses some of the characteristic themes emerging from religious

1. I wish kindly to acknowledge the efforts of Albert Rabil, Margaret King, and Maia Rigas in strengthening this chapter through their prudent editing.

2. See the wave of recent anthologies and monographs in many disciplines, including Letizia Panizza and Sharon Wood, eds., *A History of Women's Writing in Italy* (Cambridge: Cambridge University Press, 2000); Elissa Weaver, *Convent Theatre in Early Modern Italy* (Cambridge: Cambridge University Press, 2002); Helen Hills, *Invisible City: The Architecture of Devotion in Seventeenth Century Neapolitan Convents* (New York: Oxford University Press, 2004); Colleen Reardon, *Holy Concord within Sacred Walls: Nuns and Music in Siena, 1575–1700* (New York: Oxford University Press, 2002). See also the older but valuable anthologies of Craig Monson, ed., *The Crannied Wall: Women, Religion, and the Arts in Early Modern Europe* (Ann Arbor: University of Michigan Press, 1992); E. Ann Matter and John Coakley, eds., *Creative Women in Medieval and Early Modern Italy: A Religious and Artistic Renaissance* (Philadelphia: University of Pennsylvania Press 1994).

texts by and about women. The third will briefly explore the paradigmatic examples of Catherine of Siena and Bridget of Sweden.

ANIMATING PREMODERN RELIGIOUS DEVOTION

When first considering medieval and early modern devotional texts, students' initial responses generally cluster around two poles. Some reject the religious practices as too foreign and too "other" and therefore of little use in understanding the development of Christian culture; others absorb the moralizing tone and biblical references into a generic "pious-speak," overlooking the idiosyncratic character of the texts. My goals in teaching these texts are thus twofold: to enable students to see the texts as accessible and relevant to understanding broad patterns of Christian practice and to discern the distinctive and at times stridently opposed viewpoints of such texts.

In trying to maintain a balance between the themes of relevance and peculiarity of these texts, I use five overlapping rubrics that can be deployed selectively, depending on the text under consideration. Together they form a malleable platform to coax out the broadest difference in approach as well as more subtle distinctions in tone.[3]

1. What is the interplay of human and divine activity?
2. What is the Christian message (the moral)?
3. What are the sources of authority?
4. What institutions guide the way?
5. What theology is implicit or explicit in the text?

These rubrics come into play only after we have considered the primary critical questions relating to the context of any document: the identity of the author(s) and the circumstances surrounding the creation of the text, the genre(s) and potential purpose(s) of the writing, the likely audience(s), the means of transmission, and so forth.

1. Interplay of Human and Divine

Devotional texts presuppose a view of how God becomes manifest in the world and why that matters to an individual soul. Before any prayer can cross the lips or meditation enter the mind's eye, devotional authors must first frame assumptions about God's receptivity, presence, and willingness

---

3. I wish to acknowledge with thanks the model of John O'Malley, SJ, in first demonstrating to me by example the organization and utility of such an approach.

to intervene in human affairs. Such considerations often lead to Platonic dualism, distinguishing between material and spiritual realms, among other solutions. How God hears and responds is central to visionary literature, which posits the most intimate contact between the human and the divine.[4] Indeed, in the hands of some Italian women mystics, such as Catherine of Genoa in her so-called treatise on purgatory, one seems never to touch the ground, so completely subsumed does the narrator/guide become in relating the nature of divine realities away from the everyday material world.[5] Intrinsic to any consideration of the nature of divinity is the question of unity or plurality, as well as the presence or importance of other spiritual beings, such as angels or devils, and their ability to affect the individual soul. Male clerical observers typically had no difficulty accepting spiritual contact but were all too concerned about discerning whether that contact came from above or below. Regardless of their religious preparation, students often do not anticipate and thus enjoy these broadest questions of the ontological machinery underlying prayer and contact with the divine.[6]

2. Christian Message

Devotional treatises often functioned as "self-help" guides. Providing counsel and strategies for combating temptations and overcoming obstacles was a staple for Italian women writers like Catherine of Bologna in her *Seven Spiritual Weapons* or Camilla Battista da Varano in her *Spiritual Works*. Providing directives for living devoutly and well was also a basic premise for successful preachers, many of whom developed notable popularity for their advice

---

4. For a concise but broad survey of mystical literature contextualizing many of these points, see Steven Fanning, *Mystics of the Christian Tradition* (London: Routledge, 2001). For the definitive and more systematic consideration, see the multivolume series by Bernard McGinn, *The Presence of God: A History of Western Christian Mysticism* (New York: Crossroad, 1991–).

5. Catherine of Genoa, 1447–1510, *Libro de la vita mirabile et dottrina santa de la beata Caterinetta da Genoa, Nel quale si contiene una utile et catholica dimostratione et dechiaratine del purgatorio* (Stampata in Genoua, per Antonio Bellono, MDLI [1551]), ed. Valeriano da Finalmarina, OFM Cap. (Genoa, 1957); Cattaneo Marabotto, *Vita della serafica s. Caterina da Genova, colla mirabile sua dottrina contenuta nell'insigne Trattato del Purgatorio, e nel Dialogo tra il corpo, l'anima, l'umanità, lo spirito, ed il Signor Iddio, composti dalla medesima santa. In questa nuova impressione, o sia ristampa esattamente corretta, e colla giunta di nuove postille in margine migliorata, ed accresciuta di notizie del concetto, stima, e culto di detta santa fino alla di lei canonizzazione* (Genova: Nella stamperia del Franchelli, 1737); L. T. Hecker, ed., *Life and Doctrine of St. Catherine of Genoa* (New York, 1874). The most accessible modern translation is Catherine of Genoa, *Purgation and Purgatory: The Spiritual Dialogue*, trans. Serge Hughes (New York: Paulist, 1979).

6. See Rosalynn Voaden, *God's Words, Women's Voices: The Discernment of Spirits in the Writing of Late-Medieval Women Visionaries* (Rochester, N.Y.: York Medieval Press, 1999).

and attention to models for women, including the Franciscan Cherubino da Siena in his *Rules for Married Life* or the Dominican Giovanni Dominici in his treatise *On the Education of Children.*[7]

Beyond pious prescriptions, this rubric invites students to question how the "good Christian" is intended to fill up a day: Is the ideal life active or contemplative? Which practices are most central, private meditation or public ritual? How important are routines and habits, and, conversely, what role is assigned to spontaneity and impulse? To what degree are ascetic practices recommended, and how are sometimes severe mortifications incorporated, advocated, and defended as ways of controlling the flesh? While advice on these questions may fall into predictable patterns, tone and style are individual and lead to other questions: How does she convey the importance of her message? Is it a warning or war cry? Is it a prophetic appeal to divine will? Does it proceed in a philosophical manner, relating a set of proofs to be affirmed by reason? The medium can be as important as the message in capturing the originality or popular success of a devotional treatise.

3. Authorities

How does the author use the Bible? The sometimes radically divergent perspectives on the Bible of premodern devotional writers can provide fruitful cognitive dissonance for contemporary students. Pointed questions can help students discern how an author reads and deploys the Bible: Which passages roll most easily off the tongue? Is the Bible mostly a book of history, wisdom, blueprints for society, moral injunctions, poetry? Is the Bible understood as an imperative, an invitation, an argument, "threats and promises," a contract, a secret codebook? The differing tone among early modern women writers is often amplified by their characteristic selections from scripture. While

---

7. Catherine, of Bologna, [Caterina Vegri], Poor Clare, 1413–1463, *Le sette armi spirituali,* ed. Cecilia Foletti (Padua: Antenore, 1985); *The Seven Spiritual Weapons,* trans. and with notes by Hugh Feiss and Daniela Re (Toronto: Peregrina Publishing, 1998); Camilla Battista da Varano, Poor Clare, 1458–1524?, *Le opere spirituali: Nuova ed. del V centenario della nascita secondo i più antichi codici e stampa con aggiunta di alcuni inediti,* ed. Giacomo Boccanera. Prefazione di Piero Bargellini (Iesi: Scuola Tip. Francescana, 1958); *My Spiritual Autobiography,* ed. and trans. Joseph R Berrigan (Saskatoon: Peregrina Publishing, 1986); Cherubino da Siena, frate (OFM), *Regole della vita spirituale e matrimoniale* (Florence, 1490; repr. 1969). *Regole della vita matrimoniale di frate Cherubino da Siena,* ed. F. Zambrini and C. Negroni (Bologna: Commissione per i testi di lingua, 1969); Giovanni Dominici, OP, blessed, cardinal, 1356?–1420?, *Regola del buon governo di cura familiare compilata dal beato Giovanni Dominici, Fiorentino, dell'Ordine de' frati predicatori.* Testo in lingua dato in luce e illustrato con note dal prof. Donato Salvi . . . (Florence: A. Garinei, 1860). *On the Education of Children, Parte Quarta della Regola del Governo di cura familiare,* trans. A. B. Cote (diss., Catholic University, 1927).

some tune in to the easy-listening melodies of the Gospel of John, others may have preprogrammed the heavy metal of Ezekiel.[8]

It is also revealing to observe the way a writer blends the authority of the Bible with other authorities. Humanistically trained writers typically turn to pagan moralists like Cicero, Quintilian, or Horace to buttress a point, while others may turn to the church fathers or scholastic theologians or more popular texts like the Golden Legend. Mystical authors also balance personal inspiration with authority, and all devotional writers functioned under the implicit or explicit authority of contemporary ecclesiastical figures. Observing a writer's characteristic maneuvering between authorities, noting which were assumed, which defended, which attacked or ignored, can provide another insight into the values an author holds most dear.

4. Institutions

It is endlessly illuminating to observe how devotional writers conceive of community, its place, role, bonds, and obligations: What images are developed to describe human relationships? What metaphors shape the Christian life? Where does one turn for guidance and devotion? Options include private meditation, inner inspiration, authority figures, sermons, sacraments and liturgy, charitable associations and confraternities, and so on. Precisely because Jesus and the apostles seemingly left behind no constitution or book of statutes for an ecclesiastical structure, it has been left to their inheritors to slug it out through their varying interpretations of a vastly divergent collection of texts.

This rubric also provides a convenient entrée into discussing church/state divisions of responsibilities: distinctions between the clergy and laity, gender roles, and the treatment and status of Muslims, Jews, and other non-Christians. Often, discussion of community can lead to a consideration of the spatial imagination of Christian society and the stage upon which community relationships are enacted: the church is the place where XXX happens... the convent provides a platform for these activities... the private chapel or oratory relates to these practices, and so on. Consideration of the physical space for the church can lead to a discussion of the spatial

8. A convenient and useful handbook for biblical commentary in an encyclopedia format is Raymond Brown, SS, Joseph Fitsmeyer, SJ, and Roland Murphy, O.Carm., eds., *The New Jerome Biblical Commentary* (Englewood Cliffs, N.J.: Prentice Hall, 1968, 1990). As a general reference tool for historical Christianity, see F. L. Cross and E. A. Livingston, eds., *The Oxford Dictionary of the Christian Church*, 3d ed. (New York: Oxford University Press, 1997).

representation of sanctity and the commemoration and veneration of saints and their relics.

5. *Theology*

Although prohibited from the advanced study of philosophy and theology, women were remarkably prolific in writing about theological matters.[9] Consideration of the nature of the godhead is often a good place to start, as the Nicene formula of three in one provides an ample playing field for variations in emphasis: To whom does one pray, God the Father, God the Son, or God the Holy Spirit, or should the Blessed Virgin Mary or the saints be one's advocate and solicitor? What are the consequences of that choice? If an author is Christocentric, then questions of high or low Christology arise: Does the divine or the human nature of Jesus come to the fore? If one focuses on Jesus the man, is the model of his life or his suffering and death of primary significance? Considerations of Jesus' many roles open into broader soteriological discussions: What *really* saves us and how?

Questions relating to *how* a text conveys its message are as important as the content itself. How does a text provide access to the story of Jesus: does it quote scripture or retell the story from a point of view or advocate the practice of meditation or contemplation of images? How are the senses and imagination engaged? What roles do poetry, rhetoric, and logic play? Considering *how* the theology is framed and presented often leads to questions of the author's relationship to the world and the interplay of nature and grace. Does the author lean toward Augustine and stress the fallen condition of humanity and the world or toward Aquinas and emphasize the unfolding consequences of Christ's redemptive sacrifice?

To help students gain command of these critical tools effectively, I always hand out these questions in outline form at the beginning of the term (and link them to the course homepage) so that students can familiarize themselves with the clusters of issues and have them at hand as they are reading each assignment. It is sometimes helpful to prompt students to focus their attention on one rubric that is especially relevant. Depending on the size of a class, I may require each student on one or two occasions to open the discussion of a text with a brief oral presentation relating to one or more of the

---

9. See Jane Howard Guernsey, *The Lady Cornaro: Pride and Prodigy of Venice* (Clinton Corners, N.Y.: College Avenue Press, 1999). Human society is too creative to prevent the opening of cracks in presumably airtight prohibitions. See Michael H. Shank, "A Female University Student in Late Medieval Kraków," in *Sisters and Workers in the Middle Ages*, ed. Judith Bennett et al. (Chicago: University of Chicago Press, 1989).

rubrics. After only a few class discussions utilizing these rubrics, students can become remarkably adept at discerning differences in the conceptualizations of religious belief and practice.

APPROACHING WOMEN'S RELIGION

In this second section, I shall review some of the characteristic issues that frequently recur in discussions of religious texts by and about women. My discussion is organized around four clusters of questions that have proven useful in prompting insightful responses among undergraduates: the context of finding a voice, the use of ideal models and archetypes, attitudes about ascetic practices, and the quest for autonomy and self-determination.

1. Finding a Voice

A central topos of religious texts by early modern women (and a central concern within the Other Voice series) is the search for an authoritative voice and a platform. Although women were systematically excluded from ecclesiastical office and access to higher education, this did not keep them from finding their own voices. They put forth new revelations or ecstatic visions (sometimes as the voice of God), and they captured the ear of the highest clerics and secular rulers, even the popes and emperors, who acknowledged (even if they did not always obey) their message.

How did women appropriate this authority? They often deftly deflected attention by casting themselves as humble instruments for God's message, emphasizing their unworthiness (in relation to God or in relation to men, as the "weaker vessel") and declaiming their unsuitability and unpreparedness for the task at hand. Another frequent tactic was to say they wrote unwillingly, claiming that, despite a revulsion toward writing, they were obliged by a higher power to do so, either God or some ecclesiastical superior. All this provides a palpable urgency to the texts, reinforced through the use of the vernacular or even dialect and the home-spun immediacy of the images and metaphors, which are often accompanied by a lament of the insufficiency of language to capture the ineffable nature of ecstatic experience.[10]

---

10. There are numerous excellent discussions of the typologies of medieval and early modern Italian women's visionary experiences, including Katherine Gill, "Women and the Production of Religious Literature in the Vernacular, 1300–1500," in *Creative Women in Medieval and Early Modern Italy*, 64–104; Marilena Modica Vasta, "Mystical Writing," in *Women and Faith: Catholic Religious Life in Italy from Late Antiquity to the Present*, ed. Lucetta Scaraffia and Gabriella Zarri (Cambridge, Mass.: Harvard University Press, 1999), 205–18; Gabriela Zarri, "Living Saints: A Typology of Female Sanctity in the Early Sixteenth Century," in *Women and Religion in Medieval and Renaissance*

To build empathy for these writers, I have sometimes asked students to write (an ungraded assignment) about a personal "mystical experience." I seek to defuse their hesitation to accept such an assignment by encouraging them to focus on a moment of inspiration, a "eureka" experience, for example, a troubling dilemma that suddenly became clarified or a moment when they became vividly aware of some life lesson. What were the circumstances and the environment leading up to such a moment? How did they become aware of it, and why has its imprint lingered in their minds more than other experiences? I have yet to be disappointed with the response from undergraduates. At the very least, the exercise introduces the complexity of explaining or relating a transcendent experience to another and presents the genre to them from the inside, so they are more intimately attuned to its nuances in later readings.[11]

2. *Ideal Models*

Special consideration should be reserved for the role of Mary the mother of Jesus as archetype. The Blessed Virgin Mary often functions as a mirror for the cultural ideals of womanhood, whether celibate or as a mother, so students should carefully observe the qualities, virtues, honors, dispositions, and gestures ascribed to her in devotional texts. Her status also modulates in relation to Jesus, so a text developing incarnational theology, which emphasizes the efficacy and significance of God becoming man in Jesus, may consequently elevate the role of Mary from mediatrix to redemptrix, as a full participant in God's salvific plan (as Jesus redeems the sin of Adam, so Mary redeems the sin of Eve). Similarly, Mary Magdalen and Martha functioned regularly in devotional literature for women as archetypes of the contemplative and active life. Identified universally as a fallen woman in premodern biblical exegesis, Mary Magdalen especially served as the model of the ideal penitent, showing how reform of one's sinful or fallen nature was possible through rigorous asceticism.[12]

Italy, ed. Daniel Bornstein and Roberto Rusconi, trans. Margery Schneider (Chicago: University of Chicago Press, 1996), 219–303.

11. An alternative to the mystical experience assignment for classes not using mystical treatises is an ungraded assignment drawn from the example of Petrarch and many other humanists: to address a letter to an admired figure from the past. The idea of correspondence with the dead is awkward and unfamiliar enough for most undergraduates to elicit some truly worthwhile results. The intimacy of a letter juxtaposed with the creative engagement with an intellectual hero (students always choose their own pen pal) creates a valuable tension and vehicle for reflection about the past and the self.

12. For a consideration of the Virgin Mary as a magnet for ideas about women, see Michael P. Carroll, *The Cult of the Virgin Mary: Psychological Origins* (Princeton: Princeton University

The importance of biblical archetypes also reinforces the value of devotional biographies and autobiographies as living or recently deceased women came to provide the models. Pious and edifying conversion narratives have an ancient and respected pedigree within Christianity, for example, Paul and Augustine, so it is not surprising that Italian women should have recorded their own spiritual lives or composed lives of other virtuous souls for emulation. While presenting ideal types for imitation may not prove inspiring to all, it certainly held a perennial place in the devotional arsenal of early modern Italian women. Indeed, the qualities modeled in hagiographies are useful to the interpreter of *mentalités* not for the accuracy of their descriptions, but for the characteristic clarity of their expectations.[13]

3. Asceticism

The practices of asceticism and mortification are a recurring theme in devotional writings for women (whether penned by women or men). The patient abiding of suffering, even unto death in martyrdom,[14] and the practice of heroic chastity provided a potent ground for the spiritual power of women religious and undergirded their claims to authority. Indeed, the male confessors and spiritual directors of pious women, both religious and lay, often sought confirmation of a woman's spiritual gifts and insights in the copious demonstration of her stamina for mortification.[15] Modern students

---

Press, 1986). For a far-reaching consideration of the symbolism of Mary and Martha, see Giles Constable, *Three Studies in Medieval Religious and Social Thought: The Interpretation of Mary and Martha, the Ideal of the Imitation of Christ, the Orders of Society* (Cambridge: Cambridge University Press, 1995). For Mary Magdalen, see the work of Susan Haskins and Katherine Jansen: Susan Haskins, *Mary Magdalen: Myth and Metaphor* (London: HarperCollins, 1993); Katherine Ludwig Jansen, *The Making of the Magdalen: Preaching and Popular Devotion in the Later Middle Ages* (Princeton: Princeton University Press, 2000).

13. For a survey of model lives, see Gabriella Zarri, "Religious and Devotional Writing, 1400–1600," in *A History of Women's Writing in Italy*, 79–93. Also exploring the utility of both positive and negative models, see Anne Jacobsen Schutte, "Little Women, Great Heroines: Simulated and Genuine Female Holiness in Early Modern Italy," in *Women and Faith*, 144–58.

14. Robert L. Kendrick, "Looking at Martyrdom in Seventeenth-Century Italian Music," in *From Rome to Eternity: Catholicism and the Arts in Italy, ca. 1550–1650*, ed. Thomas Worcester, SJ, and Pamela Jones (Leiden: Brill, 2002): 121–41. For a brief survey of recent literature on Martyrdom, see Simon Ditchfield, "Martyrs Are Good to Think With: Review Essay," *Catholic Historical Review*, 87, no. 3 (2001): 470–73.

15. Rudolph M. Bell develops a chapter in relation to Catherine of Siena's severe physical mortifications in his *Holy Anorexia* (Chicago: University of Chicago Press, 1985). Bell's monograph should be read in concert with Caroline Walker Bynum's treatment of related themes in *Holy Feast and Holy Fast: The Religious Significance of Food to Medieval Women* (Berkeley: University of California Press, 1987). See also the discussion of penitent women, especially in the care of Dominican friars: Maiju Lehmijoki-Gardner, *Worldly Saints: Social Interaction of Dominican Penitent*

may frequently commence with little empathy for the ascetic expressions of early modern European women (and men), but with further consideration of contemporary practices of dieting and exercise (no pain, no gain) largely for aesthetic ends, they can interpret in a more nuanced fashion the ascetic goals of tempering the will and promoting detachment.

4. Self-Determination

The formation of numerous new religious orders and devotional confraternities in the fifteenth and sixteenth centuries underscores women's restless search for new means to live and interact in communities with like-minded individuals.[16] Besides attending to such new opportunities, students should also focus on the imaginative constructions of community, opportunities for leadership, and the exercise of roles prohibited outside the community.[17] Internal letters can also disclose the place of charisma within the communities, as they reveal the more diffused sensibilities of devout women in their correspondence with family, friends, mentors, protégés, and peers.

TWO CHARACTERISTIC CASES

Two paradigmatic figures who embody many of these themes are Catherine of Siena (1347–80), and Birgitta (also and better known as Bridget) of Sweden (ca.1303–73). Their origins were vastly different. Catherine was near the last of twenty-five children of a prosperous Sienese dyer, pursued a celibate life as a *mantellata*, and became the protégé of Raymond of Capua, the master

---

Women in Italy, 1200–1500 (Helsinki: Suomen Historiallinen Seura, 1999). See also *Dominican Penitent Women*, ed. and trans. Maiju Lehmijoki-Gardner, with Daniel Bornstein and E. Ann Matter (New York: Paulist, 2005).

16. For some considerations of the new orders, see Anna Esposito-Aliano, "S. Francesca Bussa dei Ponziani e le communità religiose femminili a Roma nel secolo XV," in *Women and Religion;* "St. Francesca and the Female Religious Communities of Fifteenth-Century Rome," in *Women and Faith*, 83–112; see also Katherine Gill, "Open Monasteries for Women in Late Medieval and Early Modern Italy: Two Roman Examples," in *The Crannied Wall*, 15–47; for a consideration of the changing models, see Gabriella Zarri, "From Prophecy to Discipline, 1450–1650," in *Women and Faith*, 83–112. See also Charmarie J. Blaisdell, "Angela Merici and the Ursulines," in *Religious Orders of the Catholic Reformation: In Honor of John C. Olin on His Seventy-Fifth Birthday*, ed. Richard DeMolen (New York: Fordham, 1994), 99–138.

17. For a consideration of preaching and leadership roles within women's communities, see Roberto Rusconi, "Women's Sermons at the End of the Middle Ages: Texts from the Blessed and Images of the Saints," in *Women Preachers and Prophets through Two Millennia of Christianity*, ed. Beverly Mayne Kienzle and Pamela Walker (Berkeley: University of California Press, 1998), 173–95.

general of the Dominican Order and her chief biographer. Birgitta was the daughter of a wealthy landowner and cousin to Sweden's King Magnus who married at thirteen and delivered eight children before her husband died and then redirected her life, pursuing pilgrimages as far away as the Holy Land, settling in Rome, and founding a new religious order. Yet both women rose to the pinnacle of pan-European authority within their own lifetimes, corresponded with princes and popes, and attracted widespread popular followings. Not long after their deaths, they each received official approbation (Birgitta was canonized in 1391, and Catherine was canonized in 1461 and declared a doctor of the church in 1970), and both became among the most widely emulated and admired models for religious and laywomen and laymen.[18]

Catherine could serve as an exemplar for each of the four rubrics discussed immediately above in subsection 2. By appropriating literally the voice of God and referring to herself in the third person throughout her *Dialogue*, she has found a voice that even Augustine did not approach in his *Confessions*. Through the countless publications of her writings and her vita by Raymond of Capua, she became the premier contemporary model of righteous Christian living, and the ascetic practices on which Raymond dilated so profusely (but which are notably downplayed in her own writings) became the new guiding star for mortification. While Catherine left no formal rule herself, she anchored and expanded by her example the active model for Dominican tertiaries, and by overtly obeying her confessor, she achieved the charismatic leadership of a group of lay and religious from many layers of society (her *bella brigata* as she called them).

But above all, both women were exemplars for finding a compelling voice, despite the obstacles in their way. Catherine's quintessential rhetorical gesture in her *Dialogue* is the layering of metaphor upon compound metaphor. In her characteristic fashion of circling back and piling image upon image, Catherine enables the extended metaphor itself to shoulder the heavy burden of explanation, so that the meaning and significance of her insight appear almost effortless. Consider her metaphor of the bridge. By making Jesus the bridge that spans the human and the divine, the pilgrim Christian is able

---

18. For their role as models, see Sara F. Matthews Grieco, "Models of Female Sanctity in Renaissance and Counter-Reformation Italy," in *Women and Faith*, 159–75; see also Pamela Jones, "Female Saints in Early Modern Italian Chapbooks, ca. 1570–1670: Saint Catherine of Alexandria and Saint Catherine of Siena," in *From Rome to Eternity*, 89–120. For the promotion of a Catherinian movement by the *paignoni*, the followers of Savonarola, see Gabriella Zarri, "Living Saints: A Typology of Female Sanctity in the Early Sixteenth Century," in *Women and Religion*, 219–303.

to cross the bridge of Christ over the rivers of sin and temptation, to arrive at paradise on the stones of the virtues held together by the mortar of the blood of Christ poured out in sacrifice. The Holy Spirit built the bridge, and the martyrs, confessors, evangelists, and doctors are the lamps that light the way, while the Holy Church is a hostel by the roadside giving a safe and secure berth. With this metaphor in place, Catherine can deliver the punch line: "how foolish and blind are those who choose to cross through the water when the road has been built for them! This road is such a joy for those who travel on it that it makes every bitterness sweet and every burden light."[19] By altering the frame of reference, Catherine removes the sense of struggle; with dazzling efficiency and economy, the battle for moral perfection is won before it is even engaged.[20]

Birgitta of Sweden's *Book of Revelations* is a compilation of many formats from prophetic and visionary material to a scholastic *summa* with logical progressions in the question and response format, all providing her an exceptional freedom of expression. In her popular fifth book, sometimes printed as a stand-alone text, she asks Jesus (both their voices being in the first person) why some babies are born healthy and others die in the womb, for instance, and myriad other questions for which inquiring minds would want an answer.[21] In her seventh book, Birgitta relates a vision of the nativity received on a pilgrimage to Bethlehem with such a powerful level of visual detail that it inspired a phalanx of artists throughout Europe in their depictions of the scene.[22] And in four prayerful meditations on the life and suffering of Christ, she develops about twenty-five sensually detailed vignettes through the eyes and points of view of Jesus' mother and Jesus himself. Still further, she walks the prayerful meditator through the vignettes two more times from the perspective of the individual body parts of Jesus and his mother, recounting the special dignity and role played by each organ or feature and involving all five senses in the most synesthetic journey imaginable—truly a tour-de-force display of creative imagination.[23]

19. *Catherine of Siena, The Dialogue*, trans. Suzanne Noffke, OP (New York: Paulist, 1980), 68.

20. On discussions of Catherine's use of metaphor, see Karen Scott, "Candied Oranges, Vinegar, and Dawn: The Imagery of Conversion in the Letters of Caterina of Siena," *Annali d'italianistica* 13 (1995): 91–108. Joseph F. Chorpenning, OSFS, *The Divine Romance: Teresa of Avila's Narrative Theology* (Chicago: University of Chicago Press, 1992), also discusses Catherine's use of metaphor as an important influence on Teresa of Ávila.

21. Birgitta of Sweden, [Bridget of Sweden], *Birgitta of Sweden: Life and Selected Revelations*, ed. M. T. Harris (New York: Paulist, 1990), 108ff.

22. Sylvia Schein, "Bridget of Sweden, Margery Kempe, and Women's Jerusalem Pilgrimages in the Middle Ages," *Mediterranean Historical Review* 14, no. 1 (June 1999): 44–58.

23. Birgitta of Sweden, *Birgitta of Sweden*, 221–35.

CONCLUSIONS

Despite the ever-present barriers blocking their entry into the usual forums for speculative thought on religious practices and devotion, a remarkable cohort of women crafted their own arenas and developed their own strategies to amplify their voices. The apostle Paul's prohibitions on hearing women in the church could not dampen the effervescent energy of their religious expression. In abundant ways, creative women in premodern Europe shined their light into the broad squares and recessed corners of the religious imagination. The insistence and elegance of their creative invention captivated their contemporaries and helped to form new patterns or to reinvigorate old patterns for model Christian living. Their efforts to be heard still resonate with new generations, which must construct their own answers to many of the same problems.

READING SISTER BARTOLOMEA

Daniel Bornstein

Since before this translation was published, I have used Bartolomea Ric-coboni's description of life in a Venetian convent as the initial reading in a seminar on women and religion in medieval Europe.[1] Later readings bring the students face to face with a variety of truly extraordinary women, who in any given year might include Margery Kempe, Angela of Foligno, Catherine of Siena, Julian of Norwich, Hildegard of Bingen, Margaret Ebner, Marie d'Oignies, and Birgitta of Sweden. However, before they encounter any of these individuals, whose behavior can, at times, seem odd, off-putting, even profoundly disturbing, I want my students to get to know a group of rela-tively ordinary women, engaged in a community of worship and devotion under the guidance of long-established rules. Sister Bartolomea's *Chronicle of Corpus Domini* records the collective life of one such religious community over the span of several decades, from its inception in the late fourteenth century through the contentious drama of the Great Schism. Her *Necrology* reports the deaths and recalls the lives and character of nearly fifty women who died in the convent of Corpus Domini during the first forty years of its existence. Taken together, they give readers a concrete sense of the daily routine of the convent, an awareness of the varied trajectories that could bring so many dif-ferent women to this common home, and some recognition of the concerns that dominate their collective life and the intrusions that can disrupt it.

1. I am most grateful to several friends and colleagues who have not only done me the honor of using Sister Bartolomea Riccoboni's *Life and Death in a Venetian Convent: The Chronicle and Necrology of Corpus Domini, 1395–1436* in their courses, but who generously shared their reflections on and insights into the pedagogical uses of this text: Alison Frazier (University of Texas), Lu Ann Homza (College of William and Mary), David Peterson (Washington and Lee University), Sharon Strocchia (Emory University), and Elizabeth Wengler (College of Saint Benedict and Saint John's University).

Medieval convent life is something strange to all of my students, especially those from Protestant or evangelical backgrounds, but even the Catholic ones as well. We start our discussion of the Riccoboni texts by exploring that strangeness. As my students set out to read the chronicle and necrology of Corpus Domini for the first time, I ask them to make note of something that surprises them, something that shocks or repulses them, and something that strikes them as silly or absurd and to reflect on why they responded as they did. At bottom, these are all ways of measuring the difference between what their world assumes to be normal and what was considered normal in a late medieval convent: things that Sister Bartolomea singles out for praise, or records without special comment, can seem odd, repugnant, or simply laughable to one or another of my students. The things that catch their eyes in these ways are fairly predictable. They find peculiar the sisters' propensity for visions, their readiness to see the hand of God at work in the most banal of events, their obsession with virginity, and their dismay when a gust of wind scatters consecrated hosts on the ground—a dismay made especially intense because one Eucharistic wafer happens to land in the gaping mouth of one sister. They are shocked by the rigor of the sisters' penitential practices, especially self-flagellation, and by the early age at which many of the sisters died, which they tend to see as related; by the prominence of disease in their obituary notices and their religious expressions, such as Sister Piera's impulsive decision to kiss a sick sister she is nursing; and by the youth of many of the sisters at the time they enter the convent, whether as virgins or (what may be even more startling) as widows. They laugh at the image of the elderly prioress hobbling away from male visitors as fast as she can, terrified for her virginity; at one sister's vision of devils eagerly waiting to pounce on every syllable the nuns let drop as they recited the Office; and at their furtive removal of the relics of Saint Lucy from a nearby church in the middle of the night. This gets students talking in an emotionally engaged way about specific passages in the readings—always a good way to start a seminar. What is more, it alerts them to issues that will recur over the course of the semester: the corporality of so much female piety; the centrality of visionary experience; imitation of and identification with Jesus, particularly (in this late medieval context) the suffering Jesus; the spiritual transformation of illness and suffering; penitential purification of the self and charitable service of others; and the religious significance of food, expressed notably through a rigorous renunciation of ordinary sustenance paired with an intense devotion to the Eucharist.

The first written assignment turns the students' attention from these general themes in medieval gender and spirituality to their elaboration in a specific institutional setting. Using the chronicle and necrology of Corpus Domini as their sources, students are asked to identify and examine one area of persistent tension that they feel is especially characteristic of the monastic life. Their task is not to resolve the tension (since persistent tension is by definition irresolvable) nor to judge either or both of the contending motivations right or wrong, but to explain why the particular tension they identify is so characteristic a feature of convent life and lay out the conflicting impulses that cause it. This exercise encourages them to reflect on the ways in which the inner life of prayer, worship, and recollection is shaped by the institutional form within which this religious life is cultivated. It thus prepares them to recognize the spiritual and cultural implications of the physical and social settings within which the various women they will encounter—the devout housewife, penitent or tertiary, cloistered nun, and anchoress—chose to pursue their different ways of life. It also presses them to read the chronicle and necrology more critically, to break the smooth surface of harmony that Sister Bartolomea was so concerned to present and grasp something of the rich complexity of monastic life and the challenge of maintaining unity in a cloistered community. With some prompting from the introduction and from class discussion of patterns of female piety, student essays fasten onto such tensions as those between affection for one's biological family and identification with one's spiritual kin, the call to sacrifice and the desire for security, pursuing individual spiritual perfection and sustaining the community, the ideal of apostolic poverty and the need for property, dedication to the ordered routine of worship and admiration for disruptive moments of religious ecstasy, the honor due virginity and the respect owed to chaste widowhood, and devoting one's time to worshiping God or serving one's neighbor.

Alison Frazier of the University of Texas makes a rather different use of the Riccoboni texts in her course on the Italian Renaissance. She gives her students a set of questions designed to alert them to the range of religious institutions and practices in Renaissance Italy and to aid them in locating Corpus Domini within that array—questions that would be equally suitable to the purposes of my course on women and religion in medieval Europe and that I may well adopt in the future. For instance, she asks them to

1.   Keep track of all the different religious orders mentioned by Sister Bartolomea. Note any evidence of friendliness or enmity between them.

2.   Consider how Corpus Domini got its name. To what order did it belong? How long had it been in existence when Sister Bartolomea began writing?

3.   Describe the internal economy of the convent. The convent was
      not endowed during Bartolomea's lifetime, so how is it supported
      by the external economy?

4.   Keep track of the miracles and visions at Corpus Domini (a kind
      of divine economy). What provokes a miracle or vision to occur?
      How does Bartolomea respond to the miraculous and visionary
      inside and outside the convent?

5.   Keep track of the variety of devotional practices used by the
      women of Corpus Domini. Do they seem to be especially *women's*
      practices? Are the practices standardized or regulated? Does
      Bartolomea criticize any of them?

6.   Note specific examples of the monastic virtues of poverty,
      chastity, and obedience in Sister Bartolomea's two accounts.

   However, in addition to these questions aimed at fostering an exact and
nuanced understanding of the religious context, Professor Frazier also asks
her students to ponder the literary form of these texts and the literary skills
Sister Bartolomea brings to them. She calls on them to reflect on the nature
of canonical texts, on the construction of authoritative canons (in particular,
of those that define the Italian Renaissance, in contrast to the Middle Ages),
and on the inclusion of various works in the Renaissance canon or their
exclusion from it.

1.   Consider the chronicle as a genre (a specific kind of writing).
      What is its purpose? What sorts of events does Bartolomea
      record? How often does she make an entry in her chronicle? Does
      she spend more time on things inside or outside the convent?
      What sorts of events does she treat most fully? What tools does
      she use for analyzing events (as in chapters 12, 13, 15)? Would
      you call her a historian?

2.   Consider the necrology as a genre. What is its purpose? What is
      the standard format for an entry? What information that you
      expect is regularly omitted? What sort of person seems to require
      a shorter and what kind a longer entry?

3.   Keep track of any mentions of literacy and learning among the
      women. Do they preach or conduct Mass (the Eucharistic service)
      or Office? Do the women run the convent themselves?

4.   Does Sister Bartolomea have anything at all in common with
      Boccaccio and Petrarch? Do her writings belong to the Middle
      Ages or to the Renaissance? On what grounds would you answer
      that question? Does Burckhardt offer any help in placing Sister
      Bartolomea?

5.   Boccaccio and Petrarch belong to the "literary canon" of the
West—that is, a centuries-long tradition that says these works are
worth reading because they not only represent important aspects
of European culture, but also have something timeless to say
about the human condition. Why is Riccoboni's work *not* part of
that canon? Should or could it be?

Professor Frazier thus uses these decidedly nonhumanist texts, which document and describe life in a monastic institution—a way of life that had been
central to the spiritual economy of medieval Europe, and an institution that
had played an essential role in the preservation of classical texts through the
thousand years of the Middle Ages and their transmission to Renaissance
humanists—to raise questions of periodization, of historical continuity and
discontinuity, and of cultural filiation. She also invites reflection on issues
of canonicity and of the cultural hegemony it sustains, in short, the very
issues that underlie the entire editorial project of The Other Voice in Early
Modern Europe, which programmatically attacks the monolithic solidarity
of the traditional canon and aspires to construct by its side a new canon,
built of women's works.

Through still other questions, Professor Frazier calls her students' attention to the reflections in this convent chronicle and necrology of some
of the great events of the church at large: the Great Schism of the Western
church; the travails of Pope Gregory XII and his supporters; and the efforts,
ultimately successful, to resolve the schism at the Council of Constance.
It is in this context that the second half of Sister Bartolomea's chronicle
really comes into play, for it is here that Sister Bartolomea widens her gaze
to take in events outside the convent walls. These passages may be largely
irrelevant to a course on women and religion such as mine, or the similar
one that Elizabeth Wengler offers at the College of Saint Benedict and Saint
John's University, since they are devoted entirely to ecclesiastical politics
and the career of Pope Gregory XII. But these issues of ecclesiastical order
are an important subtopic for Professor Frazier's class on the Italian Renaissance and absolutely crucial to a course like the one David Peterson teaches
at Washington and Lee University on the history of the medieval church.
Reading Sister Bartolomea's vernacular narrative alongside the learned arguments of conciliar theorists effectively brings out the interplay of events and
ideas. When the city of Venice (where their convent was located) and the
Dominican order (to which it belonged) decided to accept as legitimate the
pope elected in 1409 by the Council of Pisa, the sisters of Corpus Domini
found their own loyalties divided. One-third of them sided with their city

and their order, and recognized the Pisan pope Alexander V as the true pope; the majority, however, remained aligned with the Roman pope Gregory XII, who to the very end was supported by the convent's founder and spiritual guide, Giovanni Dominici. A central chapter of Sister Bartolomea's chronicle describes how the sisters of Corpus Domini struggled to maintain the unity and harmony they so valued in a convent that was itself now divided by the schism that for decades had split the church at large. Professor Peterson uses this chapter to demonstrate how intimately and urgently ideas of church order could matter to cloistered nuns as well as to theologians, canon lawyers, and prelates. What is more, by pairing the convent chronicle and necrology with selected letters of Saint Catherine of Siena, Professor Peterson helps his students understand the unprecedented prominence that female mysticism, political visions, and prophetic authority came to assume during this period of prolonged institutional crisis.

Lu Ann Homza of the College of William and Mary opens her course on Reformation Europe with an extended consideration of the institutional travails, intellectual currents, and spiritual concerns of late medieval Christianity, which she presents as the essential context for understanding both the Protestant Reformation and the Catholic response to it. Again, Sister Bartolomea's description of the final phase of the Great Schism helps to ground and inform class discussion. But Professor Homza also pairs this reading with Thomas à Kempis's *The Imitation of Christ*, as evidence for late medieval spiritual ideals. This holds the potential of raising questions of canon formation analogous to those addressed by Alison Frazier, although in this case the canon comprises spiritual classics, not literary masterpieces. It certainly allows students to see how the ideals of the *imitatio Christi*, described by Thomas à Kempis as open to all, become active in the lives of particular individuals. And because the individuals in this case happen to be women, this pairing lends itself to a discussion of the gendering of that ideal and of late medieval piety in general. Students are invited to consider in what ways the sisters of Corpus Domini seem to be engaged in an imitation of Christ, how their various imitations of Christ were facilitated or hampered by their gender and/or their commitment to a cloistered religious life, how their gender affected their identification with and love for a God who is gendered male, and, more broadly, how their gender (and that of the author of *The Imitation of Christ*) shaped their religious outlook and experience.

One key function of religion is to provide comfort and meaning in the face of suffering, illness, and death. This aspect of faith is very much to the fore in the necrology of Corpus Domini, whose more or less brief biographies of the sisters who lived in the convent are occasioned by their deaths. Fortitude in the face of death was a standard virtue of martyrs, as bearing pain and disease with cheerful patience was commonplace in the lives of innumerable saints; these attitudes were particularly prominent in the passional spirituality characteristic of late medieval saints—especially female saints, in whose lives illness loomed disproportionately large. But the sisters of Corpus Domini were not saints: however much she may have thought their lives admirable and their deaths exemplary, Sister Bartolomea never presumed to cast them as anything more than devout and dedicated nuns, like the many thousands of others to be found in European convents. In gathering nearly fifty portraits of fairly ordinary religious women at the moment of their deaths, the necrology of Corpus Domini amounts to a manageable database—small but significant—for the historical sociology, as well as the spirituality, of death and dying. This is precisely how Sharon Strocchia of Emory University uses the necrology, in a freshman seminar on medicine in the age of plague. She assigns a variety of primary and secondary texts, such as recipe books based on herbal medicine, a physician's casebook, a gynecology tract, and contemporary accounts of plague. The necrology is included to give students a firsthand look at how contemporaries approached illness and death from a spiritual standpoint. Professor Strocchia reports an initial concern that students would fall back on stereotyped assumptions about powerless acceptance and resignation in the preantibiotic age, but that turned out not to be the case. Instead, the students picked up on the soaring transcendence of Sister Bartolomea's text and grasped her presentation of suffering as ennobling and redemptive. Their encounter with this unexpectedly inspiring text challenged their preconceptions in several respects. The sheer fact that Sister Bartolomea kept such a systematic record shook their assumption that medieval women were uneducated and illiterate. Her positive representation of women's lives and deaths called into question the misogynistic traditions, derived from humoral medicine and Aristotelian biology, that informed many of the other readings for the course. And the sheer variety of the religious institutions and devotional practices she described forced them to discard the notion of late medieval Christianity as oppressively monolithic.

The examples adduced in this brief conspectus show how Bartolomea Riccoboni's *Life and Death in a Venetian Convent* might be used in a variety of courses: on Renaissance Italy, the medieval church, women and religion, and illness and death. One could easily imagine other uses as well, in classes on the history of monasticism or of medieval and Renaissance Venice or of the operations of memory and the writing of history. This convent chronicle could be paired with the urban chronicles of Dino Compagni or Giovanni

Villani as examples of medieval historiography. The chronicle and necrology could be juxtaposed with the *Paternal Tyranny* or *Monastic Hell* of Arcangela Tarabotti, to give voice to two sharply different experiences of female monasticism. They could be read alongside Thomas of Siena's "Life of Maria of Venice,"[2] using these two records of women's lives in early Renaissance Venice—Thomas's biography of a Dominican penitent and Bartolomea's collective biography of Dominican nuns—to point up the intersections of household and convent, religion and society. It might even be read profitably by professed nuns, or by future nuns during their novitiate, as a source of information about their forebears and reinvigoration of their spiritual calling, as I learned to my surprise when I received an appreciative note from one such nun. Sister Bartolomea might have been no less surprised by such a note of thanks, coming from a reader nearly six hundred years after her death, on a continent unknown in her lifetime; but she would surely have been as pleased as I was to think that her works continue to serve the goal she had in mind as she wrote, "in order that those sisters who follow after us may be properly edified, and that they may have reason to praise the Lord for so many good things and be inspired to live well and follow through on this good beginning" (25). In contrast, the other academic uses to which my colleagues and I turn her humble records would have been utterly unimaginable to her, as conscious as she was of producing writings that were—in their vernacular language, popular format, and concern with women's lives—so completely extraneous to the world of formal learning in her day.

I use *Life and Death in a Venetian Convent* not only to open my seminar on women and religion in medieval Europe, but to close it as well. At the end of the course, I ask students to return to the very first source we read and reflect on how their perception of Bartolomea Riccoboni's chronicle and necrology of Corpus Domini has changed over the course of the semester. Rereading Sister Bartolomea's chronicle and necrology in this manner gives the students a chance to note and articulate something that university education is supposed to foster, but standard course evaluation forms are not designed to elicit: intellectual growth. Some choose to organize their reflections around a reconsideration of the issue they addressed in the first short essay, in which they identified a particular tension as characteristic of the monastic life. Others focus on something they had *not* noticed when

2. In *Dominican Penitent Women*, ed., trans., and introd. Maiju Lehmijoki-Gardner, with contributions by Daniel Bornstein and E. Ann Matter and preface by Gabriella Zarri (Mahwah, N.J.: Paulist Press, 2005).

they first read Sister Bartolomea's chronicle and necrology but that they had become sensitized to as they learned more about women and religion in medieval Europe. Many report a sort of desensitization: the penitential practices that had so shocked them at first sight now appear quite ordinary. In part, this may be nothing more than a sign that familiarity has succeeded novelty, as they have become inured to accounts of flamboyant asceticism. (As more than one student remarks, it is hard to be shocked by *anything* after reading about Catherine of Siena.) More often, however, this new outlook testifies to the very opposite of any dulling of their sensibilities. Their initial puzzlement and revulsion have been replaced by empathetic insight and understanding, by respect and even admiration for the life that the sisters of Corpus Domini have chosen for themselves. Among a student body not noted for its sympathy for modern feminism, and still less for premodern protofeminism, this is no small achievement. And it is certainly counterintuitive that it should result in good measure from reading texts in a conservative format, describing the traditional lives of women cloistered in an Observant Dominican convent, who looked resolutely backward to an idealized past.

II

Elite Women of the High Renaissance

TEACHING TORNABUONI'S
TROUBLESOME WOMEN

Jane Tylus

I have now shamelessly taught my translation of Lucrezia Tornabuoni's *Sacred Narratives* three times since its publication in 2001. Given the content of the narratives and the prominent stature of their author, Tornabuoni's work can probably be taught in any number of contexts—courses in art history, religion, women's studies, and Italian and comparative literature might all make use of her poems. Based on my own classroom experiences, I think that Tornabuoni's writings provide the most scintillating introduction to gender and religion in pre-Reformation Italy of any work I know, and students find that these almost cinematic *storie sacre* serve as points of reference for many of their other readings. In particular, they help to refine a question that haunted Tornabuoni's contemporaries: how could one best practice an authentic Christian life within the Renaissance city?[1]

As the stories show, this question haunted Tornabuoni too, Florence's prima donna for over two decades. Fifteenth-century Italy witnessed a renewed emphasis on the *vita mista*. This was a life that embraced the values of contemplation and action alike, opening up new possibilities for laymen and laywomen of the early Renaissance, while causing headaches for civic and ecclesiastical authorities attempting to regulate public actions. As David Cast has commented, this active life of Christians is represented in much of

---

1. One could introduce a number of works at this point as useful guides to the religious and spiritual dimensions of Florentine Renaissance life. Let me just restrict myself to two very helpful recent texts that can be nicely used to set the stage for class discussions on religion and the Florentine Renaissance: Gary M. Radke, "Masaccio's City: Urbanism, Architecture, and Sculpture in Early Fifteenth-Century Florence," in *The Cambridge Companion to Masaccio*, ed. Diane Cole Ahl (Cambridge: Cambridge University Press, 2002), 40–63; and Dale Kent, *Cosimo de' Medici and the Florentine Renaissance* (New Haven: Yale University Press, 2000), particularly chap. 9, "Expiation, Charity, Intercession."

the artwork of mid-quattrocento Tuscany in which Jesus is portrayed constantly engaging with others, ministering, preaching, and healing: a life, in short, of *ministrare*, during a moment when secular thinkers such as Leonardo Bruni and Leon Battista Alberti were advocating a return to the *vita activa* as a legacy of classical writers such as Cicero.[2] The famous frescoes painted by Masaccio and Masolino in the Brancacci chapel in Florence's Church of the Carmine dramatize the idea of exemplary Christians at work in the community, with their depictions from the Acts of the Apostles of early Christians ministering to the poor through alms and the sick through the laying on of hands. Thanks to the recognizably contemporary dress and familiar buildings from the artisans' neighborhood where the Carmine is located, this community is clearly Florence. Painted shortly before Tornabuoni's birth in 1427, the frescoes reflect not the conscious archaizing of Byzantine paintings, but a quotidian, urban landscape inhabited by Florentines that creates a new kind of immediacy and, indeed, urgency. Saint Peter administering alms or the healing of Tabitha gave spectators a link with the past, to be sure. But it was clearly in the present where such piety could live again. The works of Tornabuoni's contemporaries—and, I will argue, her own poems as well—seek to renew if not the actual events themselves, at least the active faith that made them possible.

In terms of Tornabuoni's poetry, this might appear a troublesome claim, especially when one considers the characters on whom Tornabuoni focused in her five *storie sacre*, or sacred narratives. Three of them are women from the Hebrew Bible (Esther) or the so-called Apocryphal books of the Old Testament (Judith and Susanna), whose unconventional female sexuality, as Athalaya Brenner has put it, leads them to avert danger "by mixing attractiveness, sense, and faith": they are heroines whose "active lives" involved killing tyrants, forcing their way into despots' courts, and defying corrupt elders.[3] A fourth is Tobias, who risks his life to bury the Jewish dead in a land hostile to the Hebrews and who charitably gives to fellow Hebrews in need. Finally, we have Florence's patron saint, John the Baptist, who, despite his attachment to Florence (or, more accurately, the Florentines' attachment to him), led an austere life that contrasted with that of a prosperous mid-fifteenth-century

---

2. "Humanism and Art," in Albert Rabil, ed., *Renaissance Humanism*, vol. 3, 416; cited in Peter Francis Howard, *Beyond the Written Word: Preaching and Theology in the Florence of Archbishop Antoninus: 1427–59* (Florence: Olschki, 1995), n. 241.

3. See the introduction to *A Feminist Companion to Esther, Judith, and Susanna*, ed. Athalya Brenner (Sheffield: Sheffield Academic Press, 1995), 12.

town. He is unconventional too, particularly in Tornabuoni's retelling. The stories dwell on characters who are in conflict with a community that in some ways resembled the one in which Tornabuoni was so prominent, and yet one that she also critiques. They thus challenge us and our students to ask what the relationship might be between these problematic figures and a Florentine society in which Tornabuoni may well have felt women deserved to play a significant spiritual role—a role she arguably wrote her *storie sacre* in order to define.

Given that most of our students are highly attuned to visual cues, the art of Tornabuoni's contemporaries can be a valuable resource with which to introduce her poetry. Tornabuoni's works are thus considerably enriched if they are placed not only in dialogue with their source texts but with the visual world that surrounded them and on which, I believe, they heavily drew. These additional resources can also help resolve a real challenge: how to capitalize on the students' inherent interest in these transgressive biblical figures while taking care to encourage them to appreciate historical and theoretical subtleties. Armed with a copy of the Bible (one containing the Apocryphal books of Judith and Tobias, as well as the twelfth chapter of Daniel) and some digital images, slides, or even serviceable photocopies of several key artistic works, one is, I believe, well prepared to delve into Tornobuoni's' works. And one is well prepared to ask why Tornabuoni and others of her era were so fascinated with generating a highly unstable model of Christian heroism, alternately gendered as either masculine or feminine. In the brief remarks that follow, I will elaborate on what that model might be, as well as on its implications for talking more generally to students about an "other" Renaissance.

AN OTHER VOICE?

How does one define an "other" Renaissance, and how might the rather privileged Tornabuoni have been part of one, with its intimations of marginality from a mainstream culture? She was, after all, the first lady of Florence during its golden age and, as recent research is stressing,[4] an undeniably central

---

4. See recent work of Natalie Tomas, *The Medici Women: Gender and Power in Renaissance Florence* (Hampshire: Ashgate, 2003); Stefanie Solum, "Women, Art, and Evidence: The Case of Lucrezia Tornabuoni de' Medici," paper given at the Annual Conference of the College Art Association, Atlanta, 2005; and Eleonora Plebani's *I Tornabuoni: una famiglia fiorentina alla fine del medioevo* (Milan: Franco Angeli, 2002).

figure in Florence's political, social, and artistic networks. Daughter-in-law of Cosimo de' Medici, wife of Piero, mother of Lorenzo "the Magnificent," she enjoyed a highly visible social role that permitted her informal if not formal access to the centers of power in "republican" Florence. To this extent, like other well-placed early modern women—Vittoria Colonna and Marguerite de Navarre come to mind—Tornabuoni wrote from a relatively privileged platform, with the charge of justifying the role of the Medici not only in Florence, but within Italy; it was she who went to Rome to interview—one can think of no better word—the young Clarice Orsini in order to discover if this member of one of Rome's most illustrious families might be a worthy mate for her eighteen-year-old son Lorenzo. She was an effective administrator who handled the family's rents in Pisa, oversaw a large family of children and grandchildren, and was responsible for much of the day-to-day running of the Medici's affairs during the period of her husband's lengthy sickness and Lorenzo's youth. Perhaps the most telling remark about Tornabuoni is that of her father-in-law Cosimo. No doubt reflecting on the debilitating illness of his son Piero, whose gout (or as recent DNA findings suggest, rheumatism) kept him confined to his room for months at a time, as well as on the youthfulness of his grandsons Lorenzo and Giuliano, Cosimo referred to Lucrezia as "the only man in the family" ("'l'unico uomo nella famiglia'").[5]

At the same time, you will want to take into account constraints on women's public and religious behavior, as articulated in contemporary writings by Matteo Palmieri, Archbishop Antoninus Pierozzi, and Leon Battista Alberti. Easily accessible in English, Alberti's restrictions on women's interventions into the public sphere as detailed in book 3 of *The Books of the Family* are a sobering backdrop to thinking about the role of patricians' wives.[6] While it is tempting to consider Tornabuoni's interactions alongside those of Isabella d'Este or Elisabetta Gonzaga who presided over the discussions in the *Courtier*, keep in mind that mid-fifteenth-century Florence did not boast the liberal courtly practices of small northern towns. Nor did its women host salons, as would famous *cortigiane* in sixteenth-century Venice. Theirs was instead a republican setting in which they were expected to subordinate their lives to their families, and they played no role in formulating Florence's political agendas. At the same time, these were only expectations; and Dante's vision in *Paradiso* XV–XVI of a community in which women were chaste,

5. Quoted in Maurizio Martinelli, *Al Tempo di Lorenzo* (Florence: FMG, 1992), 17.

6. Leon Battista Alberti, *The Family in Renaissance Florence*, trans. and introduced by Renée Neu Watkins (Columbia, S.C.: University of South Carolina Press, 1969).

modestly dressed, and subservient is a nostalgic one grounded less in reality than in idealizing norms of the sexes.[7] You might then play the ideology of republican Florence against the details of Tornabuoni's life as found in her letters (many translated by Yvonne Maguire) and from the accounts in the introductions to Patrizia Salvadori's edition of the *Lettere* and in my introduction to *Sacred Narratives*, F. William Kent's excellent article on Tornabuoni, and chapters 2 and 3 of Natalie Tomas's *Medici Women*.[8] Is Tornabuoni the subservient and obedient wife? Or do subservience and obedience take on different valences when one belongs to a city's most influential family—and thus is in the position to perform distinctive, even exceptional roles within the community?

GENDER TROUBLES: IMAGE TO NARRATIVE

Indeed, how unique are Tornabuoni's women, particularly in her two lengthy *storie sacre*? Are Judith and Esther meant to stand out as inimitable, or as exemplary—and if the latter is the case, what then are they exemplary of? As Paola Tinagli has noted, representations of Esther and Judith abound in Renaissance culture: in public sculptures and paintings as well as on *cassoni*, or wedding chests, utensils such as tankards, and bedroom furniture. Tinagli sees few reasons to question the ubiquity of these figures; after all, both women saved their people "and were [therefore] seen as exempla of civic behavior . . . Chastity, courage, and desire for justice are the recurring themes of these stories, which show no clear boundaries between private and public virtues."[9]

Such an interpretation argues for what one might call the "genderlessness" of an Esther or Judith particularly when they serve as strictly allegorical figures. When Botticelli, Pollaiuolo, and other midcentury Florentine artists were asked to depict the cardinal and theological virtues for the Mercanzia, they produced seven women seated magisterially on thrones; some

7. See the lines spoken by Dante's ancestor Cacciaguida in canto 15, particularly stanzas 112–26, in which he praises women who went about with their faces "unpainted" and praises those "happy wives" who "watch with loving care the cradle" and, drawing "threads from the distaff," tell stories of Trojans, Fiesole, and Rome. *Paradiso*, trans. Allen Mandelbaum (New York: Bantam, 1994).

8. Yvonne Maguire, *Women of the Medici* (London: Routledge, 1927); *Lettere: Lucrezia Tornabuoni*, ed. Patrizia Salvadori (Florence: Olschki, 1993); F. William Kent, "Sainted Mother, Magnificent Son: Lucrezia Tornabuoni and Lorenzo de' Medici," *Italian History and Culture* 3 (1997): 3–34; and Tomas, *The Medici Women*.

9. Paola Tinagli, *Women in Italian Renaissance Art* (Manchester: Manchester University Press, 1997), 31–32.

scholars have suggested that Botticelli modeled his figure for "Fortitude" on Judith herself. Other depictions of Judith are more evocative of her grisly role in the biblical narrative. Consider the Judith of Donatello, a sword in her upraised hand, who inhabited the courtyard of the Medici palace where Tornabuoni lived, or the fierce Amazon found in Baccio Baldini's engraving in London's British Museum. Here Judith may be reflective not of a cardinal virtue, but of an earlier Old Testament figure: the young David, slayer of Goliath, who was frequently paired with Judith in late medieval and Renaissance iconography as a weakling who with God's help defeats a tyrant.[10]

To what extent, however, do such monumentalizing representations "rob the Old Testament heroine of her seductive and potentially subversive power as a female exemplar," as Patricia Lee Rubin and Alison Wright have suggested?[11] How, that is, do these isolated images remove Judith from her troubling story in order to render her an abstraction or an innocuous double for David? Placing Judith and, as we will see, Esther back *into* their respective narratives will reintroduce questions that these single moments may serve to silence. And you can generate some interesting discussion on the differences between artistic examples that freeze their subject in time and those that encourage you to contextualize their subject within complex narratives.

Thus you might compare Donatello or Baldini with the fabulous small panel in the Uffizi of Botticelli's Judith painted in 1470, strolling dreamily through the countryside with a maid who balances Holofernes' head on her own head as though it were a basket of laundry (and some renditions, such as one of Artemisia Gentileschi's paintings, do place the head in a basket). As Ronald Lightbown has suggested, this early work of Botticelli's gives us a Judith who moves; and she moves, moreover, through a narrative that is elucidated below and behind her, as the Israelites leave the walled city of Bethulia to rout the Assyrians after Holofernes' death.[12] Unlike the static, statuary poses of Donatello's or Baldini's Judiths, this Judith is fluid, and she holds the paradoxical emblems of her action, a sword and an olive branch symbolizing the peace she will ensure for the Hebrews. And unlike the solitary Judiths of Donatello and Baldini, she is accompanied by her

---

10. For informative background on Judith and a good selection of illustrations, see Margarita Stocker, *Judith: Sexual Warrior, Women and Power in Western Culture* (New Haven: Yale University Press, 1998).

11. *Renaissance Florence: The Art of the 1470's* (New Haven: Yale University Press, 1999), 271.

12. Ronald Lightbown, *Sandro Botticelli, Life and Work* (New York: Abbeville Press, 1989), 37.

Figure 1: Donatello, *Judith and Holofernes* (1456). Bronze, 7′ 9″ (including base). Piazza della Signoria, Florence, Italy. Photograph © Alinari / Art Resource, New York.

maid—suggesting, as the Bible makes clear, that she has not performed her heroic deed alone. In fact, subsequent illustrations of Judith (those of Artemisia Gentileschi from the early 1600s, for example, or the gruesome Caravaggio painting on which Gentileschi based one of her works) show this as the work of *women*, not just a single woman. Holofernes is slain by a female community working together rather than by an Old Testament cipher modeled on King David. He is slain, moreover, by an attractive young woman dressed in contemporary Florentine garb, who might just as easily have appeared in Botticelli's later *Primavera* or *Adoration*—and who does, students quickly realize, appear in Tornabuoni's *Storia di Iudith*.

For if one prevailing iconographical tradition isolated Judith, capturing her in a heroic posture that desexualizes her and marks her in every way as unique, Tornabuoni, like Botticelli, does something different. Compare the opening of Judith 8 with stanza 87 of Tornabuoni's poem, where we first hear about Judith. The biblical Judith fasts, wears sackcloth, and mourns for three years; shut up in her tower, she is utterly isolated from her community, forcing the elders of Bethulia to visit her when it is time to reveal God's plan. Tornabuoni's Judith has none of these singular characteristics. Tornabuoni mentions only that "for three years [Judith] had lived alone as a widow," and after debating with herself as to whether or not she can "come up with some remedy" to the Hebrews' plight, she "rose up and instantly went out,/ going off to find her superiors." As students have observed, Tornabuoni refuses to isolate Judith in the exceptional ways we find in the Bible or in images that turn her into a solitary and sexless warrior. She works, rather, as part of the community, as is clear from her dealings with her trustworthy maid: she posts her as guard to Holofernes' chambers, instructing her to keep quiet, and then hands her the head. Afterwards Judith will not neglect to reward her with a dowry for her assistance, a detail not present in the Bible. Described as a *vedovetta*—a little widow, rather than just a widow—Judith in Tornabuoni's text does not possess the mysterious and aloof stature the Apocrypha or Donatello gives her. Nor does she retain her separateness at the text's end or have a special feast day commemorated in her name, as happens in Judith 16. It is true that Tornabuoni has Judith disappear— rather abruptly, it seems—from her *storia sacra*. Yet students have argued that she is simply reabsorbed into the community as Tornabuoni returns to the story about Nebuchadnezzar that occupied her for the first half of the poem, prompting us to reflect here as elsewhere on Tornabuoni's creativity vis-à-vis her source.

Tornabuoni's and Botticelli's Judiths offer an alternative to the iconographical tradition that made Judith abstract and unapproachable. Both

Figure 2: Sandro Botticelli, *Judith* (late fifteenth century?). Uffizi, Florence, Italy. Photograph © Scala / Art Resource, New York.

Florentines in fact can be said to have depicted Judith from Holofernes' perspective: the attractive, pleasant, modest Jewish widow who represents not war, but love: "When Holofernes saw her, he was set aflame: that ferocious heart of his became human" (97). They thus open up the discomfiting possibility that Professor Gerry Milligan noted during his class discussion of the text: "If women's beauty can deceive men and bring about disaster, then the Judith story marks a precarious territory in the biblical stories about women, since the biblical story seems to show God sanctioning the castrating potential of women's sexuality."[13] Does Tornabuoni try to guard against such a "sanction" by making Judith an allegorical figure for humility who vanquishes the pride displayed not only by Holofernes, but by Nabuc, with whom so much of her poem is concerned? Here you might look to Tornabuoni's opening about the sin of pride first embodied by that "handsome man" Lucifer. Other handsome men—the proud Nabuc, Holofernes who carefully dresses himself before the banquet—will obviously follow suit and suffer the same fate as the fallen angel. Yet Tornabuoni's details about Judith's life—her attentiveness to her maid's dowry, her willingness to meet the elders within the city, her own agitations when it comes time to kill Holofernes—give us a more complicated psychological portrait of the heroine than allegory would allow. As with Botticelli's painting, the movement from statuesque icon to beautiful young woman uncertain about how to proceed has the effect of humanizing Judith. While Tornabuoni does embrace the allegory of Judith's humility in severing a "proud neck," she does so in a way that implies that Judith's humility consists not only in her dependence on God, but in her lowly knowledge of the ways in which society works and her ability to insert herself within that society.

Esther too becomes more problematic when we move from the realm of iconography to that of narrative detail—and from the Hebrew Bible to Tornabuoni's retelling. Again, a contrast with an artistic work is instructive. You might use an image from Michelangelo's Sistine ceiling, his juxtaposition of the crucified Haman and virtuous Esther, or a panel from a *cassone* that opposes the "proud Queen Vashti"—it is Tinagli's phrase—to "virtuous Esther." On the surface, Tornabuoni too seems to sanction such static oppositions; Haman is clearly the despicable villain who tries to send the entire Hebrew community to its death, and Vashti the disobedient wife whose actions must be avoided at all costs: "Women, learn nothing from this queen:/ be prudent, and listen to my words/ with great care and discretion.// And if

13. Personal communication, February 2005, from a class taught at CUNY–Staten Island titled Women and Literature in Medieval and Early Modern Europe.

you do not think that what I say is right,/ consider Vashti; I myself would guess/ that much wretchedness befell her" (chapter 3). This was the standard interpretation of the consort who "responded in a strange and disrespectful manner" to her husband's request, which Ahasuerus links to "anger, or pride." Yet while Esther can hardly be accused of acting pridefully, students are genuinely puzzled as to why Vashti's act of disobedience is so very different from that of Esther in chapter 7. When it comes time, three chapters after Vashti's refusal, for Esther to enter Ahasuerus's court unannounced and thus violate the king's command, Tornabuoni adds disturbing lines not found in the Bible: once Ahasuerus admits that he is willing to listen to her, she says "to herself: 'Now I will have vengeance. / O my Lord, teach me how to speak / So I will know how to utter words that will persuade'" (chap. 6). Given that Esther's name in Hebrew derives from "I will hide" or "I am hiding," one might ask what Esther in fact conceals.[14] Is it more than just her Jewish identity—perhaps a forceful expression of will that arguably links her to Judith—and to Vashti?

I have found Mieke Bal's comments to be helpful here:

> Vashti is eliminated only to be restored as Esther, who takes her place and avenges her by reformulating disobedience as achieving power. Vashti's refusal to be an object of display is in a sense a refusal to be objectivized . . . Esther appears not for show but for action, not as mere possession but as self-possessed subject.[15]

Bal is speaking of the biblical book of Esther, but one can use her remarks to prompt a thoughtful discussion of Tornabuoni: Does her own narrative work against her warning to women in chapter 3 that they should avoid acting like Vashti? Or could it be that the real difference between the two women consists in their ability to "please" their consort and disguise their real intentions—a manipulation at which Esther is adept and Vashti is not? Might the story of Esther offer a model for women's participation within the court, through indirection, masquerade, and strategic "pleasing"? Such has been the suggestion of several students, while others go further and note that the importance of being "pleasing" characterizes not just the women's relationship to the court, but the men's as well. Ahasuerus works hard to ensure that the barons who dine with him in chapter 1 have all that they wish: "to make his guests even more contented/ the king chose singers who

---

14. For an interesting meditation on Esther's name, see Timothy K. Beal, *The Book of Hiding: Gender, Ethnicity, Annihilation, and Esther* (London: Routledge, 1997).

15. Mieke Bal, "Lots of Writing," in *A Feminist Companion to the Bible: Ruth and Esther*, 233.

could please them; all/ with sweet melodies and skillful harmonies / . . . don't ask if there was anything there that displeased them" (chap. 2). Later he will do everything he can to make Esther happy. Haman, like the disrespectful Vashti, becomes the anticourtier, the would-be tyrant who "did not know how to be liberal and kind."

As one of my students, Tracey Citron, has suggested, to find such emphasis on "kindness and liberality," one does not have to go to Castiglione's *Courtier*. In her final paper on Esther, Citron cites the putative deathbed advice of Giovanni de' Bicci de' Medici to his son Cosimo, future patriarch of the Medici family and father-in-law of Lucrezia Tornabuoni: "Never hold an opinion contrary to the will of the people. . . . Do not speak with the air of giving counsel, but prefer rather to discuss matters gently and benevolently. Do not turn the palace into a shop; on the contrary, wait for the people to invite you . . . Be as inconspicuous as possible."[16] As Bicci's words suggest, such "pleasing" overtones can be fundamentally deceptive, a way of masking one's interests in gaining power. But it also suggests that the code of (apparent) submission and pleasure to which Esther has subscribed is a mark not only of wifely obedience: did not men have to be Esthers too? Such a stance does not necessarily mean that the men of the court are feminized, as has been argued for the courtiers in Castiglione's text. It may simply mean that the art of "pleasing" was a function of the courtly society the Medici were trying to introduce into Florence; and Tornabuoni goes to great trouble to depict an ideal court in her first two chapters, expanding at what may seem to be tedious length the terse description in the Bible.[17] Why, Tornabuoni may be asking, should the expression of courtesy detract from the greatness of a king—or queen? Is courtesy not rather the hallmark of a civilized society, and why should it conflict with a Christian one or be used as a distinction of gender?

The "active lives" that Tornabuoni's Judith and Esther pursue as "self-possessed subjects" reflect an intimate knowledge of the communities in which they live—in contrast to their stature in the Bible and in a later iconographical tradition: "only by remaining unique and apart can Judith be

16. Quoted in J. Lucas Dubreton, *Daily Life in Florence at the Time of the Medici* (New York: Macmillan, 1961), 52.

17. Envisioning Ahasuerus's court as a Florentine palazzo was not only Tornabuoni's feat. A beautifully preserved *cassone* panel at the Metropolitan Museum of Art has Esther celebrating her feast in Medicean Florence. Ahasuerus's cortege processes to Esther's house on the left side of the panel, passing in front of Florence's baptistery, and the ensuing banquet is held in a loggia similar to that where Tornabuoni's daughter Nannina and Giovanni Ruccellai's son held their wedding festivities in 1466—the Rucellai's imposing loggia across from their palace.

tolerated, domesticated, and even treasured by Israelite society."[18] Yet these are communities in which they are not always at home, as one of Esther's remarks to God in her despairing prayer of chapter 6 makes clear: "I have always been timid and shy, / I would not have been happy as queen/ had I not kept my mind, Lord, fixed on you." Esther's timidity may be questionable, but her critique of the pagan court in which she lives is not. And it is such a critique that might link these troublesome Jewish heroines to the outspoken male characters in Tornabuoni's other poems.

JOHN THE BAPTIST AND HIS "PESSIMA LINGUA"

One of the most fascinating documents of mid-fifteenth-century Florence is the *"Facezie"* of the parish priest known as "Arlotto," who recorded anecdotes about the city's rich and powerful as well as its downtrodden over a period of years. One story he relates was told to him by Piero de' Medici, Lucrezia's husband, about a poor shoemaker whose prayers to Florence's patron saint, John the Baptist, went unanswered. In anger, the cobbler chides the saint for what he calls his *"pessima lingua,"* or cursed tongue: "When you were alive, you never said anything that wasn't unpleasant, and it was because of your cursed tongue that Herod cut off your head!"[19]

The phrase is not from Tornabuoni's life of the Baptist, but it might have been. When Herodias, Herod's scheming wife, tries to convince her husband to have John killed, she asks him, "Why on earth do you listen to this critic, / this barking dog who has riled up the entire nation?"—a man who "loves [only] to look like a great saint" rather than be one (99–100). In criticizing a Herod who has taken his brother's widow as his wife, in demanding that Herod's contemporaries change their lives—the proud Pharisees, the stingy publicans, the violent knights—John uses his *"pessima lingua"* to full effect. The austerities of his life, moreover, on which Tornabuoni spends numerous stanzas, contrast starkly not only with the comforts of his home and the tenderness of his parents, but with the sumptuous banquet at Herod's court where Herodias's daughter will dance: "The banquet was elegantly prepared, / with beautiful cloths and valuable ornaments; and each lord came with his ministers and servants / . . . and they were seated at the table to dine, / where

18. Amy-Jill Levine, "Sacrifice and Salvation: Otherness and Domestication in the Book of Judith," in *Feminist Companion to Esther, Judith, and Susanna*, 218–19.

19. ("tu non dicesti mai altro che male e per la tua pessima lingua ti fue tagliato il capo da Erode.") Piovano Arlotto, *Motti e Facezie*, ed. Gianfranco Folena (Milan and Naples, 1953), 40, facezia 23.

every sort of food was prepared in abundance" (126–27). John's tongue will be silenced during this very banquet, but in a grotesque image original to Tornabuoni's account, the queen, still haunted by John's words, "weeps for the trials she had suffered—too many/—and hurls the head about her, here, and there, / and did nothing else under the sun" (145–46). The chastisements of this *pessima lingua* have driven Herodias mad.

Tornabuoni's retelling of the story of John is her most marked departure from a biblical narrative, while it also relies on contemporary treatments drawn from medieval saints' lives, such as the fresco cycle in nearby Prato's cathedral. Painted in the 1450s by Filippo Lippi, it depicts John's departure from his aging parents, his lonely sojourn in the desert, and Salome's seductive dance before Herod and his guests. Yet it is clear that Tornabuoni herself, as she remarks at the end of her poem, had a "special devotion" to the Baptist. She was the patron of another work of Filippo Lippi's, *"Adoration in the Woods,"* originally painted for the private Medici chapel in their palazzo on the Via Larga.[20] It is a nocturnal scene in which Mary kneels devoutly before the infant Jesus, a youthful John in desert garb looks out to the spectator, and the background emphasizes the austere landscape into which Christ was born. No doubt Tornabuoni's devotion to John was prompted largely by his status as Florence's patron. Yet the severity with which Lippi portrays him in both the *"Adoration"* and in the fresco cycle in Prato and Tornabuoni's insistence on John as a man apart from his society indicate the extent to which their Baptist would have been at odds with the comfortable and colorful world in which contemporary Florentines lived. The head of John presented to Herodias in Lippi's fresco shows a gaunt and enfeebled face. Tornabuoni will stress rather his youthfulness and strength of purpose, although it is a purpose—as was no doubt that of Lippi's Baptist—clearly in conflict with that of his era. As her husband's shoemaker found out, he was not a saint who necessarily told people what they wanted to hear.

Neither did Judith or Esther. Connections with their stories abound, and they seem to coalesce around fateful and, for some, fatal banquets. Like Judith standing before Holofernes, Herodias's daughter "seemed as though she was sent from heaven" (131); like the banquet Esther serves to Haman

20. See Maurizio Martinelli's comment that the larger *Adoration* by Gozzoli in the chapel is suggestive of Tornabuoni's shorter poems, her *laude* (*Al tempo di Lorenzo*). Although I have not focused on them in this article, these poems can be used to discuss more private forms of devotional literature connected in most cases to feast days in the liturgical year: Epiphany, Holy Week, Pentecost, Christmas. Professor Stefanie Solum is currently working on a full-length study of Tornabuoni's artistic commissions, including the Lippi painting. It may be possible that Tornabuoni was the guiding spirit for the chapel as a whole.

Figure 3: Filippo Lippi, *The Virgin, Adoring the Child, with Saints John the Baptist and Bernard of Siena* (The Adoration in the Forest; ca. 1459). Oil on poplar, 129.5 × 118 cm. Inv. 69. Photograph by Joerg P. Anders. Gemaeldegalarie, Staatliche Museen zu Berlin, Germany. Photograph © Bildarchiv Preussischer Kulturbesitz / Art Resource, New York.

before she reveals his plotting against the Jews—"I will not mention all the wines that were suited to each dish" (200)—the meal Herod offers his neighboring princes is rich and resplendent. In each example, a character specifically *unsettles*, through word and deed, a festive occasion on which Tornabuoni lavishes fond details, and the result is, in all three cases, death: for Haman, for Holofernes, for John. Tornabuoni's other two *storie sacre* might be brought in here as well. When Susanna protests the elders' demand, she contests societal order by revealing the corruption of the Hebrew authorities, choosing her own death over submission to the elders' desires: "She began to shriek loudly / and the elders began to cry out too, / uttering against Susanna the [false] accusation" (64). Her impassioned prayer to God after she is sentenced to death allows the young Daniel to utter his first prophetic words and overturn the corrupt judges. Tobias rejects the king's orders that the bodies of the Jewish dead be left unburied. In fact, when he hears that a Hebrew youth has been killed and his body left in the piazza, he leaves the banquet in which he is feasting "and [takes] that body, darkened and stained, / and secretly carrie[s] it to his house" (82). And in a line that can be said to resonate throughout all of Tornabuoni's work, once Tobias returns to eat his bread, he remembers, in sorrow and fear, "the words that God himself had uttered/ through his prophet Amos, who said,/ 'The days of your feasting will turn / to lamentation.'"

Tornabuoni's protagonists are all, in effect, troublemakers who either speak out against the contemporary mores and injustice of their time—and pay, as in John's case, the price—or deftly use those mores in order to lure their enemies into a false sense of security and ultimately defeat them. And yet students note that John is different from Tornabuoni's other figures, all of whom, in one way or another, end their difficult stories with feasting, real or metaphorical, their lamentations over. Susanna is vindicated, and her family and townspeople rejoice; Tobias's reunited family holds a "great banquet" for seven days (112); upon Judith's return to Bethulia the people "feast and take pleasure" (146); in *The Story of Esther* the Hebrews hold great festivities once Haman's family and associates (75,000!) are killed in a massive vendetta, thus initiating the festival of Purim (213). John is restored in a way to his own people, as his disciples bury his body "with much reverence and care" (158), but the close of the story is understandably muted. We know, of course, that John will "live again" in the heaven that his cousin Jesus promises his followers and in the poem that Tornabuoni writes. Yet his lightning-like movement through the course of the narrative, his willful isolation from everything reasonably resembling society—"my home must be the desert" (44)—and his insistence on changing one's life, all suggest a figure resolutely outside of the social networks in which Tornabuoni's other heroes and heroines find their raison d'être, their beginning and their end.

Why is this the case, and what, finally, is its meaning for Tornabuoni's work with regard to its religious contexts? Students have suggested that the unique characteristics in *The Story of John* may reflect the difference, in Tornabuoni's mind, between the Hebrew narratives and the New Testament one, and thus between rewards enjoyed in this life—a particular focus of the story of Tobias—and those that must be delayed to the afterlife. The Old Testament and Apocryphal stories are about the earthly survival of an individual and of a people. John's New Testament story discounts survival in this life as an option because the next life offers the only true paradise. Others suggest that the tales are not necessarily happy endings: does not Susanna have to live with the shame of what she has suffered? But Susanna returns to her family, while John finally cannot be absorbed into any earthly community; his only home is the desert. That Florence should have had such a figure as John for its patron saint is worthy of comment. Is he not potentially a continual critic of Florentine society? And does the fact that the other protagonists in Tornabuoni's texts eventually return to "feasting" mean that their own tongues and deeds are more acceptable than John's? Does John's very presence in Tornabuoni's oeuvre help to normalize her troublesome women, rendering their stories quaint histories with which the urgency of John's mission effectively contrasts? Finally, does John's forthrightness throw a potentially negative light on the "performances" of Esther and Judith? What is being said about the power of the bodies and words of these women who seduce their audiences, while John lashes out at his?

Unanswerable as these questions are, they nonetheless focus discussion on the rationale for Tornabuoni's poems, no doubt considered by her to be for private rather than public dissemination, unlike the *sacre rappresentazioni* or sacred plays written by Feo Belcari (whom she patronized), Antonia Pulci, and her own son Lorenzo.[21] As such, they could invite reflection and rereading and were not required to represent or invite any sympathetic response on behalf of the powerful family to which Tornabuoni belonged. She herself, we must imagine, was thus free to puzzle, and to ask her readers or listeners to puzzle, over the problematic sacrifices the individual might

21. A class that focuses on Italian Renaissance literature could bring these three figures together, or, if taught in English, the last two: Pulci's *sacre rappresentazioni* are available in James Cook's translation from the University of Chicago Press (revised edition in preparation), and Lorenzo's *Rappresentazione di Ss. Giovanni e Paolo* can be found in the University of Manchester edition of his works. Pulci's works, like those of Tornabuoni, feature strong-minded women prepared to go to their deaths, such as Domitilla, or to work on behalf of their society, such as Saint Guglielma. Lorenzo's play also features an outspoken female character, the emperor's daughter Costanza, who, saved from leprosy, converts to Christianity and refuses to marry the general her father has chosen for her; see my "Charitable Women: Hans Baron's Civic Renaissance Revisited," in *Rinascimento* 43 (2004): 287–307. In "Adjusting the Canon for Later Fifteenth-Century Florence: The Case of Antonia Pulci," in *The Renaissance Theatre: Texts, Performance, Design*, ed. Christopher Cairns (Aldershot: Ashgate, 1999), Judith Bryce suggests that it is not at all unlikely that Tornabuoni and Antonia Pulci knew each other. See her suggestion on page 141 that Pulci's and Tornabuoni's "appropriation and rewriting of authoritative texts which would enable them to speak, however problematically, as women," could and should be conceived as a challenge to traditional authorities.

be asked to make in order to assist the *bene comune*. While any sacrifices
Tornabuoni herself might have made would obviously pale in comparison
with those of her biblical protagonists, she was repeatedly asked by her
own people to serve as an advocate, a go-between, an intercessor like Mary
(and, for that matter, like Esther herself)—even to the point where an ex
voto statue of her was found in the Duomo despite ecclesiastical roles
forbidding such statues in Florence's central church.[22] Her poems stage the
demands imposed on apparently ordinary individuals, demands dictated as
much by present and immediate dangers—the cases of Judith and Esther and
arguably Tornabuoni herself at times of trouble in the Florentine community,
such as after the Pazzi conspiracy of 1478—as by a sense of loyalty and
responsibility to a tradition, as in the *storie sacre* about Tobias and John. Less
spectacular modes of intervention involve prayer, traditionally associated
with women, and successful intercessions are made by both Susanna and Sara
in the Book of Tobias. Yet prayer is also the vehicle of Mordecai and
Tobias (as it is in the stylized yet intimate *laude* of Tornabuoni herself,
particularly "O Signor mio" [269] and "Contemplate my sufferings, O sinner"
[275]). These very different figures, in short, presented Tornabuoni and
her contemporaries with a wide range of possible responses to individual
and communal crisis. Perhaps because of that range, Tornabuoni chose to
translate the lives of mostly late-first-century personalities who were far more
developed and complex than their Deuteronomic predecessors. As Amy-Jill
Levine has noted, "they are rarely ideal figures; they are morally ambiguous
and not always clearly motivated; they are torn between secular and divine
interests."[23]

   Was Tornabuoni so torn? And does her portrait of John—probably her
most sophisticated poem, and perhaps her last one—reveal her unease with a
worldly life that attempted to embed Christian practice comfortably within
it rather than making such practice a radical force questioning from without?
To return to where I began and to where one might wish to begin with
one's students: in the 1420s, Masaccio's and Masolino's frescoes gave us one
response to the question as to how and whether Christian action might fit
neatly within the modern world. So do the frescoes from the life of John the
Baptist painted by Domenico Ghirlandaio in the Tornabuoni chapel in Santa
Maria Novella a few years after Tornabuoni's death in 1482—one of which

22. Noted in F. William Kent, *Lorenzo de' Medici and the Art of Magnificence* (Baltimore: Johns
Hopkins University Press, 2004).
23. Amy-Jill Levine, "'Hemmed in on Every Side': Jews and Women in the Book of Susanna,"
in *Feminist Companion to Esther, Judith, and Susanna*, 305.

Figure 4: Domenico Ghirlandaio, *Zachariah and the Angel* (late fifteenth century?). S. Maria Novella, Florence, Italy. Photograph © Scala / Art Resource, New York.

portrays Tornabuoni herself, presiding over John the Baptist's birth (an allusion to her having given "birth" to John through her poem?). In another scene, in which the angel announces to Zachariah John's imminent birth, Ghirlandaio has inscribed on a Roman arch the inscription, "Painted in the year 1490, when the most beautiful city, with its riches, victories, activities and buildings, was enjoying well-being and peace."[24] Unlike Donatello's gaunt John or Filippo Lippi's frescoes in Prato's cathedral, there are no indications here of penitence and renunciation; John's life unfolds within the walls and sublime architecture of a beautiful city. Yet within four years, the "well-being and peace" of Medicean Florence gave way to the autos-da-fé and an attack on the supposed balance between classicizing and Christian norms to which Ghirlandaio's serene frescoes lay claim as Savonarola, like John, took up the cry of repentance for Florence's sins. Do Tornabuoni's writings possess the serenity and self-confidence of Ghirlandaio's paintings, in which she herself is figured? Or do they suggest a different relationship between the individual and the community of which he or she is—and sometimes, is not—a part?

24. "An. MCCCCLXXXX quo pulcherrima civitas opibus victorus artibus aedificiis que nobilis copia salubritate pace per fruebatur."

ANTONIA PULCI (CA. 1452–1501), THE
FIRST PUBLISHED WOMAN PLAYWRIGHT
Elissa Weaver

Antonia Pulci[1] published at least five religious plays in Florence in the 1490s, three of which were included in an important anthology that contained plays by Feo Belcari and her husband Bernardo Pulci along with a number of anonymous plays, some, possibly two, of which may also be hers. Her plays all belong to the genre of *sacra rappresentazione*, one-act verse plays whose subjects are biblical and hagiographical; one is a moral allegory. I have taught her plays in courses on Italian theater, on Italian women's literature, and on the writing of women in Europe and New Spain in the early modern period. Her plays could also be included in a course devoted to religious theater or to the literature and culture of Florence at the time of Lorenzo de' Medici. The volume of the Other Voice series devoted to Antonia Pulci[2] has been revised and now includes the Italian text as well as the English translation of the plays; the corpus of plays has also been

---

1. Antonia Pulci was known in her time by her own name, Antonia Tanini; however, since she married Bernardo Pulci, an important literary figure in late-fifteenth-century Florence, and because little was known about her until recently, modern scholars have rechristened her with the anachronism. Based on an incorrect identification of her family made by Francesco Flamini in the late nineteenth century, she has been called Antonia Giannotti by the few twentieth-century scholars who have made reference to her or edited her work. Archival documents prove that she was instead Antonia Tanini, the daughter of Francesco d'Antonio Tanini and a woman from Rome, Jacopa Torelli. See Elissa Weaver, "Antonia Tanini (1452–1501), Playwright, and Wife of Bernardo Pulci (1438–88)," in *Essays in Honor of Marga Cottino-Jones*, ed. Laura White, Andrea Fedi, and Kristin Phillips (Fiesole [Florence]: Edizioni Cadmo, 2003), 23–37 .

2. Antonia Pulci, *Florentine Drama for Convent and Festival: Seven Sacred Plays*, ed. James Wyatt Cook and Barbara Collier Cook, trans. and annotated by James Wyatt Cook, The Other Voice in Early Modern Europe (Chicago: University of Chicago Press, 1997).

modified to include only plays that can be securely attributed to her, one of which was unknown at the time of the earlier edition (1997) of Pulci in the Other Voice series.[3] The new edition includes the *Saint Domitilla Play*, *Saint Guglielma Play*, *Saint Francis Play*, *The Prodigal Son*, and *The Death of Saul and the Tears of David.*[4]

The *sacra rappresentazione* was a theatrical form that flourished in Florence in the latter half of the fifteenth century, following on a tradition of public religious spectacles that dramatized the history of redemption from the Creation and Fall to the Resurrection, Ascension, and Pentecost. The new tradition translated these mysteries into words and actions that sought to entertain fifteenth-century Florentines in order to educate them to be good Christians and good citizens. To the biblical repertoire, playwrights added morality plays and saints' lives, which, as the century wore on, were characterized increasingly by frightening representations of martyrdom and elements of romance, which contributed to their entertainment value.[5] The course that would best put Pulci's work in perspective would be one devoted to religious theater in Florence or in a broader European context. Since there were remarkable similarities among the religious theatrical traditions throughout Europe, the course could easily include examples of mystery, miracle, and morality plays from other European traditions. I have, however, also taught her plays and other *sacre rappresentazioni* in the first segment of a general survey of Italian Renaissance theater.

3. Antonia Tanini Pulci, *Saints' Lives and Biblical Stories for the Stage (1483–92)*, ed. Elissa Weaver, trans. James Wyatt Cook, The Other Voice in Early Modern Europe (Chicago: University of Chicago Press, forthcoming).

4. In Italian, *Rappresentazione di Santa Domitilla*, *Rappresentazione di Santa Guglielma*, *Rappresentazione di San Francesco*, *Rappresentazione del figliuol prodigo*, and *Rappresentazione della distruzione di Saul e del pianto di Davit.*

5. On how scenes of torture and death may have been staged, see Nerida Newbigin, "Agata, Apollonia, and Other Martyred Virgins: Did Florentines Really See These Plays Performed?" in *European Medieval Drama 1997: Papers from the Second International conference on Aspects of European Medieval Drama, Camerino, July 4–6, 1997*, ed. Sydney Higgins (Camerino: Centro Audiovisivi e Stampa Università di Camerino, 1998), 175–97. The *Saint Guglielma Play* best exemplifies the romance element in Pulci's opus; its sources and analogues have been studied by Alessandro D'Ancona in the introduction to his edition of the play. See A. D'Ancona, ed., *Sacre rappresentazioni dei secoli XIV, XV e XVI*, 3 vols. (Florence: Successori Le Monnier, 1872), 3: 199–208; see also the excellent recent study by Judith Bryce, "'Or altra via mi convien cercare': Marriage, Salvation, and Sanctity in Antonia Tanini Pulci's *Rappresentazione di Santa Guglielma*," in *Theatre, Opera, and Performance in Italy from the Fifteenth Century to the Present: Essays in Honour of Richard Andrews*, ed. Brian Richardson, Simon Gilson, and Catherine Keen, Occasional Papers, 6 (Leeds: Society for Italian Studies, 2004), 23–38.

MYSTERY, MIRACLE, AND MORALITY PLAYS:
ENGLAND AND ITALY

If the course on this genre is to be taught in English, then it would be help-ful, and productive of new insights, to study the Florentine tradition of *sacre rappresentazioni* in the context of European medieval theater, looking at texts and also their performance history: the occasions, the convents, monaster-ies, guilds, confraternities, and other religious and civic organizations that sponsored and staged the plays, the actors and (sometimes) actresses who performed them, their audiences, the music that accompanied the action, the costumes, and the stages on which they were performed. Modernized texts and general information on English medieval theater are readily available and could serve as a useful comparison to highlight shared characteristics and local differences in the traditions. Theatrical festivals that staged the story of Redemption from the Creation of the world through the Final Judgment were part of both early vernacular traditions; in each an *Abraham and Isaac* play has survived that could be used to illustrate the dramatic potential of the biblical story (Gn 22).[6] Other late-fifteenth-century English plays could be read together with the five plays by Antonia Pulci that appear in the Other Voice series and Lorenzo de' Medici's *Rappresentazione di San Giovanni e Paolo* (*The Play of Saints John and Paul*), also available in a bilingual Italian/English edition.[7] Morality plays replaced the mystery and miracle plays in England; in Italy it was the miracle play that enjoyed greatest popularity.

This would ideally be a multimedia course using recordings of modern performances of medieval plays and slides showing drawings and models of sets (some excellent ones have been made for exhibitions in the recent past). A class project could be the performance of one of Pulci's plays. In my theater courses I always stress recitation of brief passages or scenes in order to provide some idea of the difference between silent reading and perfor-mance. A dramatic reading of the texts reveals subtleties of the action and of the interrelationship of characters that can be missed in silent reading; and to appreciate the literary and dramatic qualities of the play, it is important to hear the music of the verse. The instructor or, preferably, a student should

6. The English text is anonymous; the Italian is Feo Belcari's *Abramo quando volse sacrificare Isaac* (Abraham When He Decided to Sacrifice Isaac). See *Nuovo corpus di sacre rappresentazioni fiorentine del Quattrocento*, ed. Nerida Newbigin (Bologna: Commissione per i testi di lingua, 1983).

7. The *Rappresentazione di San Giovanni e Paolo* in the original and in an English verse translation is published in *Lorenzo de' Medici: Selected Writings*, ed. and trans. Corinna Salvadori (Dublin: Belfield Italian Library, 1992).

occasionally read aloud a stanza of the Italian text so the class can hear the rhythm of the narrative octaves, their six-line development, and the concluding couplet.[8] The *Santa Guglielma* would be a good choice for a dramatic reading or a full performance, not only for its religious message but also its entertainment value. It portrays betrayal, peril, a heavenly apparition, miraculous cures, scenes of prayer, and an argument for the superiority of a celibate life of contemplation and prayer over matrimony, which is seen as a life fraught with physical and spiritual dangers. The class could also recite or perform scenes from different plays chosen to highlight the themes characteristic of Pulci's work: the value of virginity in this life and for salvation, the importance of almsgiving and caring for the poor, and faith and the power of prayer. Women became important protagonists of the *sacre rappresentazioni* in the late fifteenth century, when the subject of virgin martyrs was one of the most often dramatized. Scenes featuring women in Pulci's plays could be selected to open up discussion of the playwright's attitude toward their social roles and the possibility of female agency. Her plays present not only virgins (the virgin martyr Domitilla and the daughter of the Philistine king), but also wives and mothers (Guglielma, the wife of the Philistine king, Saul's wife and the mother of his martyred sons, and the mother of Saint Francis), and widows (Saul's widow and Jacopa, a friend of Saint Francis).

THE FLORENTINE SACRA RAPPRESENTAZIONE

Antonia Pulci's plays would have a place of importance in a course devoted exclusively to the *sacra rappresentazione* in Italy, since her work was known and published in her lifetime and had a lasting legacy. Her plays were read and performed throughout the sixteenth century and well into the seventeenth. Moreover, they are representative of all the variations of the genre popular in the late fifteenth century. Even such a course taught entirely in Italian (or in English but using Italian texts)[9] should begin with a general discussion of medieval religious theater in Europe. Then, following an overview of the situation in northern and central Italy, areas in which similar traditions were cultivated, I would move quickly to Florence, where the particular form of religious theater we call *sacra rappresentazione* was developed and flourished.

8. James Cook has included some rhyme and assonance in his translations and an occasional octave with the original rhyme scheme.

9. Until such time as a sufficient number of English translations are available.

In this version of the course I would choose to stress the historical context, especially the religious history of fifteenth-century Florence. Since students are likely to be unfamiliar with the structure and organization of religious life in the fifteenth-century city, readings should be assigned to familiarize them with the Florentine Church: the reformers, Bishop Antoninus and Girolamo Savonarola; and the parish churches, convents and monasteries, confraternities, and youth organizations, many of which sponsored theatrical events.[10] I would assign Nerida Newbigin's account of the celebration of the city's patron saint, Saint John the Baptist, on June 24, and two of the texts in her collection that were written and performed for that occasion: Piero di Mariano Muzi's *Festa del vitello sagginato* (The Play of the Fatted Calf), which takes its subject from the biblical parable (Lk 15:11–32), and Feo Belcari's *Abramo quando volse sacrificare Isaac* (Abraham When He Decided to Sacrifice Isaac).[11] Except for its opening scene in which the prodigal son plays and loses at cards, Pulci's *Figliuol prodigo* follows rather closely the structure of Muzi's play, and Castellano Castellani's play on the same subject seems to take from both his predecessors. All three plays are available in modern Italian editions. Their analysis and comparison can be used to elicit class discussion of the different interests and personal styles of the three authors and to raise the issue of audience. Can we demonstrate the interdependence of the texts? How do they relate to one another? How does each play address its audience, both directly and indirectly? Do all three plays imagine a similar audience? The publication of the plays and especially of two collections of them in the 1490s has led some scholars to think that they were being written for devotional reading purposes rather than performance.

The subjects of Antonia Pulci's plays are primarily biblical and hagiographical. The *Rappresentazione di Santa Domitilla*, her earliest play, dated 1483, is taken from the *Legenda Aurea* life of Nereus and Aquileius, the two servants who converted the Roman gentlewoman Flavia Domitilla to Christianity and who, like her, were martyred. The *Santa Guglielma* follows rather closely,

10. I have assigned general introductions such as Gene Brucker's chapter "The Church and the Faith," in *Renaissance Florence* (Berkeley: University of California Press, 1983), and Richard Trexler's chapter "Institutions" in his *Public Life in Renaissance Florence* (Ithaca: Cornell University Press, 1991); and I have found quite useful two articles that appeared in the collection edited by Charles Trinkaus and Heiko Oberman, *The Pursuit of Holiness in Late Medieval and Renaissance Religion* (Leiden: Brill, 1974): Marvin Becker's "Aspects of Lay Piety in Early Renaissance Florence" and Richard Trexler's "Ritual in Florence: Adolescence and Salvation in the Renaissance."

11. *Nuovo corpus*, ed. Newbigin. The festival for the patron saint's feast is discussed, ix–l.

but with some significant differences, a prose life of the saint that survives today in two manuscript copies held at the Florentine Biblioteca Nazionale. Domitilla is a virgin martyr who has chosen a heavenly spouse over an earthly one, and the play denounces marriage as a state characterized only by disappointment and suffering. Guglielma is a wife falsely accused of infidelity and persecuted, who vindicates herself, converts her accuser, and persuades both him and her husband to join her in a life of prayer and contemplation. These two exemplary lives indicate paths to virtue and salvation for the two principal *stati*, or categories of women of the time, the virgin and the wife. Another model for women can be found in a long scene at the end of Pulci's play the *Rappresentazione della distruzione di Saul e del pianto di Davit*. Following the dramatization of the Old Testament story of Saul's battle with the Philistines, the death of his sons, his suicide, and David's grief (1 Sm 31 and 1 Chr 10:10, 13–14), there is an episode that finds no precedent in scripture: it is the torture and martyrdom of Saul's wife. This scene is the most original in all of Pulci's work. The wife of Saul is represented as a strong-willed, clever, and verbally agile woman, who will not be intimidated by the king of the Philistines; she challenges the questions and offers he puts to her, and her faith in God is unshaken by his threats of torture and death. Even the *Saint Francis Play* includes two active and compassionate female characters: the saint's mother, who disobeys her husband to show kindness and love for her son, and Jacopa da Settesoli, a Roman widow and friend of the saint, who attends to him on his deathbed.[12] For her *Rappresentazione di San Francesco*, Pulci turns to both the *Legenda Maior*, the canonical biography by Saint Bonaventure, and the *Fioretti* of Saint Francis; she selects some of the best-known episodes but also others that appear more rarely in brief depictions of his life. She may have been guided in her choices, at least in part, by autobiographical concerns: Francesco was her father's name, and Bernardo, one of the few companions of Francis who is mentioned by name in the play, may be an homage to her husband, Bernardo Pulci. Finally, she chooses to close the story of Francis's life with the visit he receives from the Roman widow, Jacopa da Settesoli, who is almost certainly an allusion to Pulci's mother, Jacopa di Lorenzo Torelli, who, like Madonna Jacopa of the play, was Roman. It is quite a departure from the norm to introduce autobiographical elements in a religious play at the time, but it seems likely in this case. Perhaps Pulci through this homage intended the play to serve as a prayer

---

12. On Jacopa da Settesoli, see Èdouard d'Alençon, *Frère Jacqueline, recherches historiques sur Jacopa de Settesoli, l'amie de Saint-François* (Paris: Société et Librairie Saint-François d'Assise, 1927; and Rome: Postulation Générale des f.f. m.m. Capucins, 1927).

for her family. The *sacra rappresentazione* was not merely a religious drama, it was truly a devotional text, and we know from an account of Pulci's life written by her friend Fra Antonio Dolciati that she was a very religious woman.

To the reading list for this course when it is taught in Italian we should add Castellano Castellani's *Rappresentazione del figliuol prodigo,* which was mentioned earlier and which is one of the many *sacre rappresentazioni* written by this prolific playwright and devoted Savonarolian. We might look for gender differences in his rendering of the female protagonists in his *Rappresentazione di Sant'Eufrasia* or *Sant'Ursula* and in Antonia Pulci's portrayals. Bernardo Pulci's *Barlaam and Josafat,* based on the story of Buddha in the account of Saint John Damascene, would add another dimension to the course, raising the issue of a husband and wife literary team and the influence of the Pulci family of writers on Antonia. Finally, the course should include Lorenzo de' Medici's *Rappresentazione di San Giovanni e Paolo,*[13] which provides a good, perhaps the best, example of the use of the genre to convey a political as well as a religious message.

ITALIAN RENAISSANCE THEATER

I begin my course in Italian Renaissance theater with works by the three most important authors of *sacre rappresentazioni,* Feo Belcari, Antonia Pulci, and Castellano Castellani; and I include the Lorenzo de' Medici play, if time permits. Then I turn to the early performances of the comedies of Plautus and Terence in Humanist schools and in signorial courts and then to the text that first introduced ancient pastoral themes to modern theater, the *Orfeo* by the humanist Angelo Poliziano. The *Orfeo* makes an important connection between the *sacra rappresentazione* and classical literature, since Poliziano adopted the narrative octaves of popular religious theater, making the indigenous form a vehicle for presenting classical culture (the story of Orpheus and Eurydice and a meditation on the difficulty of reconstructing the classical tradition from the fragments that survived). From the discussion of texts and performances, I turn to other aspects of the theatrical event, primarily to the stage and set, which was at first simple and moveable like that of religious theater. I illustrate this aspect of early theater with a slide show (PowerPoint presentation) consisting of modern reconstructions and early book illustrations of the medieval stage and of drawings and prints that document its gradual transformation under the influence of classical studies

13. See above, note 7.

and the demands of modern audiences, ending with the permanent theaters built in sixteenth-century Italy (in Ferrara, Parma, Florence, Sabbionetta, and Vicenza). I also devote one lesson to the actors and actresses and to early theatrical audiences. Throughout the course, I present what is known of individual productions of the plays and the audience response to them.[14] For the rest of the course we study examples of comedy, tragedy, pastoral drama, *commedia dell'arte*, and the development of religious theater in post-Tridentine Italy. The discussion of spiritual comedy (and tragedy), a sixteenth-century development that drew its form and themes both from classical comedy and from *sacra rappresentazione*, is a good place to end the course. We can at this point ask what light the history of Renaissance theater can shed on the long-debated issue of the coexistence in Renaissance culture of the process of secularization and religious faith.

In order to review the long and complex theatrical tradition in a ten-week term (in a fourteen-week term this could be done more adequately), I can only assign a few examples of each theatrical genre. I teach the course entirely in Italian, but it could also be taught in English, since a good number of representative plays, except for spiritual comedies, are available in translation.

EARLY MODERN WOMEN WRITERS: EUROPE AND NEW SPAIN

I teach a special topics course on early modern women writers that is an optional third quarter component of a humanities core sequence called Readings in World Literature. I vary the reading list as new translations become available, but I always begin the course with Christine de Pizan's *Book of the City of Ladies* and end it with the *Response to Sor Filotea de la Cruz* and selected poems by Sor Juana Inés de la Cruz. Between the two classics of the *querelle des femmes* I have taught a number of texts, written by English, French, Italian, and Hispanic women. I choose them also to represent different literary genres, especially letters (by Alessandra Macinghi Strozzi and/or Suor Maria Celeste Galilei), plays (by Antonia Pulci and Elizabeth Cary), dialogues and orations (I use Laura Cereta, but texts by Cassandra Fedele and Isotta Nogarola are also available), and autobiography (Saint Teresa of Avila and the autobiographical letters and poetry of various women writers).[15]

14. Much information of this sort is available in the series Il Teatro Italiano, published by Einaudi.

15. The following are some of the editions I have used: Christine de Pizan, *The Book of the City of Ladies*, trans. Earl Jeffrey Richards (New York: Persea Books, 1982); Laura Cereta, *Letters of*

I have taught Antonia Pulci's *Saint Francis Play* in past versions of this course because the subject is well known and therefore requires little contextualization to get a good discussion going. It also includes a very subtle defense of Eve and an indictment of Adam for the Fall, a recurrent theme of protofeminist literature. However, having begun the class with Christine de Pizan's *City of Ladies*, whose third book is replete with examples of virgin martyrs, the *Santa Domitilla Play* or the *Death of Saul and the Tears of David* would also work well. I have found that students who are unfamiliar with Catholic martyrology are surprised and fascinated by saints lore, especially the stories of virgin martyrs. The principal themes that emerge from the readings in this course are the authority of women to speak and write and the defense of their sex (the *querelle des femmes*). Faith is a given in these texts, but how it is lived and the power of prayer are central concerns of most, if not all of them. I have not yet introduced the writing of Protestant women, but much is now available and it would be a good way to interest more students and enlarge the scope of debate.

THE HISTORY OF WOMEN'S LITERATURE IN ITALY, THIRTEENTH TO SEVENTEENTH CENTURIES: LETTERATURA FEMMINILE

I have generally taught this course in Italian, but it could be easily taught today in English as well. I proceed chronologically, beginning with the vexed question of Compiuta Donzella, who, if she actually existed and was not a literary hoax, would be the first known Italian woman writer. We read some of the letters of Saint Catherine of Siena and selections of the writing of humanists, men and women, on the subject of women's role in the family and in society and the education deemed appropriate for them. For the fifteenth century I concentrate on the work of three Florentine women: Alessandra Macinghi Strozzi, Lucrezia Tornabuoni, and Antonia Tanini Pulci.

a Renaissance Feminist, ed. and trans. Diana Robin, The Other Voice in Early Modern Europe (Chicago: University of Chicago Press, 1997); Suor Maria Celeste Galilei, *Letters to Father: Suor Maria Celeste to Galileo, 1623–1633*, trans. Dava Sobel (New York and London: Penguin Books, 2003); Saint Teresa of Avila, *The Book of Her Life*, in *The Collected Works of St. Teresa of Avila*, rev. ed., vol. 1, trans. Kieran Kavanaugh and Otilio Rodriguez (Washington, DC: Insitite of Carmelite Studies, 1987), 53–365; Elizabeth Cary, *The Tragedy of Mariam the Fair Queen of Jewry*, ed. Barry Weller and Margaret Ferguson (Berkeley: University of California Press, 1994); and Sor Juana Inez de la Cruz, *The Answer/ La Respuesta Including a Selection of Poems*, ed. and trans. Electa Arenal and Amanda Powell (New York: Feminist Press, 1994); for several poems I have also used translations by Alan Trueblood and Frank Warnke.

I have found it useful to pair the discussions of Pulci and Tornabuoni, since both wrote religious verse in which they propose models of female sanctity and agency. Together with Pulci's plays we read Lucrezia Tornabuoni's *Ystoria di Judith* (*The Story of Judith, Hebrew Widow*), a short narrative poem in *ottava rima* (151 narrative octaves), and a few *laude* (religious poems of praise).[16] Pulci is also known to have written *laude*, one on the subject of the *Corpo di Cristo* (Corpus Christi, or the body of Christ); however, none has yet been found that can be attributed with certainty to her.[17] I center class discussion on the models for female virtue proposed by the two authors and on the question of how these two women writers came to have a public voice at a time when it was thought to be inappropriate, even scandalous, for women.

Antonia Pulci (ca.1452–1501) and Lucrezia Tornabuoni (1425–82) may have been personally acquainted. Lucrezia was the wife of Piero de' Medici and mother of Lorenzo Il Magnifico. The Pulci family poets, Luca, Bernardo, and Luigi, all had close ties to Lorenzo, and Luigi was especially close to Lucrezia, to whom he dedicated his chivalric epic, the *Morgante*. Antonia, who married Bernardo in 1470 or 1471, must have been introduced to that society; there is also an extant letter written by her mother to Clarice Orsini, Lorenzo's wife, who was, like Jacopa, a Roman. These ties may have little to do with the literary production of either woman, but the Pulci connection to the Medicis surely helps to explain Antonia Pulci's access to the printing press. She published her plays in the 1490s, and they continued to be reprinted often in the sixteenth and early seventeenth century. In contrast, Lucrezia Tornabuoni's poetry circulated in manuscript, but it was also widely known. The issue of a public voice does not arise in the case of Alessandra Macinghi Strozzi, since her letters were private and never intended for publication, and she handled all her business dealings through her son-in-law.

When we turn to the sixteenth century, the situation changes, but even then, the first woman to open the doors of the public literary world and to publishing for women was Vittoria Colonna, a widow who belonged to the Roman aristocracy and whose poetry lamented the death of her famous

16. Some of Tornabuoni's works are available in modern editions. *I poemetti sacri di Lucrezia Tornabuoni*, ed. by Fulvio Pezzarossa (Florence: Olschki, 1978), contains the texts of the *Ystoria di Judith* and the *Vita di Sancto Giovanni Baptista*. Jane Tylus has published Tornabuoni's narrative poems and *laude* in English, in *Sacred Narratives*, The Other Voice in Early Modern Europe (Chicago: University of Chicago Press, 2001).

17. See Fra Antonio Dolciati, "Pistola del auctore," in *Esposizione della Regola di Sant'Agostino*, Florence, Biblioteca Laurenziana, MS Gaddi 132, cc. 2r–4v.

warrior husband, another female voice that could be heard in public without a breech of decorum or scandal. After Colonna's success, the publishing industry and many of the most influential literati of the time, for many different reasons to be sure, embraced the new feminine literature, the new Saphos and Corinnas discovered by the Renaissance, the Lauras responding to the Petrarchan appeal. For the sixteenth and seventeenth centuries, women's voices, secular and religious, are many, and texts are available to teach lyric poetry, the prose romance, pastoral theater, spiritual comedies and tragedies, and treatises, many that were published at the time, many more only in recent years.[18] I end the course with what might seem a paradox: the secular writing, diatribes, and defenses of women by a woman religious, the Benedictine nun Arcangela Tarabotti (1604–52), whose *Paternal Tyranny* is a manifesto against the oppression of women by fathers, the church, and the Venetian state, perhaps the first full-blown feminist work written by an Italian woman.[19]

This course too has as a central focus how women in early modern Italy assumed the authority to write and to publish, how they found and exploited an entry into male, literary society and built a literary tradition of their own.[20] Antonia Pulci, the first woman to see her work to press, occupies a place of importance in that tradition.

18. Some of the texts I adopt are Gaspara Stampa, *Rime*, introduction by Maria Bellonci, annotated by Ridolfo Ceriello (Milan: Rizzoli, 1994); Isabella Andreini, *Mirtilla*, ed. Maria Luisa Doglio (Lucca: Pacini Fazzi, 1995); Francesco Buoninsegni /Arcangela Tarabotti, *Satira Antisatira* (Rome: Salerno Editrice, 1998); Giulia Bigolina, *Urania*, ed. Valeria Finucci (Rome: Bulzoni, 2002).

19. Arcangela Tarabotti, *Paternal Tyranny*, ed. and trans. Letizia Panizza, The Other Voice in Early Modern Europe (Chicago: University of Chicago Press, 2004). For the Italian text I rely on copies I print from the microfilm of the 1654 edition that was published in Leiden [pseud. Galerana Baratotti], *La semplicità ingannata* (Leiden: Sambix [but Jean and Daniel Elzevier], 1654), now available online at http://www.lib.uchicago.edu/efts/IWW/.

20. I also assign a number of short critical and historical essays to help students think about these issues and to stimulate debate. Some of those I use most frequently are Carlo Dionisotti, "La letteratura italiana all'epoca del Concilio di Trento," in *Geografia e storia* (Turin: Einaudi, 1967), 227–54; Joan Kelly, "Did Women Have a Renaissance?" and "Early Feminist Theory and the querelle des femmes, 1400–1789," in *Women, History and Theory: The Essays* (Chicago and London: University of Chicago Press, 1984), 19–49, 65–109; and chapters from Ann Rosalind Jones, *The Currency of Eros: Women's Love Lyric in Europe, 1540–1620* (Bloomington: Indiana University Press, 1990).

VITTORIA COLONNA, SONNETS
FOR MICHELANGELO

Abigail Brundin

There is little need to "sell" a writer like Vittoria Colonna to students of Italian literature. If they have not already heard of her, they are generally fascinated to learn that there existed in the sixteenth century a woman writer who commanded the status and respect that she did and whose work went through so many editions during her lifetime and after.[1] They are keen to learn of the ways in which a secular woman was able to market herself in the literary arena with so much success and to study the tradition of writing by women that grew up in her wake and reached a peak by the end of the century.[2] Any study of women writing in Italy must begin with Colonna as its founding figure.

It is more difficult, however, to move beyond the general appreciation of Colonna's status and importance at the forefront of a groundbreaking female literary canon to a nuanced and contextualized study of her poetry itself. And yet this move needs to be made if we are to avoid the repetition of stock platitudes and stereotypes, and more particularly because there are

1. Colonna's collected poetry went through thirteen published editions during her lifetime and a further nine editions between her death in 1547 and the end of the sixteenth century. For a full publication history of the *Rime*, see Vittoria Colonna, *Rime*, ed. Alan Bullock (Rome: Laterza, 1982), 223–462. She also composed two prose meditations that were published in a single volume together with works by other authors four times in the sixteenth century; see Eva-Maria Jung-Inglessis, "Il Pianto della Marchesa di Pescara sopra la Passione di Christo. Introduzione," *Archivio italiano per la storia della pietà* 10 (1997), 115–47; see also, in a collection of three letters to her cousin that was published twice, Maria Luisa Doglio, "L'occhio interiore e la scrittura nelle 'Litere' di Vittoria Colonna," in *Omaggio a Gianfranco Folena*, 3 vols. (Padua: Editoriale Programma, 1993), 2: 1001–13.

2. For a list of published works by Italian women writers in the sixteenth century that is almost comprehensive, see Axel Erdmann, *My Gracious Silence: Women in the Mirror of Sixteenth-Century Printing in Western Europe* (Luzern: Gilhofer and Rauschberg, 1999), 206–23.

other equally fascinating sides to Vittoria Colonna that can only be revealed through detailed attention to her works themselves. Most importantly in the context of the present volume, Colonna's poetry can be used as a case study of the way in which the ideas of the Reformation percolated through Italian society, leaving traces in the most unexpected places, including coloring a genre that has long been considered closed to the effects of any outside influences.[3] This concentration on the religious aspects of the work need not be divorced from broader gender considerations, as the particular slant of Colonna's approach to reform was so clearly gendered, and also raises interesting questions about the appeal of reform to aristocratic women in this period.[4]

Various barriers present themselves to those studying Colonna's poetry in class, not the least of which is the intrinsic linguistic and thematic difficulty of the material that can leave students dispirited if it is not handled with care. In addition, it is vital to equip students with some understanding of a number of contexts—historical, religious, and literary—if they are to do justice to material that has all too often been dismissed by the critical establishment for all the wrong reasons. What is beyond doubt, and what a closer study of Colonna's *Sonnets for Michelangelo* will reveal, is that her poetry is of the very highest order and thus of immense literary interest, and at the same time it is historically fascinating for its religious significance that takes it far beyond the confined, inward-looking world of the courts to which Petrarchism has traditionally been confined.[5]

LITERARY CONTEXT

Any study of Colonna's poetry must begin with a clear and historically accurate review of the aims and ideas governing the practice of the Petrarchan genre in the sixteenth century, its role and status within the emerging canon of vernacular literature, and the linguistic debates underpinning that

3. For a discussion of Petrarchism as a "closed" genre, see Thomas M. Greene, *The Light in Troy: Imitation and Discovery in Renaissance Poetry* (New Haven: Yale University Press, 1982), 174–76.

4. Studies on women and reform in this period include Natalie Zemon Davis, "City Women and Religious Change," in *Society and Culture in Early Modern France: Eight Essays* (Stanford: Stanford University Press, 1975), 65–95; Nancy Lyman Roelker, "The Appeal of Calvinism to French Noblewomen in the Sixteenth Century," *Journal of Interdisciplinary History* 2 (1971–72): 391–418; and Merry E. Weisner, "Beyond Women and the Family: Towards a Gender Analysis of the Reformation," *Sixteenth-Century Journal* 18 (1987): 311–21.

5. See the comments by Lauro Martines, who regards the genre as creating "mini-utopias" into which the courtier can escape from problematic realities, in *Power and Imagination. City-States in Renaissance Italy* (London: Pimlico, 2002), 323–28 at 325.

phenomenon. Such groundwork is particularly vital when dealing with this much-maligned genre, famously dismissed by Arturo Graf at the end of the nineteenth century as "a chronic malady of Italian literature."[6] Graf's scorn stemmed primarily from his post-Romantic view that the genre engendered a fashion for repetitive, unoriginal, cold lyric "game playing," devoid of emotion or passion.

By reexamining the aims and ideologies underpinning the Petrarchan genre in a more historically accurate manner, students are able to appreciate the wrongheadedness of such a dismissal. This lesson is driven home forcefully by the interesting results of Amedeo Quondam's study into anthology collections of Petrarchism through the ages.[7] As poetic tastes and expectations have shifted over the centuries, so Petrarchists who were not considered outstanding in their own age (Michelangelo Buonarroti, Gaspara Stampa, to name the most famous examples) have gained prominence, while the masters of the genre in the sixteenth century (Colonna, Pietro Bembo) have fallen by the critical wayside.

Petrarchism was enormously popular during the sixteenth century itself. Petrarchan anthologies and individually authored collections of *Rime*, such as those by Colonna and Bembo, were among the vernacular "best sellers" of the new printing industry during this period.[8] Produced in small and affordable editions, they circulated widely, and there was seemingly no end to the public's appetite for "new and improved" editions of the lyrics of "various very noble gentlemen and ladies," often organized according to geographical regions, such as the series of anthologies published by Giolito and edited by Ludovico Domenichi that were issued between 1545 and 1560.[9] It can be fruitful to ask students to consider the reasons for the genre's great popularity at the time. Various suggestions have been offered in class in the past that have led to interesting discussion and analysis, including the excitement connected with having access to a vernacular literary movement

6. Arturo Graf, *Attraverso il Cinquecento* (Turin: Loescher, 1926), 3. Cited in Klaus W. Hempfer, "Per una definizione del Petrarchismo," in *Dynamique d'une expansion culturelle. Pétrarque en Europe XIVe–XXe siècle. Actes du XXVIe congrès international du CEFI, Turin et Chambéry, 11–15 décembre 1995*, ed. Pierre Blanc. Bibliothèque Franco Simone 30 (Paris: Honoré Champion, 2001), 23–52 at 24.

7. Amedeo Quondam, *Petrarchismo mediato: per una critica della forma "antologia": livelli d'uso del sistema linguistico del petrarchismo* (Rome: Bulzoni, 1974).

8. Similarly popular were the collections of vernacular letters by prominent men and women: see Anne Jacobson Schutte, "The *Lettere Volgari* and the Crisis of Evangelism in Italy," *Renaissance Quarterly* 28 (1975): 639–88.

9. The first edition is *Rime diverse di molti eccellentiss. auttori nuovamente raccolte. Libro primo* (Venice: Gabriel Giolito di Ferrarii, 1545).

apparently aristocratic in its genesis and yet available to readers with no classical training or education; the linguistic importance of the genre as a means of standardizing vernacular usage across society; the voyeurism of reading the seemingly personal and heartfelt love laments of locally known and respected figures; and of course, in Colonna's case, the particular appeal of work written by a famous aristocratic woman in a genre that had not previously seen a female practitioner. In addition, it is worth pointing out to students the fact that, given their wide reach and appeal, collections of Petrarchan poetry had great potential as evangelizing tools in spreading a message of reformed spirituality, as was indeed the case with the lyrics of Vittoria Colonna.[10]

In considering the general appeal of Petrarchism to a Renaissance audience, some time also needs to be devoted to building a good understanding of the Renaissance practice of literary *imitatio*, in the context of Pietro Bembo's pronouncements on the subject. Thankfully there are good secondary sources on this topic, so that students can prepare themselves for seminars by reading up on the theory, and class time can then be used to examine the practice in more detail.[11] A fun way to start is with the genre of *centones*, as a means of illustrating the most extreme ends to which the practice of *imitatio* can be pushed in a Petrarchan context. A *cento* by Colonna herself, "Occhi miei, oscurato è il nostro sole" ("O my eyes, our sun has been obscured"), can be used to demonstrate the poet's early training in lyric writing, her playful negotiation with her poetic model.[12] A good discussion has grown up in the past around this text concerning the difference between literary imitation and plagiarism, and other texts can be brought into play in resolving the issue, including Petrarch's and Bembo's pronouncements on the practice of *imitatio* in their theoretical writings.[13]

The potential spiritual implications of Bembo's Ciceronian model of literary imitation can also be introduced into this discussion to useful effect. There is a clear connection between the notion of imitation of the perfect

10. Anne Schutte makes the same point about vernacular letterbooks in her article, "The *Lettere Volgari*."

11. Good recommendations for initial student reading are Greene, *The Light in Troy*; Martin L. McLaughlin, *Literary Imitation in the Italian Renaissance: The Theory and Practice of Literary Imitation in Italy from Dante to Bembo* (Oxford: Oxford University Press, 1996); and Amedeo Quondam, *Il naso di Laura. Lingua e poesia lirica nella tradizione del Classicismo* (Ferrara: Panini, 1991).

12. Colonna, *Rime*, ed. Bullock, 10, sonnet A1:15.

13. See for example the citations provided in Thomas Greene at 95 and 174. For Castiglione's criticism of Bembo's position on *imitatio*, which is also useful for this discussion, see *Il cortegiano* I, xxv–xxvi.

"divine" literary model advocated by Bembo and his peers and imitation of the divine example of Christ through the Franciscan practice of *imitatio Christi*.[14] This connection confers extra ethical and moral weight upon the practice of literary *imitatio* in a Petrarchan context, affording it a gravitas and importance that has generally been overlooked by the critical world. It is noteworthy that the quality of gravitas was one of the key elements that Bembo looked for in successful sonnets and found in abundance in Colonna's oeuvre, as he states clearly in his response upon reading her work for the first time. "I received a sonnet by the Marchioness of Pescara," Bembo wrote in 1530, "it truly is beautiful, ingenious, and serious, such as one would not expect from a woman: it has far surpassed my expectations."[15]

RELIGIOUS CONTEXT: THE ITALIAN "REFORMATION"

A discussion of the textual ethics of *imitatio* opens the way to an exploration of the broader historical and religious contexts that feed directly into Colonna's poetic texts. To my surprise, even advanced students in Italian literature know little about the European Reformation and its impact on Italy. I devote a preliminary lecture to a brief summary of the development of the Reformation in a specifically Italian context and direct students to the wealth of secondary literature on this topic.[16] I also devote particular attention to the reform-minded circles that Colonna moved in during her own lifetime in Naples and Rome, the texts she was probably exposed to (including, most importantly, the *Beneficio di Cristo* [1542/3], which functions as a useful poetic foil for Colonna's sonnets), and the specific doctrinal ideas that leave such clear traces in her mature poetry.[17]

14. On this see Dina de Rentiis, "Sul ruolo di Petrarca nella storia dell' *Imitatio auctorum*," in *Dynamique d'une expansion culturelle*, 63–74.

15. "Ebbi il sonetto della Marchesa di Pescara, di vero egli è bello e ingenioso e grave più che da donna non pare sia richiesto: ha superato la espettation mia d'assai," cited in Carlo Dionisotti, "Appunti sul Bembo e su Vittoria Colonna," in *Miscellanea Augusto Campana*, ed. Rino Avesani et al. (Padua: Antenore, 1981), 1: 257–86 at 261–62.

16. Good places to start are as follows: John Bossy, *Christianity in the West, 1400–1700* (Oxford: Oxford University Press, 1985); G. R. Elton, *Reformation Europe 1517–1559*, 2d ed. (Oxford: Blackwell, 1999); Michael A. Mullett, *The Catholic Reformation* (London: Routledge, 1999); Bob Scribner et al., eds., *The Reformation in National Context* (Cambridge: Cambridge University Press, 1994).

17. All of this is summarized in more detail in my introduction in *Sonnets for Michelangelo* (Chicago: University of Chicago Press), 13–18. A useful text to recommend to students for further reading is Salvatore Caponetto, *The Protestant Reformation in Sixteenth-Century Italy*, trans. Anne C. Tedeschi and John Tedeschi. Sixteenth-Century Essays and Studies, vol. 43. (Kirksville, Mo.: Thomas Jefferson University Press, 1999).

It is important to ensure that students understand the implications of the Lutheran doctrine of justification by faith alone, or *sola fide*, for a poetic project like Colonna's. One of the most significant outcomes of a belief in *sola fide* is of course the increased responsibility that it bestows upon the individual Christian for developing an active faith through contemplation, meditation, and study of the word of God through the Bible. Yet this increased responsibility came about in the context of a negation of the effectiveness of good works and thus the impossibility of "earning" or "buying" salvation through any human actions. Responsibility for study and contemplation is thus accompanied by the acceptance of a preordained fate and a joyful certainty of salvation that has already been enacted. We can consider this to be a form of prescribed freedom, that is, the Christian is encouraged to read, learn, and understand for herself but is also safe in the knowledge that none of her personal failures or inadequacies will affect the final outcome that God has decided for her.

This seeming conundrum inherent in *sola fide* appears to have far-reaching implications for poetry like Colonna's that seeks to express her personal spiritual journey as a "reformed" Christian (one who has been convinced of the validity of the doctrine), and her choice of genre comes to seem particularly apt in this context. The sonnet itself is a prescribed form of poetry, that is, before the poet ever begins to write, certain properties of her finished product have already been decided, its duration and structure are predetermined. Yet far from inhibiting the poet, this very prescriptiveness appears to act as a positive support, a formula by which to order her experience during composition.[18] These qualities of the sonnet, its limited space and controlled freedom, offer an ideal forum in which to explore new and challenging ideas (such as, for example, aspects of a reformed spirituality) while remaining within accepted boundaries and rules. So too the arrangement of sonnets into a *canzoniere* can be seen to contribute positively to the endeavor of expressing a reformed spirituality in poetry. By its nature a Petrarchan *canzoniere* is cyclical and intimate, beginning and ending with the consciousness of the individual poet and the state of his soul. Thus it provides the perfect forum for a process of questioning, of love or faith; and while Petrarch's faith may prove weak in opposition to the overwhelming power of his unrequited love, so that his own *canzoniere* ends with an anguished plea to the Virgin to rescue him from the cycle of entrapment and longing that threatens to begin again even as it draws to a close, one can see how the

18. See Michael R. G. Spiller, *The Development of the Sonnet: An Introduction* (London: Routledge, 1992), 2.

format could lead instead to a more positive outcome as the poet is able to arrive at a new understanding of faith. The very circularity of the *canzoniere* has the potential to become a cause for celebration instead of a form of entrapment, if one links it to the doctrine of *sola fide* and the notion that the individual can cease to seek to control her fate and abandon herself to the action of God's grace on her soul, so that her powerlessness to change her fate becomes a testament to the depth of her faith in her status as one of the elect. This quality, a celebration of powerlessness and a joyful surrender to the will of God, recurs frequently within Colonna's sonnet cycle for Michelangelo.[19]

It appears then that there is potential for an intimate link between Petrarchan poetry and reformed spirituality in this period in Italy so that Colonna's use of the genre as a means of exploring her new faith is not as unexpected as might initially have been supposed. Once the importance of *sola fide* and predestination for an understanding of the sonnets in this collection has been established, the real work and pleasure of reading and analyzing the poems themselves can begin in earnest.

THE SONNETS FOR MICHELANGELO

In a small group seminar we can now turn to a close reading of a selection of sonnets, generally beginning with the opening one of the collection, "Poi che 'l mio casto amor gran tempo tenne" ("Since my chaste love for many years," 1). This opening sonnet is particularly useful as a means of dispelling the impression that Petrarchism is a dry and "soulless" enterprise. Replete with rich, sensual, and corporeal imagery evoking the body of Christ, this opening sonnet surprises and delights students, who recognize in the poet who expresses her "great thirst" in such unapologetic terms a bolder and more dynamic presence than they expected to find. If they have not already encountered the poems addressed to Colonna by Michelangelo Buonarroti, this can be a useful moment to introduce one or two as a means of illustrating the surprising consonance of style and mood between the two writers and their shared religious concerns.[20] The status of the manuscript

---

19. See, for example, sonnets 21, 22, 55, 73, and 78 in *Sonnets for Michelangelo*.

20. On this topic, see Emidio Campi, *Michelangelo e Vittoria Colonna. Un dialogo artistico-teologico ispirato da Bernardino Ochino, e altri saggi di storia della Riforma* (Turin: Claudiniana, 1994); Roberto Fedi, "'L'immagine vera': Vittoria Colonna, Michelangelo, e un'idea di canzoniere," *Modern Language Notes* 107 (1992): 46–73; Carlo Vecce, "Petrarca, Vittoria, Michelangelo: Note di commento a testi e varianti di Vittoria Colonna e di Michelangelo," *Studi e problemi di critica testuale* 44 (1992): 101–25. A good edition of Michelangelo's sonnets with parallel text translations is

for Michelangelo as a private gift from Colonna, prepared with her personal input, is relevant to this discussion in the sense that this manuscript appears to contain a more personal and unmediated selection of poems, many of them unpublished in 1540 at the time of the manuscript's preparation, than can be found in any of the published editions of Colonna's *Rime* at this time.[21] In the past in class we have examined slides showing some of the frontispiece images of Colonna kneeling in prayer before a crucifix that accompanied the published editions of the sonnets in the 1540s, in order to gain an impression of the public face of the poet that can be compared to the freer, bolder, more sensual "private" voice that is expressed throughout the sonnets for Michelangelo and in this sonnet in particular.[22]

A question that is often raised during a discussion of the opening sonnet is, How did she get away with this? Astounded by the assertiveness of the poet's poetic persona and the overt sensuality of the imagery she deploys in writing of Christ and her relationship with him, students wonder about the seemliness of such an approach and note the apparent lack of decorum and modesty they might have expected from a woman writer establishing a place for herself in new and uncharted literary territory. An astute student will cite Ariosto, in his famous eulogy to Colonna in the *Orlando furioso*, canto 37, who appears to praise Colonna above all for her poetic self-effacement in breathing new life into the defunct body of her husband through her poetry. This sonnet seems very far from such praise.[23] How did a poet whose abiding reputation was for piety and wifely devotion manage to compose such sensual verses, in which the poetic voice is unabashed in its appropriation of Christ's body for its own literary purposes in order to satisfy its longing? Other sonnets in the collection add to this impression and can usefully be brought into the discussion, for example, "Debile e 'nferma a la salute vera" ("Weak and infirm I run towards true salvation," 21) and "Tra gelo e nebbia corro a Dio sovente" ("I often run through cold and mist toward God's," 22), both of which will be discussed in more detail below.

The context for the sensuality of her poetic voice in writing of Christ is Colonna's earlier amorous poems in praise of her deceased husband, Francesco D'Avalos, in which she expressed her longing for him and her

---

The Poetry of Michelangelo, ed. and trans. James M. Saslow (New Haven: Yale University Press, 1991).

21. On the contents of the gift manuscript for Michelangelo, see *Sonnets for Michelangelo*, 33–39.

22. Examples of such images can be found in *Vittoria Colonna. Dichterin und Muse Michelangelos*, catalogue to the exhibition at the Kunsthistorisches Museum, Vienna, curated by Silvia Ferino-Pagden, February 25 to May 25, 1997 (Vienna: Skira, 1997), 146.

23. There is a fuller discussion of Ariosto's praise of Colonna in *Sonnets for Michelangelo*, 1–2.

admiration of his many virtues. The close and loving relationship with Christ established in the later spiritual sonnets grows directly out of this earlier marital poetic context, and therefore the great degree of intimacy and a notably "human" loving bond is sanctioned from the start of the poetic process. In addition, a reader needs to be aware of the sensuality of religious writing more generally in this period. John O'Malley used the term "incarnational theology," in the context of papal sermons in the period spanning the late fifteenth and early sixteenth centuries, to describe the tendency to view the Incarnation of Christ as the key moment in the Passion sequence, the moment when the Redemption of man was guaranteed.[24] Such a theological approach inevitably places emphasis on the body of Christ as the proof of God's bounty in offering his son for the salvation of humankind, so that a celebration of that very body is allowed a clear theological justification.[25] And such "incarnational theology" feeds too into the long-standing tradition of mystical and sensual religious language stemming from the sermons of a figure such as Bernard of Clairvaux in the twelfth century.[26]

The reform movement also draws directly upon these mystical vernacular traditions in evangelizing its own message. Bernardino Ochino, the Capuchin preacher who strongly influenced Colonna and many others in her circle, including Pietro Bembo, was famed for his evocative and uplifting sermons on the New Testament that inspired his audiences to new heights of piety. The potency of his message was such that he was eventually forced to flee Italy on suspicion of heresy.[27] The *Beneficio di Christo* is also a text that clearly draws on these traditions of religious mysticism in inspiring its readers to contemplate a reformed faith, and its success was such that the book was swiftly and vigorously repressed by the Catholic authorities and included in Della Casa's Index of Prohibited Books in 1549.[28] In the *Beneficio,*

24. See John W. O'Malley, *Praise and Blame in Renaissance Rome: Rhetoric, Doctrine and Reform in the Sacred Orators of the Papal Court, c. 1450–1521* (Durham, N.C.: Duke University Press, 1979), 138–50.

25. Interesting, if controversial, work by Leo Steinberg has found an emphasis on Christ's genitals in Christian art of the period, which acts as proof of God's descent into manhood and thus of the salvation of humankind. See *The Sexuality of Christ in Renaissance Art and in Modern Oblivion*, 2d ed. (Chicago: University of Chicago Press, 1996).

26. A good introduction to the saint's life is Gillian R. Evans, *Bernard of Clairvaux* (Oxford: Oxford University Press, 2000).

27. On Ochino, see Carl Benrath, *Bernardino Ochino of Siena: A Contribution towards the History of the Reformation* (London: James Nisbet, 1876).

28. Details of the publication and circulation of the *Beneficio di Christo* are contained in "Nota critica" to Benedetto da Mantova, *Il Beneficio di Cristo con le versioni del secolo XVI, documenti e testimonianze*, ed. Salvatore Caponetto (Florence: Sansoni, 1972), 469–98. See also Tommaso

Christians are encouraged to shake off the servile Old Testament fear of God that has encumbered them for centuries and embrace instead a loving God and a brother in Christ whose very body experiences the pain they feel when they are hurt by their fellow Christians.[29]

There clearly exists, therefore, a religious precedent for the sensuality expressed in a number of Colonna's sonnets in describing her relationship with Christ, yet nonetheless, her female gender seems interesting in this context. A number of critics have in the past pointed out the influence on her work of the writings of the fourteenth-century religious mystic Catherine of Siena, which were published four times in the sixteenth century and display a language and style that offer a clear precedent for Colonna's approach.[30] In addition, it should be borne in mind that such sensual and evocative religious language was curiously ungendered in the period, so that it was equally acceptable for Michelangelo, for example, to describe himself as a bride of Christ in his own poetry or for Christ himself to be represented as a mother lactating through the wound in his side.[31] Nonetheless, we should not underestimate Colonna's own careful negotiation with the tradition, in establishing so early on in her poetic oeuvre the "wifely" relationship that she would later come to explore in relation to the Son of God himself.[32]

A reading of the opening sonnet alone then can easily lead to a lengthy and highly informative discussion of contexts and themes. Subsequently, time can usefully be spent analyzing various poems that best reflect the influence of Colonna's belief in *sola fide* upon her poetic project. A

Bozza, *Nuovi studi sulla Riforma in Italia I. Il Beneficio di Cristo* (Rome: Storia e letteratura, 1976); Dermot Fenlon, *Heresy and Obedience in Tridentine Italy: Cardinal Pole and the Counter Reformation* (Cambridge: Cambridge University Press, 1972); and Carlo Ginsburg and Adriano Prosperi, *Giochi di Pazienza: Un seminario sul "Beneficio di Cristo"* (Turin: Einaudi, 1975).

29. See *Il Beneficio di Cristo*, 55, 81.

30. See Maria Luisa Doglio, "L'occhio interiore e la scrittura nelle 'Litere' di Vittoria Colonna," 13. Also *Le Lettere di S. Caterina da Siena*, ed. Piero Misciatelli, 6 vols. (Florence: Marzocco, 1947); Suzanne Noffke, "Caterina da Siena," in *Italian Women Writers: A Bio-Bibliographical Sourcebook*, ed. Rinaldina Russell (Westport, Conn.: Greenwood Press, 1994), 58–66.

31. See Michelangelo's sonnet "Vorrei voler, Signor, quel ch'io non voglio," in *The Poetry of Michelangelo*, 208, and the reference to the poet as "[il] tuo bella sposa" ("your beautiful bride"). See also Fiora A. Bassanese, "Vittoria Colonna, Christ and Gender," *Rivista della Civiltà Italiana* 40 (1996), 53–57.

32. It is this quality of consistency—that her eventual spiritual aims were in place from her very earliest verses and governed every aspect of her presentation of D'Avalos and her relations to him—that has led previous critics to accuse Colonna of repetitiveness and dryness. Such readers have, I believe, generally overlooked the important spiritual ends governing her poetic project from its earliest beginnings.

compelling example is sonnet 22, "Tra gelo e nebbia corro a Dio sovente" ("I often run through cold and mist towards God's"), which draws directly on Petrarch's poem number 189 in the *Rime sparse*, "Passa la mia nave colma d'oblio" ("My ship full of forgetful cargo sails"), and can usefully be employed to demonstrate the distance that Colonna has moved in her mature poetry from her apparent poetic source.[33] Petrarch's sonnet alludes to the amatory frustrations experienced by the poet that prevent him from reaching port, representing satisfaction and resolution. Colonna's rewriting of this theme (one that occurs frequently throughout the collection[34]) is far more radical than might at first be apparent, and this quality comes to the fore as soon as students begin to contemplate the influence of *sola fide* upon the poetic conceit. The key to interpretation in this vein is contained in the final lines: "his waves are always smaller and more gentle/ for those who, in a bark of humility upon the great ocean/ of his divine grace, freely abandon themselves."[35] Christ is the sea upon which the elected soul, certain of the joyful outcome of the act of faith, launches itself with abandon and unwavering optimism. Unlike Petrarch, who despairs of his continuing distance from the safety and shelter represented by the port, in Colonna's sonnet the port is no longer even an issue. The ocean itself, with all its potential dangers and uncertainties, is the poet's end, and she is happy to drift upon it without direction or aim, guided by God's will.

Such close reading and analysis allows students to gain a clearer impression of the ways in which this collection of sonnets by Colonna constitutes a "reformed *canzoniere*" and affords them some greater appreciation of its groundbreaking qualities as a sustained exercise in submitting the Petrarchan format to the new imperatives of a reformed spirituality. As a closing exercise, I have in the past asked students to come to a seminar prepared to give a ten-minute presentation on a sonnet of their choice, why it appeals to them and what it can tell us more generally about Colonna's poetic project. The results have to date always been hugely heartening. Having come to this study of Colonna uncertain about their commitment to conducting a sustained reading of "difficult" and "boring" Renaissance poetry, they conclude the course filled with enthusiasm for the subtleties of such poetic analysis and more convinced than ever of the interest of this extraordinary

---

33. Colonna's sonnet is in *Sonnets for Michelangelo*, 72–73. For Petrarch's sonnet see Francesco Petrarca, *Canzoniere*, ed. Alberto Chiari (Milan: Mondadori, 1985), 314. William J. Kennedy looks at an earlier amorous sonnet by Colonna in relation to this Petrarchan precedent, in *Authorizing Petrarch* (Ithaca: Cornell University Press, 1994), 114–34.

34. See, for example, sonnets 35 and 79.

35. *Sonnets for Michelangelo*, 75.

woman writer, only now furnished with the concrete evidence to back up
their earlier assumption.

CONCLUSION

I hope that the preceding discussion has demonstrated the ways in which
Vittoria Colonna defies the limitations traditionally imposed upon her by
the critical world in this manuscript gift for her friend Michelangelo by composing poetry that goes well beyond the parameters established by Petrarch
in his earlier *canzoniere*. The resulting poems can usefully be categorized as a
vivid and appealing example of the manner in which a reformed spirituality
can influence a literary enterprise in this period before the convocation of
the Council of Trent, and they illustrate clearly the particularly happy marriage of Italian reform with Petrarchan lyricism that took place in Colonna's
oeuvre. Furthermore, and equally important, this text serves definitively to
overturn previous misconceptions about Colonna as a dry and uninteresting
poet by demonstrating the many compelling and beautiful ways in which
she found poetic expression for her concerns as a Christian and as a woman
writer. Indeed, perhaps the most important result of this study will be the
conviction of Colonna's sheer worth and talent as a poet and the recognition
that she was lauded by her contemporaries not because, like a dancing dog,
she amazed them by performing in an unnatural way, but because they were
able to respond to the quality and beauty of her verses directly and enthusi-
astically and were not hampered by the many centuries of misunderstanding
that have clouded our judgment since then.[36]

36. The allusion here to Samuel Johnson is cited by Germaine Greer in *Slip-Shod Sibyls: Recognition, Rejection and the Woman Poet*, 2d ed. (London: Penguin, 1996), xxi.

MARGUERITE DE NAVARRE:
RELIGIOUS REFORMIST[1]

Rouben Cholakian

THE ISSUE

Those who have some familiarity with the works of Marguerite de Navarre will be inclined to see in her a divided writer, creating on the one hand profoundly religious texts like *Le miroir de l'âme pécheresse* (Mirror of a Sinful Soul) and, on the other, secular ones, like her anthology of stories, the *Heptameron*.[2] But scratch the surface of even as earthy a text as the latter work and, more often than not, you uncover the author's religious orientation. The following teaching guide aims to make that point by looking at these two essential texts.

CULTURAL CLIMATE

Although Marguerite de Navarre (1492–1549) has slowly and begrudgingly been allowed access to the pantheon of Renaissance writers, she is still not so well known that a brief review of her place in her cultural world would be amiss for most students.[3] At the very least it is significant to point out that at a time when women's education was very limited, Marguerite's mother saw to it

1. I wish to thank Corona Machemer for her intelligent editorial reading of this text.

2. The standard bibliography is H. P. Clive, *Marguerite de Navarre: An Annotated Bibliography* (London: Grant and Cutler Ltd., 1983), which can be updated by the annual Modern Language Association bibliographical listings.

3. Marguerite de Navarre's canonization is primarily a twentieth-century phenomenon. Two books published in the 1930s established her place in French letters: Pierre Jourda, *Marguerite d'Angoulême, duchesse d'Alençon, reine de Navarre (1492–1549): Etude biographique et littéraire*, 2 vols. (Paris: Champion, 1930), which remains the biographical bible for students of Marguerite; and Emile Telle, *L'Œuvre de Marguerite d'Angoulême, reine de Navarre et la Querelle des Femmes* (1937; repr., Geneva: Slatkine, 1969). Interest in women writers has stirred great interest in her work since the 1970s. For the most recent life story in English see Patricia F. Cholakian and Rouben C. Cholakian, *Marguerite de Navarre: Mother of the Renaissance* (New York: Columbia University Press, 2006).

that she and her brother François, who in 1515 would become king of France, were both thoroughly grounded in classical and contemporary languages, philosophy, and modern and ancient literatures. They also had access to what in those days would have been considered a substantial private library.

Marguerite was a political figure, a humanist, and an important instigator in efforts to reform the Roman Catholic Church. For that reason, any serious understanding of her texts requires some introductory comments on the political, cultural, and religious environment of her time. The literature in all of these areas is understandably vast, but the novice student does not need to be lost in a maze of details. How much time is available and how the class is set up will determine the extent of background reading that is required. This is a case where less is often more. Any good encyclopedia essay on the Renaissance would not, I think, be out of place.[4]

From the very start, Marguerite had the humanist's passion for learning and the arts, and as a grown woman and wealthy member of the royal family, she surrounded herself with important literary figures, such as the poet Clément Marot, the novella writer Bonaventure Des Périers, and the translator Antoine Le Maçon.

So in the class's introductory comments, the teacher might want to review essential humanistic ideas: love of classical texts, the learning of Latin and Greek, increased cosmopolitanism, and, in a general sense, a greater appreciation of the human intellect.[5] The creator may still be at the center of the universe, but more room is certainly being made for his most important creation.

The student will also require some elementary understanding of what is meant by religious reform. Although the literature is again overwhelming and growing all the time, I believe that a modest volume like Greengrass's study is intellectually accessible to the yet untutored and a good place to begin.[6]

---

4. I myself do not share the ubiquitous disdain among most teaching scholars of a substantial encyclopedia article. An intelligent overview offers a general frame into which the learner can slowly make detailed accretions of information. But of course teacher and student could make good use of more ample studies. Here are but a few suggestions: Frederic Baumgartner, *France in the Sixteenth Century* (New York: St. Martin's Press, 1995); George Holmes, *Renaissance* (New York: St. Martins, 1996); Robert J. Knecht, *The Rise and Fall of Renaissance France: 1483–1610.* 2d ed. (London: Blackwell, 2001); Margaret L. King. *The Renaissance in Europe* (New York: McGraw-Hill, 2005). Finally, the now classic publication by Natalie Davis offers a more gender specific orientation: *Society and Culture in Early Modern France* (Stanford: Stanford University Press, 1977).

5. Margaret King's chapter 3, "Human Dignity and Humanist Studies," in *The Renaissance in Europe* is a good preamble to this entire discussion.

6. Mark Greengrass, *The French Reformation* (London: Blackwell, 1987).

By Marguerite's own time the reformist movement was splitting into two quite distinct camps. On the one hand, in Germany, Martin Luther (1483–1546) saw no way out of the conflicts with Rome and eventually separated himself from papal jurisdiction. On the other, the Dutch humanist Desiderius Erasmus (1466–1536) persisted in believing there was still room for reform and conciliation. Marguerite decidedly allied herself with the latter sentiments.

And what in fact were the fundamental ideas of this reformist group to which Marguerite so energetically gave her support?[7] Encouraged by the humanistic emphasis on the primacy of the individual human soul, they aimed, through translations into the vernacular, to make sacred texts available to a fast-growing reading public and to favor individual conscience over clerical authority and interpretation. Like Luther, they attacked the practice of granting indulgences by which one might buy, as it were, years of freedom from purgatorial confinement after death. They disapproved too of what they perceived to be the idolatrous veneration of saints. They deplored priestly abuses of power and corruption and especially found fault with mendicant friars, many of whom had fallen so far from Saint Francis's ideal that they had come to exemplify lascivious and lustful behavior. They challenged the custom of handing out clerical offices and proprietorship over monastic lands essentially to the highest bidder, who all too often rarely visited the sees and abbeys from which he garnered considerable wealth.

In a more theological vein, they argued that salvation depended less on good deeds and more on the generous gift of a generous God, which they called grace. They urged private spiritual practices, not as a substitute for the Mass, but as an important supplement to it. In some cases, as with Marguerite, this gave birth to a new mysticism, which preferred direct contact through prayer with God's son, from whom came all strength and ultimate redemption.[8]

---

7. In his biography on Francis I, Robert J. Knecht offers a good review of the political implications of the heresy issue: *Renaissance Warrior and Patron: The Reign of Francis 1* (Cambridge: Cambridge University Press, 1994).

8. There is currently some discussion as to how much and which mystic writers Marguerite actually read and knew. Here is what Jourda has to say on the subject: "It would be difficult to be precise about her readings . . . whether she read Plotinus, Proclus, Hermès Trismegiste or Denys the Areopagyte." He goes on to posit the idea that much of her mystical education was most likely acquired directly through conversations with contemporaries like Briçonnet and Jacques Lefèvre d'Etaples" (*Marguerite d'Angoulême* 2:1022).

Marguerite was a diligent and prolific correspondent,[9] and her four-year exchange, from about 1521 to 1524, with Guillaume Briçonnet, Bishop of Meaux, about theological matters is important to mention, at least in passing, not only because it is evidence of her keen interest in these issues and her training in the mystical tradition, but because it is the place where she learns something about what she later affectionately calls *la doulce escripture* (sweet writing).[10] Over the years, Marguerite came to realize that while she was all these things—court personality, humanist, and reformist—she was also a writer.

Thus, as part of the classroom introduction, it might be appropriate to present students with a chronological list of all Marguerite's publications, including brief summaries of their contents,[11] and to point out that when, at the end of her life, she chose to compile an anthology of her writings, she significantly divided them into more or less distinct categories of religious and nonreligious works.[12] So one comes full circle, back to the discussion's primary question: just how "distinct"?

The Mirror of the Sinful Soul

Le miroir (1531), the author's first publication, is a carefully wrought defense of Marguerite's reformist religious views.[13] Composed in over a thousand

9. It was not until the nineteenth century that Marguerite's immense correspondence was published in two separate volumes by F Génin. *Lettres de Marguerite d'Angoulême* (1841) and *Nouvelles lettres de la reine de Navarre à son frère le roi François Ier* (1842). More recently, one can consult with profit Elizabeth Goldsmith and Colette Winn, eds., *Lettres des femmes, texts, inédits et oubliés du XVe au XVIIIe siècles* (Paris: Champion, 2004). It is useful in this regard to look also at Jourda, *Répertoire analytique et chronologique de la correspondance de Marguerite de Navarre, duchesse d'Alençon, reine de Navarre (1492–1549)* (repr., Geneva: Slatkine, 1973).

10. Although there now exists a two-volume edition of this correspondence under the direction of Martineau et al., there is no English translation as yet, a daunting task if anyone has the courage to undertake it. In the meantime, one could prepare a few select passages by way of example for the student from *Guillaume Briçonnet/Marguerite d'Angoulême: Correspondance*, ed. Christine Martineau, Michel Veissière, and Henry Heller, 2 vols. (Paris: L'Imprimerie Lahure, 1975–79).

11. A useful guide is Pierre Jourda, "Tableau chronologique des publications de Marguerite de Navarre," *Revue du seizième siècle* 12 (1925): 209–31.

12. That she published this two-volume anthology, *Marguerites de la Marguerite des princesses* and *Suite des Marguerites de la Marguerite des princesses* (1547) indicates that the diplomat, royal sister, philanthropist, and reformist wanted also to be remembered as a writer. See Clive, *Marguerite de Navarre*, 22.

13. By contemporary standards, Marguerite's first publication was hugely successful, producing several editions in her own lifetime. In 1545, when she was only twelve years old, the future

dense, decasyllabic couplets, it is a good introduction to both the language and thought of the movement. Indeed, nearly everything else that Marguerite wrote afterwards about her beliefs has its roots in this early publication.

She begins on a note of unremitting self-deprecation, and students should be led to discover the characteristics of this chest-thumping, masochistic style, which to the uninitiated will seem preposterously hyperbolic but which was an important component of mystical writing (lines 1–55, 1,126).[14]

So degenerate and unworthy is the narrator (Marguerite), that no mortal can bring salvation (67), only a merciful and redemptive God. The weak and undeserving sinner cannot be saved except through his unmerited and magnanimous grace (91–92). Marguerite pleads for mercy but at the same time understands that grace is granted, unsolicited, at birth. The sinner acknowledges God's unconditional divine love and likens it to the love of family members (170–73). Again, to the modern reader the language seems strange, a curious fusion that by turns defines the narrator as daughter (60, 358, 392, 408), spouse (600, 612, 703), sister (499, 527, 565), and mother (262, 347, 417) of a loving God, who is father, husband, brother, and child. The instructor could initiate here a sociological digression on the changing meanings of family relations.

Reformists of the sixteenth century were Christ-centered. Marguerite finds enormous comfort in the love of a redeemer to whom she pours out her heart (469–75). These are passages well worth reading aloud, not only for the poetic movement of the text, but also for its significance. Such recitations should spawn comment on parallel sentiments in modern Christianity.

The poem concludes with thanks and praise to one of the reformists' major biblical heroes, Saint Paul (1,382, 1,422). The instructor will find this an appropriate moment to talk about contemporary translations of Paul's letters and how the first-century letter writer's theology eventually came to mold much of what Protestantism proclaims today, especially in regard to the primacy of faith over works.

Before leaving *le Miroir*, it would be desirable to take a moment to speak of some other stylistic features: the use of paradox (885, 1,081, 1,199), for example, and dramatic repetitions (980–95). These owe much to a tradition

---

queen of England, Elizabeth, was inspired, probably as an exercise in French as well as a devotional meditation, to translate Marguerite's work.

14. My edition here is the 1972 publication edited by Joseph L. Allaire (Munich: Wilhelm Fink Verlag).

of poetic writing produced by court poets of the early Renaissance known as the *Rhétoriqueurs*.[15]

Depending on available time, the instructor may wish to draw attention to some other of Marguerite's religious texts, for example, her *Dialogue en forme de vision nocturne*, written before *le Miroir*, but published later.[16] Marguerite's response to the death of her young niece Charlotte, the *Dialogue* is in fact a good digest of reformist ideas because the deceased, transformed into a learned theologian, comes back from death to console and instruct her aunt. The list also includes the *Oraison à notre seigneur Jesus* (Prayer to our Lord Jesus) and the *Pater Noster* (Our Father), illustrations of the popular devotional tendency among reformists;[17] her four nativity plays, which are heavily laden with reformist speeches;[18] her long poem on redemption, *Le triomphe de l'Agneau* (The Lamb's Triumph);[19] and some of her shorter poetic pieces published together as *Chansons spirituelles* (Spiritual Songs).[20]

If in fact the syllabus would allow for a reading of any of the above, my inclination would be to prepare short, telling snippets. There are any number of appropriate passages from the *Dialogue*, for example, that could demonstrate how deftly the author makes use of the theatrical format. As for the verse prayers, a small section would readily suffice to give students a taste of the tone of these meditative and highly introspective poems, nurtured by reformist thinking.

Le Triomphe de l'Agneau, on the other hand, more complex and important for the emotional evolution it conveys in nearly two thousand decasyllabic

15. These poets (Clément Marot's father, Jean, was one) were noted for their elegant, but often overplayed, verbal gymnastics.

16. It appeared in 1533. A good modern edition has been prepared by Renja Salminen, *Dialogue en forme de vision nocturne* (Helsinki: Suomalainen Tiedeakatemia, 1985).

17. At least two authors ought to be consulted on the general theme of Marguerite's religious verse: Robert Cottrell, *The Grammar of Silence* (Washington, D.C.: Catholic University Press, 1986), and Gary Ferguson, *Mirroring Belief: Marguerite de Navarre's Devotional Poetry* (Edinburgh: Edinburgh University Press, 1992).

18. See Marguerite de Navarre, *Les comédies bibliques*, ed. Barbara Marczuk (Geneva: Droz, 2000). Marguerite's secular theater was edited by V. L. Saulnier in 1963 and reedited and translated in 1992 by R. Reynolds-Cornell. In my view, the so-called religious theater would have little to say to the modern student. On the other hand, the instructor could cull out of the "profane" plays—often, however, very theological—scenes that would corroborate the essential argument here, namely, that Marguerite rarely strayed very far from her religious convictions.

19. See volume 1 of H. P. Clive's anthology, *Oeuvres choisies: Marguerite de Navarre* (New York: Appleton-Century-Crofts, 1968).

20. See *Chansons spirituelles*, ed. Georges Dottin (Geneva: Droz, 1971). One might also consult the essay by Ehson Ahmed, "Marguerite de Navarre's *Chansons spirituelles* and the Poet's Passion," *Bibliothèque d'Humanisme et Renaissance* 52 (1990): 37–52.

lines, should be read in its entirety, if at all. For some, it represents the epitome of Marguerite's mystical style, what Lefranc has called a "grandiose moral drama."

THE HEPTAMERON

If there is any one work that has made Marguerite famous, it is this extraordinary French "decameron," inspired in fact by Boccaccio's work of the fourteenth century. Marguerite had not only read Boccaccio in the original Italian, but in 1544 commissioned Antoine le Maçon, to translate it into French.[21] The instructor can profitably introduce a general digression at this juncture on the entire novella tradition, forerunner of today's "short story," pointing out its essential ingredients and offering some samples, if time permits.[22]

The fundamental question is whether religion plays any role in this conspicuously secular work. The answer is decidedly affirmative: first, in the prologue that sets up the literary frame for the work; second, in the subject matter of many of its stories; and finally, in the fiery discussions among the narrators that follow them.

Let us begin with the frame device. This literary technique, the most famous example of which is the *Thousand and One Nights*, creates a narrative excuse to tell stories. In the "Arabian Nights," we recall, Scheherazade (Sharazad) postpones her execution by entertaining the king with nightly tales. In Boccaccio's *Decameron* it is the calamity of the plague that brings together ten escapees from the city, who choose to while away the time by exchanging stories. Like Boccaccio, Marguerite uses a crisis—in her case flooding at a Pyrenees spa—in order to create a frame.

Pertinent to our discussion is the fact that as the narrators set up their daily schedule, Marguerite has one of her characters, Oisille, lead the stranded travelers to the Abbey of Our Lady at Sarrance, although, we are told, she was not motivated by any "superstitious" notion that the Virgin

---

21. While there are more recent editions coming out, Michel François's careful and scholarly edition of 1960 remains a reliable source. As for critical commentary, there is no way of doing justice here to that huge output. A good collection of essays can be found in John Lyons and Mary B. McKinley, eds., *Critical Tales: New Studies of the 'Heptameron' and Early Modern Culture* (Philadelphia: University of Pennsylvania Press, 1993). Depending on the level of scrutiny desired, the instructor can consult Clive and the Modern Language Association bibliographies to establish a list of recent studies on Marguerite's most famous work.

22. See *The Early French Novella: An Anthology of Fifteenth and Sixteenth-Century French Tales*, trans. Patricia F. Cholakian and Rouben C. Cholakian (Albany, N.Y.: State University Press, 1972).

would intercede on their behalf. Clearly, Marguerite is taking a swipe at Roman Catholic Mariology. But that is not all.

Later, when the group approaches the abbot of the local sanctuary, we are told that he offers them room and board only reluctantly, because, as the narrator is quick to emphasize, "he was not an especially likable person." Marguerite here echoes contemporary attitudes toward monks, especially Franciscans, who were perceived to be corrupt. She goes on to denounce the abbot as a "hypocrite" who merely feels "obliged" to play the good person (65).

When it comes time to establish a program of activities, the group once again turns to this venerable older woman, Oisille, who notes that she had spent her entire life in search of the appropriate way to deal with "tedium and sadness" and then happily announces that she has finally found the one and only truly meaningful comfort, the reading of Holy Scripture. Marguerite thus puts into the mouth of this character an essential feature of the reformist doctrine: general access to sacred texts, preferably in the vernacular. Oisille goes on to describe her personal morning devotions: regular reading of scripture and "meditation on the Almighty's essential goodness," since, "for our sakes, He sent his son to earth to proclaim his holy word and to redeem our sinful natures." In the end, she also sings God's praises in the form of the Psalms (66–67).

This is an appropriate moment to remind students of how important Marguerite was in sponsoring vernacular translations, including that of the Hebrew songbook. It was she who encouraged her favorite poet Clément Marot to put these poems into French; many still appear to this day in French Protestant hymnals.

And so it is decided that every day will allow time for prayers and that each morning Oisille will read from the gospels to the assembled party of five women and five men. All this in addition to spending the hottest time of the day—from noon to four—in a "delightful meadow" nearby, where the newfound friends will entertain themselves by recounting tales that have either been personally "witnessed" or told to them by a "trustworthy" person. In this way, after ten days they will have accumulated the "entire one hundred!"[23] (68–69).

And of what do these tales consist? Do they have a "religious" dimension? Marguerite, although she sets out to tell only *true* stories, like so many of the

---

23. Of course, as we know, Marguerite never actually completed the work. Was it because she died? Was it because she did not find enough stories to satisfy her? Critics are divided in their reasoning, and interested students can consult the bibliographies for additional information on this thorny issue.

novellistes (short story writers) of her time, draws from many different sources, written and oral. The setting can be bourgeois and down-to-earth (novellas 2, 8, 36, 45, 50, 55, 61, 68, 71) or courtly (novellas 3, 6, 12, 17, 26, 30, 39, 44, 53, 70). The tone can be vulgar (novella 11), or delicate and refined (novella 10). The reader may laugh heartily (novella 28) or weep profusely (novella 12). At least two important tales recount incidents of sexual assault that may have been autobiographical in origin (novellas 4, 10).[24]

Incontestably, a major component is stories of infidelity and sexual abuse, many of them involving clerics or monks. Here Marguerite joins the ranks of contemporaries who enjoyed ridiculing oversexed members of religious communities.[25] But while in other cases—Boccaccio, Chaucer— such stories were meant merely to invite laughter, there is rather a more bitter edge with this reformist author, who borrows from a venerable, comic tradition, but with a more serious, didactic purpose. Marguerite, we know, was a principal in a campaign to improve the quality of religious life in France, and so her tales of wayward monks have to be seen as more than commonplace jokes.

In some instances, her aim is to show that a resourceful woman can out-wit the devious stratagems of monks up to no good, most often Franciscans. In novella 5, for example, two of these plot to rape a boatwoman but are finally made fools of when she cleverly evades their lecherous advances and reports them both to the Father Superior of their monastery. Novella 23 is a tragedy in which a crafty and dishonest Franciscan not only takes advantage of a trusting and naive woman, but by his terrible misdeed brings about the deaths of the victim, her child, and her grieving husband. Lest there be any question concerning the intentions of the narrator of this dreary tale, the teller (Oisille) at one point interrupts the story long enough to inform us that the unfortunate woman had foolishly believed in false Franciscan preaching on fasting and chastisement, while ignoring the significance of God's divine grace and the "remission of sin" through Christ's death on the cross. In short, the story has an emphatically reformist flavor.[26]

Not all of the *Heptameron*'s badly behaved clerics are mere monks; there are also tales that expose abuse by loftier members of the church hierarchy.

---

24. This is the basic argument in Patricia F. Cholakian, *Rape and Writing in the* Heptaméron *of Marguerite de Navarre* (Carbondale, Ill.: Southern Illinois University Press, 1991).

25. It should be noted that an important contemporary writer, François Rabelais, devotes many pages of his giant stories to poking fun at the monastic life style. See especially the section on the *Abbaye de Thélème* (*Gargantua*, chaps. 52–58).

26. See in this regard Cholakian, *Rape and Writing*, the chapter on "Rape and Religious Reform."

The sexual aggressor of novella 1 is the "Bishop of Sées," and the guilty party of novella 61 is "a canon of Autun." Marguerite, sister after all, of a mighty monarch, did not hesitate to criticize even those in important places.

The uniqueness of Marguerite's frame is that her storytellers are not narrators alone, like those in the *Decameron*, but also *devisants*, conversationalists, who happily engage in the courtly ideal of witty, educated, and sophisticated discourse.[27] This is by no means idle, empty-headed chatter, for the lively dialogue following every narrative soon transforms these raconteurs into very real people with very real opinions.

The *Heptameron*'s postnarrative commentaries often serve as a forum for airing religious views, and the prevailing outlook is almost invariably negative. Like the reformists, who inveighed against members of the church hierarchy for their shameless hypocrisy, many of Marguerite's discussants vent their disgust at clerical corruption. There are a few exceptions. Saffredent, for example, apologetically notes that monks are after all human and thus subject to the same passions as others (novella 41). Oisille at one point is made to say that "they are not all bad" (novella 22) and later hopes that the *devisants* can go beyond talk about badly behaved monks alone (novella 48).

Such protestations are the exception not the rule, however. Most often, corroborating the tales of clerical duplicity in the collection, the commentary is hostile to monks. Nomerfide confesses that the mere sight of one "fills her with disgust" (novella 22). Geburon says they "talk like angels, but are as aggressive as devils" (novella 5). Nor is the negativism limited to the clergy. Saffredent broadens the criticism to say that the church is haunted by the works of Satan (novella 61). In a later discussion, this same character gives voice to another common reformist criticism: that veneration of saints is dangerous idolatry (novella 65).

Reformist that she is, Marguerite also finds appropriate moments in these discussions to speak in more positive, constructive terms about the reformist program. It is clear, for example, that many of these narrators have a good acquaintance with sacred texts, proof that the reform is taking hold and that lay people are choosing to read biblical texts on their own, instead of having scripture spoon-fed to them by priests. Several readily cite the Bible. At the close of novella 22, Geburon quotes Jesus when he says, "Everyone who exalts himself shall be humbled, and he who humbles himself shall be

27. It was Baldasare Castiglione, in *Il cortegiano* (The Courtier), who included superior conversational skills as part of his definition of the perfect Renaissance courtier. For a good summary of the work, see Margaret L. King, *The Renaissance in Europe*, 234–40.

exalted" (Lk 14:11). In another instance, Saffredent bolsters his argument with reference to the gospels (novella 65). In that same discussion, Oisille offers another reflection characteristic of reformists' thinking: that greater glory goes to the humble and unpretentious.[28]

Two other precepts, central to reformist thought, come into the text. At the close of novella 33, Simontaut advocates the doctrine of salvation through faith, and later in that same discussion, Parlamente, who almost certainly represents Marguerite herself, is made to say, "For the sake of our own well-being, it would be wonderful if through faith in Him [Christ] . . . we could make a show of that faith to all those around us" (novella 33).

Part of this same doctrine, as we have noted, is the gratuitousness of God's grace. Geburon tells the others that there is no goodness without the indwelling of God's grace (novella 22), and in the discussion following novella 56, Simontaut asserts that those who do not put their faith in the grace of God often end up very badly.

These tales and their storytellers' commentaries are so engrossing and thought-provoking that they cannot fail to inspire discussion on gender and religion. If the instructor needs further stimuli, however, the scholarly bibliography is rich with motivating ideas.[29]

EPILOGUE

With these two contrasting texts in mind, the instructor will invite closing arguments: What is Marguerite's religion? How does she express it and where? What is the tie-in between the "religious" ideas she brings into a secular text like the *Heptameron* and her more self-conscious theological

28. In her play *L'inquisiteur* (The Inquisitor), Marguerite sets up a religious contest between a learned "inquisitor" and a group of unsophisticated children. In the end, it is the children who carry the day. A similar exchange is found in *La Comédie de Mont-de-Marsan*, probably the last play Marguerite wrote, in which the allegorical figure *La Ravie de Dieu* (God's Ravished), whose religious expression consists of singing and praise, triumphs over her three rivals, *La Sage* (The Wise), *La Supersticieuse* (The Superstitious), and *La Mondaine* (The Worldly).

29. A classic study on love and religion in the *Heptameron* is Lucien Febvre's *Autour de 'L'Heptaméron': Amour sacré, amour profane* (Paris: Gallimard, 1944), to be supplemented, however, by more gender-oriented and modern reinterpretations written by women scholars like Carla Freccero and Colette Winn. See especially Carla Freccero, "Gender Ideologues, Women Writers, and the Problem of Patronage in Early Modern England and France: Issues and Frameworks," in *Reading the Renaissance*, ed. Jonathan Hart (New York: Garland, 1996), 65–74; and Colette Winn, "La Loi du non-parler dans *L'Heptameron* de Marguerite de Navarre," *Romance Quarterly* 33 (1988): 157–88. It would also be helpful to examine Telle, *L'Œuvre de Marguerite d'Angoulême*.

pronouncements elsewhere?[30] To put minds at rest, it is probably worth noting that generations of so-called specialists in Marguerite's life and works have themselves gone at it tooth and nail trying to put a single label on her.[31]

In the end, using these texts as reference points, the most interesting question to raise is how gender and religion interface as themes in Marguerite. To be sure, while an outspoken critic of the established church, the queen of Navarre would never have directly accused Christianity of being the cause of gender bias, although, knowledgeable as she was about sacred texts, she most certainly could have found justification in biblical literature. At the same time, she could not have been unaware—having been herself persecuted—that being a woman made her that much more vulnerable in the eyes of church authorities.

Her consolation and her defense strategy were twofold. She, first of all, maintained a lifetime of meaningful female friendships, many of which came of deeply shared religious convictions: her favorite aunt, Philiberte; Renée, Duchess of Este, to whose Italian court she sent Clément Marot when the Faculty of Theology at Paris came after the poet; Madame d'Étampes,[32] François's official mistress and Marguerite's closest ally at the French court; her own namesake niece, for whom, at the time of her marriage, she wrote her cautionary tale against male aggression, *La Fable du faux cuyder*; the Italian poet Vittoria Colonna, with whom she carried on a mutually admiring correspondence[33]; and Marie Dentière, whom she greatly inspired as another dedicated woman reformist. Moreover, in her collection of stories now known as the *Heptameron*, the queen of Navarre made much of clerical abuse of innocent women.[34] Thus both as a significant political figure and as a writer, Marguerite challenged her two favored grievances: church and gender abuse.

30. See Jourda, *Marguerite d'Angoulême*, 2:904, and Carol Thysell, *The Pleasure of Discernment: Marguerite de Navarre as Theologian* (Oxford: University Press, 2000).

31. The major argument is over whether Marguerite was a proto-Protestant. For some the answer has been emphatically yes (Abel Lefranc). Most, however, have not been willing to go that far.

32. It is noteworthy that she sent her important poem about female bonding, *La coche*, to Madame d'Étampes so that she might submit "a woman's work" to the king's judgment.

33. See in Jourda's *Repertoire*, letters 797–800 and 983–84.

34. The instructor may here make reference to her allegorical poem *La Fable du faux cuyder* (1543) in which Marguerite warns her namesake niece—about to be married—against bad male behavior.

III

Women and the Reformation

MARIE DENTIÈRE: AN OUTSPOKEN
REFORMER ENTERS THE FRENCH
LITERARY CANON

Mary McKinley

Marie Dentière intrigues students. Much of her life (1495–1561) is shrouded in mystery, but the few historical records of her reveal a determined woman whose religious convictions often led her against the grain.[1] She left the security of her convent and her family in Tournai in the early 1520s in order to follow French religious reformers to a safe haven in Strasbourg. From there she went with her husband, a former Catholic priest, to Switzerland, where the couple preached the new reformed religion. She took part in the takeover of Geneva in 1535–36 before John Calvin arrived there, and she reappears fleetingly in the Reformed Church's history up to the year of her death in 1561.

My students read Marie Dentière's *Epistle to Marguerite de Navarre* in conjunction with a work written by the woman to whom she addressed the letter, the *Heptameron*, a collection of seventy-two novellas.[2] Although the *Epistle*, appearing in 1539, predates the *Heptameron*, which was composed for the most part in the 1540s, I introduce it after students have read Marguerite's tales.[3] The *Heptameron* gives students a context for the *Epistle*. Its tales and

---

1. Here and throughout this article I refer readers to the bibliography in my translation. To the list of biographical sources about Dentière in that Other Voice volume, in the volume editor's introduction (2, n. 2), I add a recent article that was not available when the book went to press: Isabelle Graesslé, "Vie et légendes de Marie Dentière," *Bulletin du Centre Protestant d'Etudes* 55, no. 1 (2003): 1–31.

2. The *Heptameron* is available in several French editions. For classroom use I prefer the edition with a very informative introduction and notes by Gisèle Mathieu-Castellani (Paris: Livre de Poche, 1999). The excellent scholarly edition of Renja Salminen, *Heptaméron* (Geneva: Droz, 1999) is a valuable guide, even if too expensive for students. For the *Heptameron* in English, see *The Heptameron*, trans. Paul Chilton (New York: Penguin Books, 1984).

3. I explain that I refer to Marguerite by her first name just as I refer to her brother, the king of France, as Francis. Members of royal families, both women and men, are conventionally known

frame story depict situations that Dentière decries in the *Epistle*: corruption in the clergy, for example, and pious devotions that have degenerated into superstitions. Almost all of its stories are set in the early years of the sixteenth century; they offer a richly varied view of life in France and its neighboring countries as the events of the Protestant Reformation were unfolding. The *Heptameron* portrays regular reading of the Bible as part of the story-tellers' daily routine. They meet every morning for scriptural readings led by the widow Oisille, their spiritual guide, and they tell their stories in the afternoon. From the beginning of the movement that became the Protestant Reformation, Holy Scripture was the authority on which the reformed churches were founded. Although there are differences in the positions taken by Marguerite de Navarre and Marie Dentière on important issues of church reform, differences that emerge in the *Epistle*'s often acerbic attack on the Roman Catholic Church, both women were influenced in the early 1520s by a movement in France that sought to reform the church from within, avoiding the kind of open break that Martin Luther had made in Germany. That movement, called *évangélique* after the French word for Gospel (*évangile*), was led by Jacques Lefèvre d'Etaples, an eminent biblical scholar, and included men like Guillaume Farel and Gérard Roussel, who like Dentière were French self-exiles in Strasbourg. There are indications that Marguerite de Navarre was the godmother of one of Marie Dentière's daughters, and although the two women may have met, there is as yet no clear evidence that they did. Whatever reformist sympathies they may have shared in the 1520s, by the 1530s they had chosen different paths to bring about religious reform. Dentière joined Farel in his efforts to proselytize French-speaking Switzerland and create the new Reformed Church, completely independent from and hostile to the Roman Catholic Church. Lefèvre and Roussel, however, returned to France under Marguerite's protection and continued to work with her for reform from within. In 1533, Marguerite obtained a bishopric for Roussel in Oloron, a town in her husband's territories in southwest France. The group in Switzerland considered their former colleagues hypocrites who compromised their beliefs by staying within the institution they both criticized. The *Epistle* often alludes to the events that created animosity between the two groups. At the same time it appeals to Marguerite de Navarre to intervene with her brother on behalf of those it considers to be the true believers.

---

by their first names. We do not refer to the reigning monarch of England as "Windsor," and I do not refer to Marguerite as "Navarre."

I begin by assigning the pages in my introduction that outline that historical background (1–21) and the opening sections of the *Epistle*: the dedicatory address and the Defense of Women (51–56). I urge students to look for the rhetorical strategies that Dentière uses when addressing Marguerite in these early sections. I explain that rhetoric, the choices a speaker or writer makes in order to persuade, was part of the medieval curriculum of the seven liberal arts. Rhetoric, along with grammar and dialectic (or logic), made up the trivium, the language arts. Rhetoric's goal was eloquence, a quality essential for men who hoped to advance in public life. Since women were excluded from public life (see the series editors' introduction, xvi–xvii), and silence rather than eloquence was the ideal society demanded of them, rhetoric was not part of a woman's education. Nevertheless, the *Epistle* is carefully crafted rhetorically.

She opens her dedicatory address by using a formula of respect, "My most honored Lady," but in the same sentence she adds the words "we women," insisting on the concerns she and Marguerite shared in common as women rather than on their difference in social rank. She then attributes her assertion that women should flee error in dangerous times to Marguerite: "as your writings have already sufficiently shown" (51). Those words suggest another affinity between Dentière and Marguerite: Marguerite was herself a published writer, and Dentière was becoming one by publishing the *Epistle*. Her tactic illustrates her awareness that women were still "the other voice," especially in matters of religion. Dentière justifies publishing a religious polemic by alluding to Marguerite's *Mirror of the Sinful Soul* (1531 and 1533), a long mystical poem reflecting evangelical beliefs that Parisian theologians had attempted to suppress.[4] Dentière points to Marguerite as an example who authorizes her own writing on religious doctrine. I point out that Dentière apparently sent the *Epistle* to Marguerite in manuscript before publishing it in Geneva. The intended audience of the *Epistle* is therefore much broader than Marguerite alone, and the address is more than a direct communication from one woman to another. Intended readers included both men and women, people in Switzerland and in France who were not free to practice their reformed beliefs, and the French clergy, especially those who believed in reform but, in Dentière's eyes, lacked the courage to profess those beliefs openly. Finally, the dedicatory address makes it clear that the message of the *Epistle* is meant to reach King Francis himself, through the intervention of his sister. I ask the students to look for indications of all

---

4. An anthology of Marguerite's writing that includes *The Mirror of a Sinful Soul* is forthcoming in the Other Voice series.

those intended readers as they read the *Epistle* and to be alert for shifts within the work where the intended audience changes.

The opening address paints a picture of a society torn asunder by dissension and violence, ruptures extending into the city of Geneva itself. In 1538, a year before the *Epistle* appeared, the Council of Two Hundred, the municipal council of Geneva, had expelled Farel and Calvin, whose approach to shaping the Reformed Church in the city they found too rigid (volume editor's introduction, 11–12). Dentière and her husband Antoine Froment were on the side of the banished leaders, whom the *Epistle* calls the "servants of God" and compares to Jesus Christ (51–52). News of the expulsion spread, and Froment later reported that Marguerite had asked for details of the affair from Dentière, prompting her to send the queen a copy of the *Epistle*.

When Dentière explicitly says that she is writing to ask Marguerite to intervene with her brother, she goes on to remind Marguerite that she too has political power and a God-given responsibility to declare her faith openly: "what God has given you and revealed to us women, no more than men should we hide it and bury it in the earth" (53). I ask students to examine the language of this passage carefully. In it Dentière tightens her rhetorical affinity with Marguerite even as she refers to a broader—female—audience. By slipping from "you" to "us women," Dentière once again draws Marguerite into a partnership where they are equal. By moving to the first person plural, she also softens a bit what would have been an implied accusation that Marguerite had compromised her reformer's convictions by staying within the Catholic Church. Then Dentière, still linked with Marguerite through the pronoun "we," broaches the question of women's speech and the exclusion of women from teaching in public about religious matters.

The series editors' introduction (especially xxv–xxvii) provides the historical context for the tradition that stifled women's voices, prizing eloquence in men but associating it with loose sexual morals in women. My students have already encountered the silencing of women in the *Heptameron*. Many of its tales show women prevented from speaking: Rolandine, temporarily, in story 21; her aunt in story 40; the assaulted princess in story 4; and the wife discovered with her lover in story 32 are just a few examples. Several women break through the rule of silence: Rolandine, Marie Héroet in story 22, and the female storytellers themselves. The frame story offers striking examples in the lively female characters who tell stories and make outspoken remarks in the discussions. One scholar has even proposed that the *Heptameron* itself is Marguerite's response to that suppression of speech in her own personal experience.[5]

The injunction against women speaking out in church was not merely tacit. The marginal reference at this point in the dedicatory address refers the reader to Paul's 1 Timothy 2:11–12, which church leaders had long cited as their authority: "Let the women learn in silence with all subjection. I suffer not a woman to teach, nor to have authority over the man, but to keep silent." At the first meeting of the Women Writers course, I give students a sheet with quotations about women made by male writers from Paul to Shakespeare. I begin with the verses from 1 Timothy, as well as similar verses from 1 Corinthians 14:34–35. Dentière clearly has these verses in mind when she writes: "And even though we are not permitted to preach in public, in congregations and churches, we are not forbidden to write and admonish one another in all charity" (53). As it unfolds, the *Epistle* becomes a written admonishment to Marguerite and, through her, to her brother the king. History records two occasions when Dentière spoke out vehemently. The first, in August 1535, was to a group of women, the Catholic nuns of the Poor Clares convent in Geneva, whom Dentière urged to follow her example, that is, leave the convent and marry. That proselytizing effort is recorded by Jeanne de Jussie in her *Short Chronicle*.[6] Eleven years later, in 1546, Calvin reports that Dentière did preach in public and had a hostile encounter with him on that occasion. Calvin reports the incident derisively in a letter to Farel (volume editor's introduction, 8–9, 19–20).

At the end of the dedicatory address, Dentière specifies some of the people in her intended audience. She mentions only women: Marguerite, but also "other women detained in captivity, and principally the poor little women (*femmelettes*) wanting to know and understand the truth" (53). "Detained in captivity," is a reference to the Jews of the Old Testament held in captivity first by the Egyptians and then by the Babylonians. Supporters of the reform were "in captivity" in France, in the sense that they were not free to express and practice their religious beliefs. Dentière encourages them not to fear leaving their French homeland, as she had done. The diminutive expression *femmelettes* refers to ordinary women, not yet actively committed to

---

5. Patricia Cholakian, *Rape and Writing in the* Heptameron *of Marguerite de Navarre*, Carbondale: Southern Illinois University Press, 1991.

6. Jeanne de Jussie, *Short Chronicle*, ed. and trans. Carrie Klaus, The Other Voice in Early Modern Europe (Chicago: University of Chicago Press, 2006). An essay on that text is also included in this volume.

the reformed ministry like Dentière, but questioning and seeking the truth.[7] The passage includes all of them in one community of women and suggests that Marguerite is one of the "other women detained in captivity." It would have been quite a coup for the Reformed Church if Marguerite had publicly rejected the Catholic Church and joined them, a move unimaginable for the sister of the king of France. The *Epistle* makes that suggestion several times obliquely and becomes more explicit toward the end. Marguerite's own daughter, Jeanne d'Albret, did publicly convert to Calvinism shortly after her mother's death in 1549. Born in November 1528, she was only ten years old when Dentière put her at the end of the list of women designated in the dedicatory address. In a few lines that appear in only one of the two extant copies of the *Epistle*, Dentière writes,

> And also to give courage to my little daughter, your goddaughter, to give to the printers a little Hebrew grammar that she has made in French for the use and profit of other little girls, above all, for your daughter, my Lady the Princess, to whom it is directed. (53)

Students are intrigued by this detail of a little girl writing a Hebrew grammar for another little girl. The religious reformers included philologists, Lefèvre d'Etaples and Erasmus prominent among them, who were striving to recapture the original text of the Bible by studying its original languages. They viewed the official Catholic Church version of the Bible, the Latin Vulgate, as having been corrupted over the centuries. The Old Testament or Hebrew Bible, and the New Testament, written in Greek, required study of those two languages if the original version of the scriptures were to be reestablished. Later in the *Epistle*, Dentière implies that she has studied Hebrew (71). The image of Dentière's daughter offering the product of her study as a gift to the young princess Jeanne adds an element of intimacy to the letter, especially since it is here that Dentière refers to her daughter as Marguerite's goddaughter.[8] Natalie Zemon Davis writes that the habit of sending books

---

7. Thomas Head examines the situations and beliefs of the women Dentière refers to here in "The Religion of the *Femmelettes*: Ideals and Experience among Women in Fifteenth- and Sixteenth-Century France," in *That Gentle Strength: Historical Perspectives on Women in Christianity*, ed. Lynda Coon, Katherine Haldane, and Elisabeth Sommer (Charlottesville: University Press of Virginia, 1991), 149–75.

8. See William Kemp and Diane Desrosiers-Bonin, "Marie d'Ennetières et la petite grammaire hébraique de sa fille d'après la dédicace de l'*Epistre* à Marguerite de Navarre (1539)," *Bibliothèque d'Humanisme et Renaissance* 60, no. 1 (1998): 117–34.

as gifts to friends was common among humanists; she cites several examples where Erasmus offered one of his books to a friend or a host.[9]

THE DEFENSE OF WOMEN

The second section of the *Epistle* belongs to an important literary tradition, works in praise of women that responded to the dominant misogynistic discourse of the Middle Ages (series editors' introduction, xviii–xx). The virtuous women in this gallery all come from the Bible. Although I provide brief identifications of these biblical women in a note (54, n. 9; 55, n. 11), I find it helpful to ask what students know about the women whom Dentière mentions. We identify the qualities that made these women exemplary and would encourage imitation from Dentière's contemporaries. The New Testament women enjoyed a privileged close relationship with Christ, one needing no male intermediaries. Dentière uses them explicitly as examples to authorize women as preachers:

> What woman was a greater preacher than the Samaritan woman, who was not ashamed to preach Jesus and his word, confessing him openly before everyone, as soon as she heard Jesus say that we must adore God in spirit and truth? Who can boast of having had the first manifestation of the great mystery of the resurrection of Jesus, if not Mary Magdalen, from whom he had thrown out seven devils, and the other women, to whom, rather than to men, he had earlier declared himself through his angel and commanded them to tell, preach and declare it to others? (55)

I bring in examples from other authors praising women, including one on which Dentière seems to have modeled her own, Agrippa's *Declamation on the Nobility and Preeminence of the Female Sex.*[10] Like Agrippa, Dentière points out the examples of evil men in the Bible and she makes a jab at the men she sees as their successors, the leaders of the Catholic Church. Our discussion of the Defense of Women usually runs over into the next class meeting, during which we also embark on the Epistle proper, the third and longest section of the work.

9. Natalie Zemon Davis, *The Gift in Sixteenth-Century France* (Oxford: Oxford University Press, 2000), 59–61.

10. Henricus Cornelius Agrippa, *Declamation on the Nobility and Preeminence of the Female Sex*, trans. and ed. Albert Rabil, Jr., The Other Voice in Early Modern Europe (Chicago: University of Chicago Press, 1996), 52–54, 85.

THE EPISTLE PROPER

In order to understand the doctrinal issues raised in the *Epistle*, students need some background. Even before arriving at Marie Dentière, while we are discussing Rabelais or Marguerite de Navarre, for example, it is not unusual for a student to ask, in effect, "What was the Protestant Reformation?" I cannot presume to teach the Reformation, but I try to anticipate their question by asking at an appropriate point, "What words or ideas do you associate with the Protestant Reformation?" I write the words that students volunteer on the board: Luther, Calvin, marriage for the ministers. If no one suggests the following words, I add them to the list: sin, forgiveness, faith, grace, good works, salvation. I explain that there is a good deal of difference even among those who wanted to reform the Roman Catholic Church, but that a few concepts are essential. I write two words side by side on the board with a little space between them: person and God. I explain that many of the disputes arose from how people understood the relationship between an individual and God. The *Epistle*, like the teachings of the French-speaking Swiss reformers (Farel, Calvin, and others), insists that salvation comes from faith in Jesus Christ alone. The reformers reacted against the Roman Catholic doctrine that an individual could help to achieve his or her salvation by doing good works (performing virtuous actions or pious practices). They also insisted on the Bible as their sole authority, thereby rejecting centuries of doctrinal accretions made by the Catholic Church through popes and papal councils and the body of canon (or church) law. One of those doctrines was that grave (or mortal) sins could normally be forgiven only after a penitent confessed them to a priest and received from the priest absolution, a formal act that constituted the sacrament of penance. In that process of reconciliation between the penitent and God, the priest was a necessary intermediate authority. The Geneva reformers denied the need for any such human intermediary and rejected the sacrament of penance. I direct students who want more information than the notes provide to some basic reference works that can be found in most libraries.[11] I ask them to be ready to explain the following words as we prepare to discuss this longest and most difficult section of the *Epistle*: canon law; shroud of Turin; Waldensians;

11. *The Oxford Encyclopedia of the Reformation*, ed. Hans Hillerbrand, 4 vols. (New York: Oxford University Press, 1995); *The Oxford Dictionary of the Christian Church*, ed. F. L. Cross, 3d ed., ed. E. A. Livingstone (New York: Oxford University Press, 1997); and *A Catholic Dictionary of Theology*, 3 vols. (New York: Nelson, 1962). Thomas Tentler's *Sin and Confession on the Eve of the Reformation* (Princeton: Princeton University Press, 1977) provides an excellent historical background for beliefs about the forgiveness of sins and reconciliation between God and the sinner.

transubstantiation, real presence; Turks; Nicodemism; Melchizedek; and demonic possession.

The Epistle proper opens by affirming the authority of Jesus Christ alone and then warns immediately of the enemies: "all those who rise up against him and his followers, trying to destroy him by tyrannies and human powers." (56) The *Epistle* presents a view of the world in cataclysmic conflict as those enemies attempt to destroy Christ. I encourage students to go to some of the scriptural passages that we find referenced in the margins in order to see how the *Epistle*'s language echoes biblical imagery. Echoing the Bible is one part of the *Epistle*'s rhetoric. Since preaching was an essential tool of the reformers' ministry, and Dentière has used the word *prescheresse,* or "female preacher," in the "Defense of Women," I suggest that we look for evidence of rhetorical choices in the *Epistle.* Its style often suggests preaching. I ask for volunteers to read some of these early passages aloud, and we appreciate the repetitions and cadences of the prose. One aspect of the *Epistle* that can confuse readers is the way the identity of the speaking voice, the "I," as well as that of the intended audience, the "you," changes. That variety could be conveyed in preaching by a change in tone of voice and would help to avoid monotony; thereby holding the interest of the congregation. Such a change occurs almost immediately in the Epistle proper when, without warning, the speaking voice becomes that of Christ: "Be therefore vigilant and ready in tribulation, for you will certainly be hated by all because of me, led before kings, princes, and lords because you give witness to truth in my name" (57). The voice of Christ continues to admonish for half a page, before the speaking voice shifts back to "we." I point out that in classical rhetoric prosopopoeia is a rhetorical figure that imports the imagined speech of an absent person, often a god, into an oration.

The *Epistle* attacks the Roman Catholic Church for having usurped the sole authority of Christ by teaching false doctrines that complicate the clear message of the New Testament. It accuses the clergy of having appropriated more and more power for themselves and made of the priests, bishops, and pope false Christs or idols. I ask the students to make a list of the specific criticisms Dentière makes of the church. Here (57–58) she attacks the Catholic hierarchy on three counts, three accusations that will recur throughout the *Epistle:* they forbid the clergy to marry; they impose dietary restrictions (especially fasting and abstaining from meat); and worst of all, they believe that bread and wine are transformed into the body and blood of Christ in the Eucharist, a major preoccupation of the *Epistle.* Those "false doctrines" are all seen as a form of idolatry. The speaking voice "we" implicates itself among those who have been taken in by those false Christs.

I draw attention to a sentence that begins, "The Lord God, knowing well that our nature is prone to evil and inclined toward all sorts of idolatry, . . ." (58). The *Epistle* reflects a view of humankind as marked by the original sin of Adam and Eve and their fall from paradise, recounted in Genesis. Their fault condemned the whole human race until the coming of Christ, told in the New Testament. The people of the Old Testament are often shown succumbing to idolatry. The Old Testament era is seen as the time of the law, the laws of Moses in the Ten Commandments but also the many prescribed rituals listed in Old Testament books such as Leviticus. Both the French evangelical reformers and the Reformed Church in Geneva taught that Christ replaced the letter of the Old Testament law with the spirit of the New. The *Epistle* depicts the history of Christianity as an ungrateful refusal of God's love and a reversion back to the idolatry that characterized the Old Testament, an error that can, however, quickly be set right: "In spite of all that . . . the spirit gives life" (58–59), a statement that conveys succinctly the reformers' view of the relationship between each individual and God.

Idolatry becomes a keyword in the following pages, covering a broad range of beliefs and practices of the Roman Catholic Church that, in Dentière's eyes, bestow on material things the honor that belongs only to Christ: "the earth is filled with idolatries" (59). These include pilgrimages, indulgences, veneration of saints, and devotions to objects such as the crucifix. The greatest idolatry, however, according to the *Epistle*, is the Catholic Mass. The Mass, with its claims to repeat the sacrifice that Christ had made by dying on the cross and to effect the miraculous change of the bread and wine into the body and blood of Christ, was a bitter bone of contention. Less than five years earlier, in October 1534, at a critical point when Francis I was negotiating with a group of German Protestant princes and hoping to achieve a peaceful compromise that would repair at least some of the ruptures within the Church, printed broadsheets (called placards) contemptuously attacking the Mass had appeared in Paris and throughout France. Francis, shaken by that affront to the order of his kingdom, had reacted by ordering a severe crackdown on perceived heretics.[12] The talks with the German Protestants collapsed, and hopes for building a common ground were dashed. The anonymous placards had been printed in Neuchâtel and were the work of Antoine Marcourt, a French expatriate like Dentière and Froment and many of the Swiss reformers. The group at Neuchâtel was closely

12. For more about this important episode in the history of the Reformation in France, see Robert J. Knecht, *Renaissance Warrior and Patron: The Reign of Francis I* (Cambridge: Cambridge University Press, 1994), 313–21. Francis Higman gives the text of the placards in *La Diffusion de la Réforme en France 1520–1565*, Publications de la Faculté de Théologie de l'Université de Genève, 17 (Geneva: Editions Labor et Fides, 1992), 72–75.

connected to the Geneva reformers and had provided crucial reinforcements during the battles that led to the Catholic clergy's expulsion in 1536. After Farel was expelled in 1538 he settled in Neuchâtel permanently, and Marcourt came to Geneva. The *Epistle*'s attack on the Mass follows closely Marcourt's in the placards, and the language of the two documents is similar.

The Reformed Church replaced the Mass with a service called the Lord's Supper. It understood that Jesus meant his actions at the Last Supper to be remembered in a service that commemorated them rather than presuming to repeat them. The *Epistle* explains the reformers' belief that the bread and wine used in the Lord's Supper are a sign of Christ's body and blood rather than a miraculous "transubstantiation." I explain that Farel and Calvin's position was different from that of Luther and different also from that of Zwingli. Again I refer them to the reference works cited above.[13]

Among the passages developing the attack on the Mass are indignant outbursts against the Catholic hierarchy and against the temporal authorities in France who keep them in power and thereby support them in their persecution of those suspected of heresy. Here the criticism targets "kings, princes, and lords," necessarily including while not naming, Francis I:

> What do you fear from the cardinals and bishops who are in your courts? If God is on your side, who will be against you? Why don't you make them support their case publicly, before everybody? They are just so many doctors, so many wise men, so many great clerics, so many universities against us poor women, who are rejected and scorned by everyone. (61)

By adding "us poor women" Dentière places Marguerite in an ambiguous position. Although Dentière seems here to be addressing men—"you seem to be completely emasculated" (61)—Marguerite was also in the circle of kings and princes. A few lines later she refers to the Lord's Prayer (62), a move that seems calculated in part to remind Marguerite of one of her earliest works, a meditation on the Lord's Prayer closely modeled on a work of Luther.[14]

---

13. See note 11. An excellent book about the reaction against the Catholic doctrine of the Eucharist among the reformers in Neuchâtel and Geneva is Christopher Ellwood, *The Body Broken: The Calvinist Doctrine of the Eucharist and the Symbolization of Power in Sixteenth-Century France* (New York: Oxford University Press, 1999).

14. Marguerite de Navarre, *Pater Noster et Petit Œuvre dévot,* ed. Sabine Lardon, vol. 1 of *Œuvres complètes,* gen. ed. Nicole Cazauran (Paris: H. Champion, 2001). For the similarities between Marguerite's *Pater Noster* and Luther's *Kurtz begreiff,* see 25–44; and W. G. Moore, *La réforme allemande et la littérature française* (Strasbourg: La Faculté des lettres à l'Université, 1930), 187–88.

The acerbic attack on the Roman Catholic hierarchy, particularly the pope and those who support him, dominates the end of the *Epistle*. The Swiss reformers saw in the history of the church under the popes a steady corruption of the pure teachings of Christ in the New Testament. They rejected the pious practices that the clergy had encouraged over the centuries—using holy water, going on pilgrimages, giving money for indulgences, fasting during Lent—as misplaced beliefs in the efficacy of good works rather than faith alone, and they related them to the rituals of the Jewish law in the Old Testament (70, 74). They expressed contempt for the clergy and certain religious orders, who, they felt, lived off the labor of the people and took concubines while refusing priests the right to marry (68, 70). Their contempt extended to the devotion shown to certain saints, some of whom are ridiculed here (74). They decried the persecutions of groups that the church viewed as infidels and heretics. The *Epistle* defends in particular the Waldensians, a sect condemned as heretics in 1215 that had survived in remote communities in the Alps (71–73). In 1532 some of their leaders had met with Farel and had moved toward a union with the reformers. Persecution of the group spread, and would culminate in 1545 in an organized massacre of the Waldensians living in the Luberon region of Provence, a massacre authorized by Francis I (71, n. 37; 73, n. 40).

These pages contain oblique references to historical events of the mid-1530s that reverberated in Geneva. Although the ostensible reason for addressing the *Epistle* to Marguerite in 1539 was to convey to her the news of the situation leading to the expulsion of Farel and Calvin, other events may have provoked the Geneva reformers to seek her attention at that particular moment and may help to explain their angry criticism of the French court. In the years before 1539, Francis I's political agenda vacillated between rapprochement with King Henry VIII of England, who encouraged Francis I to follow his example and break with the pope, and with Pope Paul III himself. In spring 1538 Francis agreed to meet with his nemesis Charles V, the Holy Roman Emperor (and staunch Catholic), for peace negotiations mediated by the pope. Francis met twice with the pope in Nice in June and met with Charles in July. Marguerite accompanied her brother on that trip and participated in the customary ceremonial festivities marking such encounters.[15] Those events could not have gone unnoticed in Geneva.

Guillaume Farel's first published work was also a commentary on the Lord's Prayer: *Le Pater Noster et le Credo en françoys*, ed. F. Higman (Geneva: Droz, 1982). See also Higman, *La Diffusion de la Réforme en France*, 27–31.

15. See Knecht, *Renaissance Warrior and Patron*, 385–88; and, for Marguerite's participation, Pierre Jourda, *Marguerite d'Angoulême, Duchesse d'Alençon, reine de Navarre (1492–1549)* (Turin: Bottega d'Erasmo, 1966), 231–34.

The *Epistle*'s caustic reference to the custom of kissing the pope's slipper as a gesture of reverence (78) raises the specter of that meeting as it targets those who believed in reform but remained in the church. Already in 1537 Calvin had written to Gérard Roussel, castigating him for hypocritically remaining among the "papists" in order to avoid persecution and to receive the benefice that his bishopric of Oloron allowed him. Without naming him, Dentière refers to Roussel and those like him as "vermin on earth" and entreats Marguerite to avoid them (78). In fact, Roussel remained under Marguerite's protection until her death in 1549, and he died in 1555 from injuries following an attack on him as he was preaching in his cathedral at Oloron. Calvin was to continue his criticism of those whom he later called Nicodemites in a 1544 treatise, and he implicated Marguerite de Navarre among them in a letter addressed to her in 1545 (volume editor's introduction, 18). As the *Epistle* draws to a close, it vituperates the conduct of Pierre Caroli, another reformer whose vacillation disgusted the Swiss reformers (86).

If the *Epistle* offended Marguerite or Francis, it did not prevent Antoine Froment from meeting with the king three years later in Lyon, according to a report from Froment to Calvin that Calvin mocked in a letter to Farel (volume editor's introduction, 17–18). Froment's name, the word for a kind of wheat in French, appears as an allusive signature in the last lines of the *Epistle* (87).

As we read these closing pages, I ask the students to notice the words "woman" and "women" (76, 77, 79, 80, 84), words that have not appeared since the "Defense of Women." Dentière anticipates animosity toward a woman who dares to criticize male church officials, both Catholic and Reformed. That animosity did not fail to flair up, both in her lifetime and more recently. The Geneva Council that had expelled Calvin and Farel confiscated the book from the printer, Jean Girard, shortly after it appeared in April 1539 and apparently destroyed most of the copies. A Reformed Church pastor in Lausanne, Beatus Comte, advised in August of that year that the book be suppressed "because the title announces that a woman (who has no business prophesying in the Church) dictated and composed it, and because that is not true" (volume editor's introduction, 15). Calvin's 1546 letter ridiculing Dentière's public preaching records another major objection.

The increased interest in women's history and literary activity during the past twenty years has led to new research on Marie Dentière and new assessments of her role in the Reformation (bibliography, 43–48). I like to end our discussion of the *Epistle* with a news item that I was not aware of when the Other Voice translation went to press. In autumn 2002, Marie Dentière's name was chiseled onto the Wall of the Reformers in Geneva, a major monument to the Reformation and one of the most frequently visited sites in the city. The new addition was officially unveiled on Reformation Sunday, November 3, 2002. Credit for this recognition of the role women played in the Reformation goes in large part to the Reverend Isabelle Graesslé, a theologian and the first woman moderator of the Reformed Church of Geneva's Company of Pastors and Deacons—the author of the article cited here in note 1.[16]

16. Laurie Sparr, "Swiss Reformation monument gets new additions—one a woman," *Ecumenical News International*, October 31, 2002.

READING JEANNE DE JUSSIE'S SHORT CHRONICLE WITH FIRST-YEAR STUDENTS

Carrie F. Klaus

Devious city councilmen who mislead trusting religious women, licentious soldiers who try to lift the nuns' veils and steal kisses, murderous Christians who break through doors with axes and smash pulpits, statues, and crosses—Jeanne de Jussie's *Short Chronicle* includes plenty of dramatic moments to pique student interest and provoke lively classroom discussion.[1] The challenge, however, is to prompt students to read the text critically, to put these compelling scenes in their proper historical context, and to see the doctrine behind the drama. I recently taught Jussie's *Short Chronicle* in a first-year seminar on early modern women writers. All participants in the course happened to be women, and all were undergraduates in their first semester at a small, residential, liberal arts college. We spent two one-hour sessions discussing Jussie, although we could easily have devoted more time to her. In the first session, we dealt with early modern monasticism and women's choice in the matter. In the second, we examined clashes between women on both sides of the Reformation in Geneva and, especially, how these women viewed their roles in the church.

Before reading Jussie's *Chronicle*, students had studied part of Arcangela Tarabotti's *Paternal Tyranny*.[2] They had read and discussed the dedication "To the Most Serene Venetian Republic," in which Tarabotti chastises much-revered Venice for "forcing more young girls to take the veil than anywhere else in the world,"[3] and book 2, in which she provides copious evidence of

1. Jeanne de Jussie, *Short Chronicle*, ed. and trans. Carrie F. Klaus, The Other Voice in Early Modern Europe (Chicago: University of Chicago Press, 2006).

2. Arcangela Tarabotti, *Paternal Tyranny*, ed. and trans. Letizia Panizza, The Other Voice in Early Modern Europe (Chicago: University of Chicago Press, 2004).

3. Tarabotti, *Paternal Tyranny*, 37.

the evils of forced monachization, drawn from classical and biblical sources, more recent literary texts (Dante, Ariosto), and events in contemporary Venice and beyond. To prepare to teach Tarabotti's work, I found Jutta Sperling's study of convent life in Renaissance Venice to be very useful.[4] Although Tarabotti (1604–52) lived a century after Jussie (1503–61), and although she was a Benedictine while Jussie was a Poor Clare, it worked well to read their texts together because, on the surface at least, there are important parallels between the two women. Both came from families that, although relatively affluent, would have had difficulty providing adequate inheritances for all children. Tarabotti, who had at least two brothers and four sisters, seems to have been destined for the convent at a young age because of a physical deformity she inherited from her father.[5] Jussie, the last born of six siblings (four boys and two girls) to reach adulthood, may also have realized at a young age that the religious life was her most likely career choice.

Students first reacted to what seemed to be a marked difference between the two writers. Whereas Tarabotti denounces fathers who force their daughters to become nuns, Jussie and her sisters in the convent fight tooth and nail to be allowed to uphold their vows. When the city of Geneva officially accepts the Reformation and the syndics (the four top elected officials in the city) tell the nuns they may remain living in their cloister as long as they abolish seclusion, stop wearing habits, and abandon the Mass,

> The city will certainly allow you to stay here in your house, as long as you are prisoners no more and are free to come and go as you wish; and we will help those who want to marry, and the others may do as they wish. But you must change your clothing and say no more office or masses. . . . (145)

the nuns refuse unequivocally and end up traveling by foot from Geneva to Annecy to live in the abandoned Augustinian Monastery of the Holy Cross rather than forsake their way of life.

After identifying the obvious differences between the two texts, however, students began to realize that these two women are not as opposed to each other as they first seem to be. Although Tarabotti says she finds no

---

4. Jutta Gisela Sperling, *Convents and the Body Politic in Late Renaissance Venice* (Chicago: University of Chicago Press, 1999). See especially the introduction and first chapter, "*Potlatch alla Veneziana*: Coerced Monachizations in the Context of Patrician Intermarriage and Conspicuous Consumption," in which Sperling discusses issues surrounding forced monachization in seventeenth-century Venice.

5. See Tarabotti, *Paternal Tyranny*, 2.

textual justification for conventual life, she is careful to note that she does not condemn monasticism universally, but only forced monachization: "I declare explicitly that there is no intention in my writings to criticize religion itself or to enter into debates—except against those fathers and relatives who act violently in making their daughters don the religious habit."[6] As for Jussie, who is clearly aware of the problem of forced monachization, she states firmly and repeatedly that all the nuns in her convent entered of their own free will. The abbess and the vicaress in her chronicle tell the Genevan syndics, "We were all brought here by the grace of the Holy Spirit, and not by force, to do penance and pray for the world" (124); and then later, the vicaress tells a Bernese councilman, "We are not forced to do any of the things we do, but each one is here out of her own will, without any compulsion or force" (151). Indeed, although the term *force* appears frequently in Jussie's chronicle, it is most often in reference to Reformed Genevans who try to make staunch Catholics change their ways.[7] There is no sign, at least according to Jussie, that any of the Poor Clares desired anything but to lead a monastic life.

Reading and discussing Tarabotti and Jussie together made the students more sensitive to the complexity of the decision (or not) to take monastic vows, gave them a fuller understanding of monasticism and its function in early modern society and culture, and better prepared them to read Jussie's *Short Chronicle* on its own terms. Still, in order to make sense out of Jussie's text, they needed quite a bit of background information. (An instructor of an upper-level course could, perhaps, assume some of this knowledge, but it is essential to provide it in a lower-level course.) At the start of our discussion, I spoke briefly to students about the monastic vows—in the case of the Poor Clares, the importance of the vow of seclusion in addition to the three basic vows of poverty, chastity, and obedience—and about daily life in the convent. I explained the main roles in the convent, especially those of abbess, vicaress, and portress, and, of course, Jussie's own role as secretary. I also mentioned the presence in the convent of confessors and lay brothers and of lay and tertiary sisters. Finally, because it is central to understanding the events Jussie narrates, I drew on the blackboard a sketch of the basic convent

---

6. Tarabotti, *Paternal Tyranny*, 38. In Tarabotti's first published work, *Il Paradiso monacale*, she describes the pleasures of convent life for women who have chosen it. *Il Paradiso monacale, con un soliloquio a Dio* (Venice: G. Oddoni, 1643).

7. See the following passages: "the monks *were forced* to leave the monastery" (49), "the sisters *were forced* to ring the bell for the sermon and to listen at the grille with the curtain raised" (64), "one father tried *to force* his young daughter to go with him to that Lord's Supper" (116, emphasis added).

layout, pointing out the turning window and grille in particular. I also gave students some very basic information on the Reformation of Geneva.[8]

Since Jussie's chronicle is long and we were covering quite a lot of ground in the first-year seminar, I asked students to focus on a few significant passages in the text. I chose some of the most action-packed scenes that I thought would be the most accessible.[9] I asked students to prepare an informal writing assignment (one-page, typed) in response to the following questions: "What is your impression of these women? How does Jussie draw the lines between good and evil?"[10]

I like to begin class with fact-type questions—"What is happening in this passage?" "Who is involved?" "What are the main themes raised by the text?"—to get students talking and to lay the groundwork for more substantive discussion (see sample discussion questions below). I then move to more open-ended, interpretive questions. Students were especially eager to talk about the vicaress. They had a lot to say about her as a character, about how Jussie portrayed her, and about the ways in which she did and did not seem to represent the "ideal" woman as seen in other religious and nonreligious texts of the early modern period that we had read in the course. They were particularly fascinated by her willingness to stand up to ecclesiastical and civic authorities and by the conviction and clarity of her speech. Some students decided that the vicaress exemplified the Renaissance ideal of the virago, which we had discussed earlier in the semester; others were not so sure.[11] In addition, they commented on her selective use of evidence, such as the fact that she tells the syndics "it is not women's place to dispute" (123) when she is trying to avoid having to attend the Rive Disputation but has no trouble speaking up later on.

8. This information may be found in the introduction to Jussie's chronicle. Other useful sources in English include Irena Backus, "Les clarisses de la rue Verdaine / The Poor Clares of the Rue Verdaine," in *Le guide des femmes disparues / Forgotten women of Geneva*, ed. Anne-Marie Käppeli (Geneva: Metropolis, 1993), 309–25; and E. William Monter, *Calvin's Geneva* (New York: Wiley and Sons, 1967), especially the first chapter.

9. "The sisters of St. Clare refuse to attend the Disputation of Rive" (122–26), "Guillaume Farel tries to preach at the Convent of Saint Clare" (129–33), "Violent entry of the Genevans into the Convent of Saint Clare" (138–40), "Sister Blaisine is led out of the convent" (140–44), and "Conclusion of the sorrowful departure of the sisters of Saint Clare" (164–72).

10. I often assign short response papers, which I then collect at the start of the next day's class. In this way, students are accountable for their work—I respond to their comments in writing—but they are not allowed to use their assignments as a crutch for discussion, that is, they cannot simply read what they have written.

11. On this topic, see Barbara Newman, *From Virile Woman to WomanChrist* (Philadelphia: University of Pennsylvania Press, 1995).

Just as they had been great admirers of the vicaress, students were appalled by the trickery used by Reformers and by leaders of the city to gain access to Jussie's convent. Here, as at other times, I had to remind students of Jussie's potential bias as a narrator. I mentioned that while we should be attentive to the seriousness of her experiences and of her account of them, we should nonetheless remain critical readers. I asked students repeatedly for what audience they thought Jussie was writing and for what reasons. (This corrective might be less necessary in an upper-level class.) Interestingly, by failing to observe Jussie's narrative bias, at least initially, students were following in the footsteps of Jussie's first editors, who called her chronicle a "naive Tableau"[12] and who suggested that it simply "fell from [her] pen—or rather, [her] heart."[13] Reading Tarabotti with Jussie was helpful in terms of sensitizing students to narrative bias and to the deliberate choices made by each writer.

On the second class day dedicated to Jussie, we considered a handful of Genevan women who spoke out for or against the Reformation, all of whom appear in Jussie's text. I asked students to focus on four passages in the *Short Chronicle* in which, after Guillaume Farel's complete failure to convince the Poor Clares to renounce their vows, leave the convent, and marry, Reformed women come to the convent to speak to the nuns about their own understanding of scripture and to try to persuade them to convert.[14] I also asked students to read the first part of Marie Dentière's own *Very Useful Epistle*, namely, the prefatory dedication to Marguerite de Navarre and the "Defense of Women" that follows it.[15]

Reformed Genevan Hemme Faulson appears often in Jussie's chronicle, as she campaigns successfully for the removal of her sister, Blaisine Varembert, from the convent and then joins Varembert in demanding restitution of a monetary contribution that they claim was made when Varembert entered the convent. Claudine Levet, another Reformed Genevan, is mentioned in

12. "A Illustrissime Prince Victor Amé, Prince de Savoye, et de Piedmont," in *Le Levain du Calvinisme ou commencement de l'heresie de Geneve. Faict par Reverende Soeur Jeanne de Jussie, lors Religieuse de Saincte Claire de Geneve, & apres sa sortie Abbesse au Convent d'Anyssi* (Chambéry: Du Four, 1611), a2v.

13. Jean-Marie-Vincent Audin, *Histoire de la vie, des ouvrages et des doctrines de Calvin* (Paris: L. Maison, 1856), 1:172–73.

14. These passages are "Hemme Faulson's visit to the Convent of Saint Clare" (100–101), "Hemme Faulson tries to remove her sister, Blaisine Varembert, from the convent" (133–34), "Marie Dentière tries to make the young sisters leave the convent" (151–52), and "Claudine Levet preaches the Gospel to the sisters" (159–60).

15. Marie Dentière, *Epistle to Marguerite de Navarre and Preface to a Sermon by John Calvin*, ed. and trans. Mary B. McKinley, The Other Voice in Early Modern Europe (Chicago: University of Chicago Press, 2004).

the text from time to time as the "apothecary's wife" (79) and then finally appears in person when she shows up at the convent to preach to the nuns. Shortly after Levet, Marie Dentière also comes to the convent in an attempt to convert the Poor Clares. A foreigner to Geneva and herself a former nun, Dentière (1495–1561) had left an Augustinian convent in Tournai in the early 1520s to marry Simon Robert, a former priest. She moved with him to Strasbourg, where the two were active in the community of French Reformers. In 1528, Dentière and Robert followed Guillaume Farel to the Valais region east of Geneva. After Robert's death in 1533, Dentière married Antoine Froment, another Reformer. Dentière and Fromment came to Geneva in 1535, in the midst of the tumultuous events Jussie narrates in her chronicle.[16] Dentière visited Jussie's convent in August 1535. Jussie records this visit in her chronicle in a memorable passage in which she calls Dentière "a false, wrinkled abbess with a devilish tongue . . . who meddled in preaching and perverting pious people" (151).[17] Reading Dentière with Jussie thus makes for evocative comparisons and again brings up the issue of narrative bias.

When studied alongside Jussie's description of her, Dentière's *Epistle* provides rich subject matter for consideration of women's self-representation in the context of the Reformation. For this second day's class, I asked students to prepare another informal written response. This time, I asked for a character sketch of Marie Dentière, based both on Jussie's portrayal of her in the *Short Chronicle* and on Dentière's presentation of herself in her own text. Dentière deals with a whole host of theological issues in the main body of her *Epistle*: she denounces traditional practices such as pilgrimages, veneration of the saints, and indulgences; refutes the doctrine of transubstantiation; and affirms the authority of scripture and the primacy of faith. However, it was on the question of women's role in the church, and particularly on the value of the monastic life, that she and Jussie clashed most directly, so our discussions focused mainly on this topic, which Dentière pointedly addresses in her dedication and "Defense of Women."

Students were especially interested in Dentière's comments on women's right to engage in theological debates, as when she writes to Marguerite de Navarre that "what God has given you and revealed to us women, no more than men should we hide it and bury it in the earth."[18] They compared this

16. Details of Dentière's life come from Dentière, *Epistle*, 2–5.

17. Madeleine Lazard has published an article on this encounter: "Deux soeurs ennemies, Marie Dentière et Jeanne de Jussie: Nonnes et réformées à Genève," in *Les réformes: Enracinements socio-culturels*, ed. B. Chevalier and C. Sauzat (Paris: La Maisnie, 1985), 233–49.

18. Dentière, *Epistle*, 53.

assertion to the vicaress's refusal to attend the Rive Disputation, which we had examined during the previous class period. By this point in the semester, accustomed to the modesty pose typical of so many texts of the early modern period, students would not have been surprised if Dentière had made some feigned excuses for her writing, perhaps asking Marguerite for indulgence in reading a theological text composed "only" by a woman. Dentière, however, makes no such excuses. In fact, she does just the opposite, telling Marguerite frankly

> as you well know, the female sex is more shameful than the other, and not without cause. For until now, scripture has been so hidden from them. No one dared to say a word about it, and it seemed that women should not read or hear anything in the holy scriptures. That is the main reason, my Lady, that has moved me to write to you, hoping in God that henceforth women will not be so scorned as in the past.[19]

It was, in fact, Dentière's bold eschewal of the modesty pose that most interested the students, perhaps because they found it refreshing after the other texts we had read, by both women and men. In our examination of the "Defense of Women," students made a list of the biblical women Dentière cites (Sarah, Rebecca, the mother of Moses, Deborah, Ruth, the Queen of Sheba, Mary, Elizabeth, the Samaritan woman, and Mary Magdalene), and we then considered why she brought in these particular figures and to what end. We compared Dentière's selections to other catalogs of exemplary women we had observed in the course of the semester, and we discussed reasons for the absence of such a catalog in Jussie's text.

Depending on the nature of the course—and the students—an instructor could make the discussion of these issues even livelier by asking students to role-play the confrontations between Jeanne de Jussie and the Reformed women who visited her convent. Students would be asked to prepare for the role-play as homework (an alternative to the written character sketch of Marie Dentière). Half of the class would be asked to play the roles of nuns; the other half would be the Reformed women who come to preach to them. Students would be asked to read the designated excerpts from Jussie's *Short Chronicle* and from Dentière's *Very Useful Epistle* carefully and to write a brief description of their characters' main motivations, drawing evidence from the texts. They would then act out the confrontations in

19. Dentière, *Epistle*, 53–54. The first part of this passage does not appear in all copies of the *Epistle*. See McKinley's notes (Dentière, 53, n. 7). See also William Kemp and Diane Desrosiers-Bonin, "Marie d'Ennetières et la petite grammaire hébraïque de sa fille d'après la dédicace de l'*Epitre* à Marguerite de Navarre," *Bibliothèque d'Humanisme et Renaissance* 50, no. 1 (1998): 117–34.

class—as a class activity or in groups, depending on course enrollment—and discuss their reactions to the activity, and what they learned from it, afterward.

Even without a role-play, students had an animated discussion of the confrontations between these intriguing women. They were especially interested in the question of marriage versus celibacy (particularly after our discussions of monachization during the previous class period), in the powerful images Jussie uses to describe her enemies (she calls them devils, serpents, and ravenous wolves), and in Dentière's admission—according to Jussie, at least—that she had taken money from the treasury of her own convent before she left it. Although we spent only two class days on Jussie's *Short Chronicle*, we could easily have devoted more time to it. In addition to their questions about Marie Dentière's assertion that she had taken money from the treasury, students were curious about the matter of Blaisine Varembert's dowry, which she and her sister (Hemme Faulson) tried to reclaim when Varembert left the Convent of Saint Clare. Jussie's account of Varembert's removal from the convent, the prolonged dispute over the restitution of her dowry, and the question of whether a dowry was ever, in fact, given, makes up another fascinating part of the chronicle that would be worth examining in a third day's discussion.[20]

Other sections from Jeanne de Jussie's *Short Chronicle* could be grouped topically to suit the needs of a variety of courses at all levels of the curriculum, particularly in history, religious studies, women's studies, and even literature. I was delighted with students' response to Jussie in an interdisciplinary first-year seminar on early modern women's writing and at how often her chronicle intersected with other works we studied in the course. Just as reading Tarabotti prepared students to read Jussie, so reading Jussie prepared them for Dentière. Taken together, these three women and their writing provided a wealth of information on early modern monasticism and the theological debates surrounding it in sixteenth- and seventeenth-century Italy, Switzerland, and France. As they worked with these texts, students not only gained familiarity with these issues, but also developed critical reading skills that will serve them well in the rest of their years in college and beyond.

---

20. The main sections on this topic are "Hemme Faulson tries to remove her sister, Blaisine Varembert, from the convent" (133–34), "The sisters' attempts to retain Blaisine Varembert" (136–37), "Sister Blaisine is led out of the convent" (140–44), "Blaisine Varembert asks the convent to return her dowry" (146–47), "Negotiations between the sisters and the Genevan authorities regarding the goods claimed by Blaisine Varembert" (147–50), and "The syndics return with Blaisine Varembert and Hemme Faulson" (155–59).

QUESTIONS FOR DISCUSSION

"The sisters of Saint Clare refuse to attend the Disputation of Rive" (122–26).

1. What is going on in this passage? What do the syndics want from the nuns?
2. What is the nuns' response? What do you think of this response?
3. What is your impression of the vicaress?

"Guillaume Farel tries to preach at the Convent of Saint Clare" (129–33).

1. How does Jussie portray the Reformers' entry into the convent?
2. What are the main points about which Farel tries to preach?
3. What happens? Who wins? Why do you think so?

"Violent entry of the Genevans into the Convent of Saint Clare" (138–40); "Sister Blaisine is led out of the convent" (140–44).

1. Again, how does Jussie portray the Reformers' entry into the convent?
2. What does Jussie have to say about free will? What is the importance of these statements in the context of the Reformation?
3. What is the importance of the nuns' bodies in this scene? What do you think about this emphasis on their bodies?

"Conclusion of the sorrowful departure of the sisters of Saint Clare" (164–72).

1. Which main details of the nuns' departure from Geneva does Jussie choose to include?
2. What is the importance of these details?
3. How would you describe the relationships among these women? Between these women and the other persons who appear in this passage?

"Hemme Faulson's visit to the Convent of Saint Clare" (100–101); "Hemme Faulson tries to remove her sister, Blaisine Varembert, from the convent" (133–34); "Marie Dentière tries to make the young sisters leave the convent" (151–52); "Claudine Levet preaches the Gospel to the sisters" (159–60).

1. Which theological issues does Jussie show these Reformed women raising? What seem to be their main interests?
2. How do the Poor Clares respond? Do they provide opposing viewpoints or refuse to engage?

3.   How does Jussie describe the Reformed women? What terms does she use? What kinds of details does she include? How do these women speak?

4.   How does Jussie represent the Poor Clares?

5.   Who else is present in these scenes? How do they react?

"Hemme Faulson tries to remove her sister, Blaisine Varembert, from the convent" (133–34); "The sisters' attempts to retain Blaisine Varembert" (136–37); "Sister Blaisine is led out of the convent" (140–44).

1.   How does Jussie portray Blaisine Varembert? Which details does she use in her description of her? Why do you suppose she chooses to portray her in this way?

2.   How does Jussie highlight the differences between Sister Blaisine and the rest of the Poor Clares?

3.   How do the Catholic ladies of Geneva show their support of the nuns? What questions do they ask them? What is the significance of these questions?

4.   How does Jussie portray the nuns during the scene in which Sister Blaisine finally leaves the convent? What do you think of this portrayal?

5.   What is the significance, for the rest of the Poor Clares, of Sister Blaisine's removal from the convent?

"Blaisine Varembert asks the convent to return her dowry" (146–47); "Negotiations between the sisters and the Genevan authorities regarding the goods claimed by Blaisine Varembert" (147–50); "The syndics return with Blaisine Varembert and Hemme Faulson" (155–59).

1.   What does Varembert demand be restored to her? What accusations does she make?

2.   How does Jussie demonstrate that she believes Varembert's claims to be false?

3.   How do civic authorities try to mediate the dispute between Varembert and the Poor Clares? Are they successful?

4.   What is the significance of the "bishop's relic"?

5.   How does Jussie portray Varembert in these passages?

TEACHING KATHARINA SCHÜTZ ZELL
(1498–1562)
Elsie McKee

Introducing Katharina Schütz Zell of Strasbourg to twenty-first-century students is a fascinating challenge.[1] This essay is divided into two parts: the first part locates her among women of her time, and the second locates her and her writings among early Protestant reformers and is thus more directly related to teaching her texts.

PART 1: KATHARINA SCHÜTZ ZELL AMONG EARLY MODERN WOMEN

Daily life is rarely something historical figures explicitly describe, but the physical circumstances and family experience, the social and gender assumptions of a culture, shape the context that helps to give resonance to any person's voice. The paragraphs that follow are very limited sketches of much larger topics, on which there is extensive literature.[2] The present introduction makes no claim to be comprehensive but aims simply "to locate" Schütz Zell in her larger context.

---

1. Katharina Schütz Zell published under both her birth family name, Schütz, and her married named, Zell; historians usually call her Katherine Zell, and Strasbourgers often continued to call her Katherina Schütz. Here she is named Schütz Zell. Throughout, I make extensive use of my biography of Schütz Zell: Elsie Anne McKee, *Katharina Schütz Zell. Volume 1: The Life and Thought of a Sixteenth-Century Reformer* (Leiden: Brill, 1999). See also *Volume 2: The Writings* (Leiden: Brill, 1999).

2. This section draws on Merry E. Wiesner, "Ideas and laws regarding women," "The female life-cycle," and "Women's Economic Role" in *Women and Gender in Early Modern Europe* (Cambridge: Cambridge University Press, 1993), 9–114; see also Wiesner, "Family, Household, and Community," in *Handbook of European History, 1400–1600*, ed. Thomas A. Brady, Heiko A. Oberman, and James D. Tracy (Leiden: Brill, 1994), 1:51–78; and Thomas M. Safley, "Family," in *Handbook of European History*, 2:93–98.

The Housewife

There are a number of common historical roles such as housewife or mother that early modern women shared almost automatically. First, women were virtually always members of households. Those who joined religious orders had a different kind of household, but except for the rare anchoress, life was still communal and the great majority of women were daughters, wives, mothers, or servants in households "in the ordinary world" of farm, village, town, or castle. Living alone, or even as a group of women (unless they followed an accepted religious rule), was either impossible or at best difficult, for both financial and social reasons. Money was often a problem; women's work was always more poorly paid than men's since it was assumed that "all women were either 'married or to be married'" and not obliged to support themselves. Social mores posed another, equally significant problem, since it was assumed that women must always be under the authority of men. Even a woman of wealth or a group of women who could earn enough to keep themselves were regarded with suspicion if they tried to live independent of male supervision.[3]

The character of housekeeping in early modern Europe is something the twenty-first-century West may not be easily able to envision. Water had to be brought in by manual labor, wood for heating and cooking found and chopped, and fires guarded. The sheer physical effort of living consumed a great deal of energy; for example, in the prosperous urban home of Martin Bucer, his wife, Elisabeth Silbereisen, had the care of eleven children and "only a half-time maid to haul water and wood, and one nursemaid" for domestic help.[4] Besides water and wood, a household needed food, but with only cellars for coolness and salt or smoking for preservation, feeding a family required constant work. In the towns, foodstuffs must be purchased, sometimes almost daily, and prepared without any "labor-saving" devices. Strasbourg held a weekly dairy market on the square behind the cathedral, where rural farmwomen brought milk, cheese, butter, and other products for sale to the city folk.[5] In rural areas where the great majority of people lived, things one could buy in the city, such as bread from the baker, had to be made at home, along with much else.

---

3. See Merry E. Wiesner, *Women and Gender in Early Modern Europe*, chaps. 1 and 3; quotation on p. 99.

4. Bucer to Margaret Blaurer, August 20, 1533, in T. Schiess, *Briefwechsel der Brüder Ambrosius und Thomas Blaurer* (Freeiburg i.B.: Friedrich E. Fehsenfeld, 1908–12), 2: no. 21, p. 801.

5. For a glimpse of this market, see the illustration in Katharina Schütz Zell, *Church Mother: The Writings of a Protestant Reformer in Sixteenth-Century Germany*, The Other Voice in Early Modern Europe (Chicago: University of Chicago Press, 2006), 8.

Houses were usually very small and crowded (by modern standards), and households were large and complex. The "family" living under one roof varied in different parts of Europe. In the northwest where the Schütz and Zell clans lived, at first marriage couples were usually in their mid or late twenties, with the husband only a few years older than the wife. They began their new life together when they had sufficient resources to found a new household, either through their own industry or parental help or both.[6] Katharina Schütz was twenty-five, the usual age for a bride, when she and Matthew Zell were married. (He was twenty years her senior, but that anomaly was owed to his having been a priest and therefore not among the candidates for marriage before he broke with Rome's law of clerical celibacy.) The finances of establishing their life together were easier for the Zells than for some couples. As a priest formally installed in a parish (not a monk or wandering friar), Matthew had a house and income, and the Schütz family was well enough established to provide their daughters with comfortable dowries.[7] A new husband and wife were not alone in their home, however, even if they did not immediately have children. Besides the nuclear family, most urban and many better-off rural households included servants (who might be poor relations but were usually young people from the countryside) and apprentices or lodgers who shared the family business, all living packed together. As a newlywed pair, the Zells had a very young girl to assist Mrs. Katharina, and in later years there were other young women of her household whom Schütz Zell remembered in her will.[8]

The household was the economic and social unit of life. The householder (paterfamilias) was master, husband, and father, but all the members

6. Marriage and household patterns were different in southern and eastern Europe. In the south, men were much older than their young wives at first marriage; in the east, both husband and wife were young and became part of the household of one set of parents. In both south and east, there were often members of several generations under a single roof.

7. See McKee, *Life and Thought*, 224. The bequests in Schütz Zell's will (KS 98, II, f78v–86v, in the Archives Muncipales de Strasbourg) indicate several kinds of household furnishings. The more notable were the fine tableware; some may have been gifts to the Zells, but some were certainly inherited from family and probably formed part of her dowry. Schütz Zell specifically designates some gifts: a silver drinking vessel gilded on top; a small gilded drinking vessel with gilded top; a child's silver cup with gold decorated cover with the name "Jesus" on it; an (old) silver bowl gilded inside; a silver bowl that had belonged to Jacob Schütz (Schütz Zell's father); six spoons with silver handles (with Jacob Schütz's mark); three silver drinking glasses with covers; a silver *Keutel* with a name engraved on it; a small drinking cup and spoon (for ordinary use). Furniture included a bed with complete equipment: straw mattress, two large pillows, a bedcover, a big brown coverlet, six linen sheets; two small chests; and three beds, each equipped with four linen sheets and a bedcover. The list of bequests also includes a number of items of clothing, especially several fur coats.

8. See Katharina Schütz Zell, *Church Mother*, 78–79; for her will, McKee, *Life and Thought*, 224.

of this *familia* had to work together. The master was expected to rule and provide for his dependents, but the housewife was a subordinate partner in the business. She trained the servants and children, seeing that babies and domestic animals as well as all the working members of the household were cared for, and she helped her husband ensure that all did their jobs. Women also participated in various aspects of the unit's economic livelihood, and they might sometimes have independent charge of a craft, although this was less common. Wives of that new Protestant invention, the minister's family, contributed to household finances and to the training of future clergy by running a boarding house for students. In addition, hospitality was one of the expected virtues of a pastor's household, so ministers' wives were likely to have unexpected guests—or refugees—for dinner or more extended visits.[9]

Households were often large for several reasons. Besides needing hands to do the work, it was a simple fact that establishing a new household required economic resources that were beyond the reach of a significant number of young men and women. If your family could not help, you must earn a dowry or the material basis for a home yourself or wait until your parents' death gave you an inheritance. If none of these means was available, you might be destined to spend your whole life as an unmarried apprentice or servant in someone else's household. With weddings delayed until long after puberty, and situations in which a number of young people could never marry, it is not surprising that out-of-wedlock babies arrived from time to time. If the mother or father was their dependent, the householder and his wife would have to oversee arrangements for the baby. If the mother died and the father could not be identified, these infants usually ended up in church or city welfare institutions or fosterage until they were old enough to learn a trade or go into service themselves.

The Daughter, Wife, and Mother

Households were the basic unit of society, but most individuals' lives were also shaped by their biological families, and family life was often precarious. Plague was only the most devastating of the many forms of ill health and disease, which every early modern household endured many times over the course of the years. Quite apart from the grief, there was the social effect

9. The best-known minister's boarding house is documented in Martin Luther's "Table Talk," comments that were often collected by students living with his family. In Strasbourg, Ludwig Rabus was counted among the Zells' household for several years before his marriage, and the Zells' guest list for occasional visitors and short or long-term refugees is a lifelong part of their story; see McKee, *Life and Thought*, 77–82, 104–8.

of frequent familial deaths. Children often grew up in "blended" families or lived with relatives,[10] and an adult might well be widowed and remarried several times. For practical reasons, widows and widowers usually remarried quickly. A man needed a housewife for his home and a mother for his children; widowers were more likely to remarry than widows and to do so more quickly. Younger widows, especially poor ones, hoped to remarry to provide for themselves and their children. Older widows, however, were less likely to find another husband; they often made up a large segment of the poor, for whom relatives were supposed to care if possible, but who not infrequently became dependent on the community (village, town, church).

Schütz Zell's longtime friend Wibrandis Rosenblatt (1504–64) and her children are a classic model of what this task of widowhood and blended families could mean for a woman.[11] Rosenblatt, an educated citizen of Basel, was married four times, suffered widowhood four times, bore children in each of these marriages, and cared for the combined households of all the blends. Her first husband was a humanist named Ludwig Keller (m. 1526, d. early 1528) with whom she had one daughter. The other three were Protestant pastors (married priests), whose somewhat risky calling added further stresses to the ordinary marital challenges. Husband number two was the Basel reformer Johannes Oecolampadius (m. late 1528), with whom Rosenblatt had three children, of whom only one daughter would survive to adulthood. Oecolampadius died in November 1531, at almost the same time the Strasbourg reformer Wolfgang Capito lost his wife Agnes. Capito's household was soon in considerable disorder so, urged on by Bucer, in 1532 Capito married the widow of their mutual friend Oecolampadius, and she moved herself, her children, and her elderly mother to Strasbourg. Rosenblatt had five children with Capito, but when the great plague of 1541 struck Strasbourg, she was widowed a third time and also lost several more children. In the same plague Bucer's wife Elisabeth and four of their remaining five children also died, but not before Elisabeth had asked her husband Martin and her friend Wibrandis to marry after her death. Thus Rosenblatt married another reformer and moved her mother, herself, and her remaining children to Bucer's home to care for him and his son Nathaneal. Two more

10. Schütz Zell's brother Jacob probably died when his three children were small. The Zells helped one nephew through school, and Schütz Zell personally looked after his handicapped brother for the rest of her life and devoted a considerable part of her will to insuring his future; see McKee, *Life and Thought*, 143–44, 172, 220–22.

11. See Roland H. Bainton, *Women of the Reformation in Germany and Italy* (Minneapolis: Augsburg Publishing House, 1971), 81–88.

babies were born of this, Rosenblatt's fourth marriage, although one died young and the other did not live to maturity. Besides the children and Rosenblatt's mother, the family also included an adopted niece. Although most widows did not remarry so often, Wibrandis Rosenblatt's story was otherwise not uncommon: she was hardly a "merry widow," but she certainly reared a blended family!

There has been much debate about the affective relationships of husbands and wives, parents and children in early modern Europe. Marriages were usually arranged with pragmatic factors such as dowries and inheritances explicitly considered. However, scholars of family history point out that love or at least affection was expected to develop over time, even if it was not the primary basis for the marriage, and often this expectation appears to have been borne out. Among those who shared the new fervor of the Reformation, marriage was normally based on common religious commitments, as the story of Katharina Schütz and Matthew Zell shows in one fashion and the successive marriages of Wibrandis Rosenblatt to three reformer colleagues illustrate in another way. With regard to relations between parents and children, it is clear that high infant mortality did not keep mothers or fathers from having a deep attachment to their children, and family ties were often affectionate. Certainly, Schütz Zell's lifelong anguish for the loss of her two babies is a theme in various writings, and her correspondence shows her sensitivity when others faced this sorrow.[12]

For many women, life and death were inextricably intertwined in a particularly intense way in their role as mothers. Women often died in childbed; it is possible that Schütz Zell's almost fatal illness in April 1531 was her own experience of this. If both mother and child survived, there was still the problem of adequate nourishment for the infant. Sometimes a woman nursed her baby herself, but often circumstances (for example, when the mother was a servant and could not keep her baby with her) or custom dictated having a wet nurse (for example, when an upper-class woman wanted to increase the number of pregnancies by avoiding continued lactation). However, physical dangers and cares were not the only problems an early modern mother faced: the spiritual loss of a child was, if anything, worse. Babies might be stillborn—a great trauma for a devout woman since a dead baby could

12. For Schütz Zell's own accounts of their marriage, see her various writings, especially *Apologia for Matthew Zell, Lament for Matthew Zell,* and *Letter to Caspar Schwenckfeld,* in Katharina Schütz Zell, *Church Mother.* For loss of her children, and care for an orphan, see *Church Mother,* 117, 189, 197. For other expressions of sorrow or sympathy about children, see McKee, *The Writings,* 99–100, 109–110, 112.

not be baptized and therefore according to traditional theology would be consigned to limbo. Many late medieval miracle stories tell of a saint, often the Virgin Mary, who resuscitates a stillborn child long enough for it to be baptized and thus saved eternally, if not temporally. Schütz Zell explicitly expressed her concern for these women and her rejection of this doctrine: omission of the rite would not condemn a child to limbo.[13]

Although her own understanding of the trauma of a stillborn child was altered by Schütz Zell's new faith, it was natural for her to interpret maternal care in spiritual as well as physical terms. For a Protestant, spiritual care meant making or keeping someone safe by teaching the gospel. It is probable that Schütz Zell's exposition of the Lord's Prayer was begun with her own children or perhaps young relatives in mind, although the completed text was offered first to other women and then to the public generally. Certainly her hymnbook publication was devoted to the goal of helping mothers and householders generally teach their children and dependents saving religious knowledge. Keeping children and households safe spiritually was both an extension of Schütz Zell's maternal activity and the calling of a "church mother."[14]

The Citizen/Member of Society

One of the factors that shaped all early modern culture was the common acceptance of hierarchy as a natural and normal—and even, in some respects, normative—feature of life. There were radical movements that denied hierarchy in various ways. The most widespread was the claim of religious reformers for spiritual equality. Some groups (most visibly in the Peasants' War) applied their radical rejection of traditional hierarchies to this-worldly

13. For Schütz Zell's illness, see McKee, *Life and Thought*, 83. Her sympathy for mothers whose babies died unbaptized is expressed in her account of the Strasbourg Reformation; see quotation in McKee, *Life and Thought*, 279: "Alas, God, how did Dr. Luther, my dear husband, Capito, Bucer, and the other old or first preachers of the gospel cast out and with great effort and work uproot the great unbelief and error which was in the papacy, i.e., the emergency baptism of children. If they died unbaptized they were not buried with other Christians but elsewhere in some other place, so that they were robbed of the sight of God (which is salvation, Matt. 18:10). They [those who taught this] have afflicted the heart of many a poor mother and driven her to great unbelief, and have so completely forgotten the precious blood of Christ, and—against all the teaching of Christ and His apostles—they have given [the power of Christ's blood] to the water, which God did not create for the salvation of souls but for the right use and knowledge of His works."

14. See Katharina Schütz Zell, *Church Mother*, 93–96, 151–56, 226.

society. The great majority of Europeans, however, regarded social distinctions as appropriate and approved of different ranks within the state or common life. As a sturdy Strasbourg citizen, Katharina Schütz speaks with respect of civic leaders like Sir Felix Armbruster or Daniel Mieg or Jacob Sturm, although she admired the first two more than the last because Armbruster and Mieg were deeply committed to defending "the gospel" with their lives and Sturm was ready to compromise.[15]

Hierarchy within the family was widely accepted, and acknowledgment of the parental right to control minor children was virtually universal. Much twentieth-century secondary literature about the family emphasizes that the early modern period strengthened the authority of the male head of the household and put corresponding restrictions on other members, including the householder's wife. Other voices caution that the task of the paterfamilias was also a major responsibility; obligations between the head and the members, the husband and the wife, the father and the dependents, were expected to be mutually beneficial, and when one side became too extreme the other might well revolt.[16] The character of Katharina Schütz's partnership marriage with Matthew Zell gives a very "liberated" idea of what the mutual ties of husband and wife could be. She happily affirms his leadership but also emphasizes that he respected, encouraged, and supported her in her vocation—including matters that most men would not have regarded as part of a wife's work! The Zells' marriage was very unusual in the character of its mutuality, but it illustrates what was possible when there was a common faith and common social rank, even accompanied by significant differences of age and education.[17]

Intellectual attainments were also an important hierarchical factor in the early modern world, but this was a more ambiguous sphere than social or familial status. In part, the ambiguity was a consequence of increasing vernacular literacy among a portion of the lay population. Traditionally, education had been a prerogative of the clergy, but that had begun to change in the later middle ages as more laity (both nobles and city people) became

15. For various definitions of "radical" and their relationships to social movements, see James M. Stayer, "The Radical Reformation," *Handbook of European History*, 2:249–82. For Schütz Zell on the civic leaders, see McKee, *The Writings*, 107, 244, 310ff.

16. For emphasis on household life as repressive for women, see Lyndal Roper, *The Holy Household: Women and Morals in Reformation Augsburg* (New York: Oxford University Press, 1989). For emphasis on the responsibility of the paterfamilias and mutuality see Safley, "Family," 95–96.

17. For the Zells' marriage, see McKee, *Life and Thought*, 441–51 et passim.

literate, usually in their own vernaculars. By the late fifteenth century there was a growing consciousness of a divide between the university-educated elite who used Latin and the great majority of the population who lived their whole lives using only their mother tongues. The elite were increasingly identified as "learned liars," and reformers of all kinds referred to the "common man" (those literate in the vernacular) as the truly educated ones, a stance that combined anticlericalism and social criticism.[18] Many "common men" contributed to the flood of vernacular pamphlets in the early 1520s, asserting their right to speak on the basis of a new intellectual attainment: concrete knowledge of the Bible. Artisans might be the lowest ranks of the literate, but under the influence of the Protestant Reformation they derived confidence from the conviction that their source (the Bible) was superior to anything the elite could command. However, the gulf between the international culture of the Latin-educated and the regional communities of the vernacular-educated was paralleled by that between those who were literate and those who were not. From the perspective of the great majority, whether the city poor or the vast rural population, those who could read and write fluently considered themselves a cut above their country cousins.[19] The point here is that the daily social, political, and intellectual life of an early modern urban citizen like Schütz Zell was shaped in both conscious and unconscious ways by the commonly accepted fact of different ranks—at least in this-worldly society.

The Woman

Recent scholarship has given more attention to issues of gender hierarchy than hierarchy in general in the early modern world. What did it mean to a girl born in 1498 in German-speaking Europe to see herself as a woman? One of the dangers that twenty-first-century readers face in reading Schütz Zell is that in some ways her language and her life both seem "very modern" in terms of feminist self-confidence and independence. That tempts the reader to interpret this Strasbourger approvingly as "far ahead" of her time and to miss the ways that her "feminism" is shaped by her historical and religious context.

18. See Robert Scribner, "Heterodoxy, Literacy, and Print," in *Religion and Culture in Germany* (*1400–1800*), ed. Lyndal Roper (Leiden: Brill, 2001), 253–58.

19. For artisan pamphleteers, see Miriam U. Chrisman, *Conflicting Visions of Reform: German Lay Pamphlets, 1519–1530* (Atlantic Highlands, N.J.: Humanities Press, 1996), 159–78. For Schütz Zell's awareness of differences between herself and peasants, see McKee, *Life and Thought*, 66, 185, 337–38.

Schütz Zell was more "liberated" than the great majority of her fellow women in the sixteenth century. She uses very little "self-deprecating" language; on the rare occasions when she seems to call herself "a poor little woman" by comparison with a man, the sense is essentially ironic—mocking the stereotypes of women. Her independent behavior caused much annoyance to her husband's colleagues, whose wives were more conventionally pious. So in both speech and action Schütz Zell seems closer to the twenty-first-century Western ideal of womanhood than do most of her contemporaries. That leads some readers to feel impatient when she calls herself "Matthew's rib" (Gn 2:21–22) or explicitly accepts Paul's restrictions on women's ordination (for example, 1 Cor 14:34).[20] Given her obvious freedom from many of the expressions of women's submissiveness that were pervasive in her own day, what stopped her from carrying her liberation further, from claiming equality in her marriage or the church? To understand this one must see Schütz Zell's religious thought in historical context.

Except for queens or other noble women whose voices have been heard because of their birth and rule, women's public speaking has most commonly been related to their society's religion, and so it has been shaped by the religious authority the women themselves accepted. The three most frequently observed means to a public role for women and others outside the formal structures of religious power have been through a claim for immediate divine inspiration or a life of great sanctity or martyrdom. The last of these, martyrdom, hallows earlier teaching after the person is dead and cannot exercise the authority personally. The holy life must be recognized by others, usually after long years of ascetic practice that authenticate the holy person's wisdom. The authority of immediate inspiration, however, is not limited by time or circumstance, age or sex, education or status. It is also acknowledged in most religions and enshrined in biblical texts of both the Old and New Testaments, such as Joel 2:28–29 (quoted in Acts 2:17–18). Logically, this source for religious authority is one claimed by Schütz Zell's best-known female contemporaries. She herself cites these verses once, at the end of the *Apology for Matthew Zell*, which is often read as her defense for public speech by women.[21]

---

20. For her views of herself, see McKee, *Life and Thought*, 419–53; for her denial of ordination and reference to herself as "Matthew's rib," see Katharina Schütz Zell, *Church Mother*, 196–97, 228.

21. See Katharina Schütz Zell, *Church Mother*, 82. For common citation of Joel 2:28, see *Argula von Grumbach: A Woman's Voice in the Reformation*, ed. Peter Matheson (Edinburgh: T & T Clark,

Somewhat surprisingly, however, Schütz Zell actually bases her obligation and justification for teaching or preaching chiefly on the grounds of her biblical learning, not immediate divine inspiration. Her affirmation of "scripture alone" helps to explain why she reluctantly but plainly does not claim ordination for women and why she accepts Matthew as the head of their marriage. As a Protestant theologian, she felt bound to the text of the Bible—the whole Bible and nothing else. Although she narrowed the sense of Paul's injunction about women's silence as much as possible, she refused to pretend that it was not there or that it did not apply to her; although she claimed partnership with Zell as their mutual choice, she can acknowledge that others (rightly) see him as her head.[22]

PART 2: KATHARINA SCHÜTZ ZELL AMONG EARLY MODERN CHRISTIANS

It is commonly known that in medieval Europe belief in God, the presence of the church, and the influence of religious language and considerations permeated all of society. Some older scholarship affirmed that the major religious upheaval called the Protestant Reformation was the beginning of the modern secular world. In actuality, Protestants clearly insisted on both the ultimate and the immediate authority of God in every situation, even as they re-formed and re-oriented some aspects of what this meant. The post-Enlightenment secular West, on the other hand, is accustomed to dealing with a world in which this earthly existence is the central and sometimes the only life human beings have and certainly the locus of what is most important. Because these sixteenth- and twenty-first-century presuppositions about religion are so divergent, one of the greatest challenges for a modern reader of Schütz Zell or her contemporaries is to make sense of what they say about their faith.

The Religious Worldview and Its Language

The people of early modern Europe inhabited a society in which religion was an intrinsic reality that affected everything from the year's calendar

---

1995), 73, 176. Ursula Weyda, *Wyder das unchristlich schreyben und Lesterbuoch des Apts Simon Zuo Pegaw* ([Augsburg] 1524), title page.

22. For a summary of her arguments for speaking out drawn from all her writings, see McKee, *Life and Thought*, 398–418. For the most interesting, see Katharina Schütz Zell, *Church Mother*, 63–66.

and the daily schedule to potential marriage partners and life vocations and everything in between.

The real existence and the power of God were beliefs accepted by virtually everyone, and most people were convinced that God's will must be reckoned with in all aspects of daily life. That meant an effort to identify and follow what they thought God wanted. Generally, for most people this included trying to find supplemental help from saints or charms or religious practices such as pilgrimages, in case their sins kept God from responding to their prayers. Yet others were eager to escape too close supervision by God (or, more particularly, representatives of God's church). Practically no one doubted the fact of a life beyond this earth, for better or worse; even the most hardened libertines were led by the approach of death to serious consideration of eternity. For the devout, obedience to God not only had to do with reaching ultimate salvation but also played a major role in ordering the present world. It was particularly for this-worldly needs that saints were invoked and charms used, although the Virgin Mary and patron saints might be especially petitioned in situations of great danger as well as daily troubles. Like other Protestants, Schütz Zell strongly rejected appeal to the saints as a denigration of the honor owed to God alone, but in the re-forming of her prayer life there were continuities as well as discontinuities.

One of the specific linguistic manifestations of continuity with the late medieval religious worldview is evident in Schütz Zell's penitential language. To modern ears, the prayers of medieval and Reformation Christians sound incredibly self-deprecating. Phrases like "You will not cast me away, miserable as I am, with others of Your miserable sinners, because I have transgressed and sinned against You"[23] make the present-day reader cringe. The language sounds extravagant and possibly insincere, and it certainly seems "unhealthy"; usually it prompts a quick response: "You need to develop your positive self-image." That is a natural reaction to the language heard particularly in Schütz Zell's *Meditations on the Psalms and Lord's Prayer,* but also in many other writings. Such a reaction, however, misunderstands the religious context and import of the words.

For medieval and early modern Europeans, this was familiar and appropriate language to address to God, in view of their perception of what was a life or death matter: salvation or damnation. It was also shaped by long practice and common habit; no one thought such language was unusual, everyone had heard it from infancy, and most would be surprised by its absence,

23. See Katharina Schütz Zell, *Church Mother,* 142.

not its use. What would have startled Schütz Zell's contemporaries about her meditations was not their penitential character but the total absence of appeal to the saints and the relative audacity of her constant direct recourse to God. To identify what is traditional and what is distinctive in the devotional language of this Strasbourg reformer it is helpful to place her writings alongside medieval or other early modern texts, such as the prayers to the saints in books of hours or the self-image of the devout person in the *Imitation of Christ*.[24]

It is notable that prayer is the one context in which Schütz Zell freely employs "self-deprecating" language with passionate sincerity. It is only in relationship to God that she affirms her own total and justified submission, but that acknowledgment of sinfulness and unworthiness is heartfelt. Indeed, it is a dimension of her sense of worth and identity because she believed that only by acknowledging her sinfulness could she receive God's mercy and grace. Paradoxically, to speak of herself as a "poor, miserable sinner" in prayer was not "running herself down" but a statement of her confidence in God—and the source of her own freedom from absolute submission to any human authority.

The Biblical Student and Protestant Reformer

Once Schütz Zell's religious worldview and language have been grasped, it is possible to isolate another difficulty in understanding her writing: her biblical Protestant theology. This faith stance illuminates in interesting ways the problem of locating her in time—and shows continuities and discontinuities that must be understood in order to interpret her (and her contemporaries). In the first place, Schütz Zell's approach to the Bible is rather different from that of the devout medieval woman, who would rarely have had access to a translation of the Bible and who would have been strongly discouraged from reading it if it were available. As a Protestant, Schütz Zell not only had a vernacular Bible at hand but also was exhorted to use it, a situation that seems more familiar to readers in the modern West. On the other hand, the sheer amount of scripture this "person in the pew" cites—and that the reader must recognize in order to follow her argument—may astonish and challenge the twenty-first-century student. Whether it appears as the substance of the

24. See *Time Sanctified: The Book of Hours in Medieval Art and Life*, ed. Roger S. Wieck (New York: George Braziller, 1998), esp. 163–66. Thomas à Kempis, *The Imitation of Christ*, trans. Leo Sherley-Price (New York: Penguin Books, 1952), esp. book 1, chaps. 21–24 et passim.

argument or the source for her illustrations or the idiom of her thought in general, the presence of scripture is pervasive in Schütz Zell's writings and significant for grasping who she was and what she thought.[25] And that means remembering that she was a Protestant of the sixteenth century.

It is natural to think that "Protestant" meant the same thing in the sixteenth century as it means in the twenty-first century. Even the student with a clearer conception of the differences between the Reformation period and today, however, is likely to have some difficulty realizing that there was development within Protestantism over the course of the sixteenth century. Comprehending the religious scene in Schütz Zell's time requires more than recognizing a multifaceted Protestantism different from the present. It demands equal awareness of the complexities of other faith communities in early modern Europe. Most significantly, the Roman Church in 1500 and the Roman Catholic Church in 2000 are two considerably different historical entities. Rome experienced a series of reforms in the early modern period, beginning even before the break with Protestants. In addition, the Second Vatican Council (1962–65) changed the face of the Rome that early modern people knew by so much that it is virtually impossible to compare the Rome against which the Protestant Reformation reacted with the Rome of the present. Furthermore, there were also many individuals and small groups in sixteenth-century Europe who were not satisfied with the reforms of either Rome or the Protestants. The internal diversity of these "Radicals" in the early Reformation is often forgotten, while the "Anabaptists" of the sixteenth century are far from identical with the Mennonites or Hutterites of the modern West. To make sense of Schütz Zell and her contemporaries, it is essential to grasp clearly the diversity of those whom modern textbooks often lump together under "Protestant" and to remember their historical development over the course of the Strasbourg reformer's lifetime. It is also vital to define in proper fashion the other Christian communities of early modern Europe, setting them precisely in their historical reality.

25. Early modern Europeans experienced a revolution in biblical studies as humanists turned to Greek and Hebrew texts. Protestants rejected the Latin Vulgate, which had been *the* authority for centuries, and made vernacular translations based on new sources, even as they also made considerable changes in interpretation. However, the biblical tradition of the sixteenth century was also quite different in both textual basis and interpretation from the post-Enlightenment biblical studies dominant today. Schütz Zell's scriptural allusions will often not correspond to the most recent English translations. For a detailed study of her scriptural arguments it is wise to consult an original (1611) version of the King James Bible or a copy of the English puritan "Geneva Bible" produced in the same religious context as her writings; see *The Geneva Bible: a facsimile of the 1560 edition,* with an introduction by Lloyd E. Berry (Madison: University of Wisconsin Press, 1969).

SOME COMMENTS ON TEACHING

The writings of Katharina Schütz Zell are both more numerous and include more diverse genres than is true for most "other voices" in this series, and that makes it difficult to suggest ways that each of her texts may be used in the classroom. Most of my personal experience has been in teaching her as one person among a number of others, in courses on women's spirituality, or Reformation history-theology, or worship and piety, for which I have selected shorter texts or excerpts appropriate to the themes. Only once, when I was a guest professor in Germany and Schütz Zell was the sole topic of the seminar, did the class read almost the whole corpus of her writings and consider issues of her theology, "voice," context among lay pamphleteers, and so on over the course of her entire life. At the end they could reflect on her spiritual development by comparing similar pieces from different periods of her life, such as the two letters of consolation (1524 and 1558), or considering how her rhetorical strategies or ways of presenting herself did or did not change over time.

Most often, selected parts of Schütz Zell's body of work are useful in classes on early modern European religion to break (into) the traditional clerical canon of "Protestant reformers" with lay voices. Theologians like this articulate Strasbourger can give a better idea of how religious teachings actually got to many persons in the pew and what the basic doctrines sounded like when passed on by the clergy's enthusiastic "ordinary" hearers. So, for example, reading Schütz Zell's exposition of the Lord's Prayer alongside Luther's in his catechism, or her hymnbook preface alongside his, gives a fuller (and more embodied) picture of what the "priesthood of believers" meant. Her polemic against clerical celibacy and for biblical authority and her arguments with her foster son Ludwig Rabus about the way he was misinterpreting Matthew Zell's heritage provide fascinating perspectives on what laity and clergy both believed was essential in the new church order and where laity disagreed and why. Schütz Zell's correspondence with Caspar Schwenckfeld and that with Rabus demonstrate not only how "ordinary" people felt freed by their faith to make up their minds about religious matters, but also that (at least some) laity considered themselves qualified to make their own judgments about the differences among the "learned."

More can be said about extending the diversity of Protestant reformers, especially the addition of women's perspectives. For example, Schütz Zell's letter of consolation to the persecuted women of Kentzingen opens a particularly feminine window on the issue of suffering for "the gospel": the men might leave town but women and children must remain behind with the persecutors. Her sermon at her husband's burial is significant for the fact that it happened at all and was preserved, but it is also a very good example of a Protestant perspective on death and dying: the words of a wife and mother about her husband and children. In addition, it shows clearly the personal engagement of laypeople in the continuing struggle for their faith; the Reformation was not just a clerical matter, even though lay and female voices were heard much more rarely after the 1520s.

Schütz Zell also provides a very interesting voice "to diversify" more general courses on early modern Europe because of the extent of her publications, her social status, and her vernacular education. Practically all lay pamphlets were published only in the early 1520s, while Schütz Zell's manuscript and printed materials cover a period of thirty-four years. Thus the body of her work is especially useful as an addition to studies of lay pamphleteers, to expand the scope of social history seminars. This Strasbourg citizen also provides a female voice from the honest "middling class" to balance the more available excerpts from royal or noble women or members of religious orders or deviants found in court records. To have such a large corpus from a "common person," a woman from an urban artisan family, literate only in the vernacular, who had never been a member of a religious order, is a rare thing for the sixteenth century. Schütz Zell also adds a very helpful dimension to discussions of early modern education. In my experience, present-day students tend to equate limited formal schooling with limited knowledge and intelligence; they forget that even semiliterate medieval and early modern people often had an amazing capacity to remember what they heard and to formulate sometimes complex ideas in oral discourse. So readers of Schütz Zell's texts are always surprised by the breadth and depth of her knowledge of the Bible and Protestant theology, as well as the facility with which a person educated only in a local vernacular school could argue sophisticated doctrines with Latin-educated men trained at a cosmopolitan university.

One aspect of Schütz Zell's polemic that always needs to be explained to modern students is the intermittent "nasty name calling," especially in the *Lament for Matthew Zell*. This text demonstrates that "ordinary" people were just as capable of polemic as the clergy, but that is not something a modern student wants to see. Generally I have found that students are horrified by the harsh language of sixteenth-century religious controversy and need assistance in putting what seems like mud slinging in theological and literary as well as historical perspective. It helps to remind them that for early modern people—lay as well as clerical—religion was a matter of life and death, so bitter attacks by Protestants on Rome or Anabaptists, or Roman Catholics on Protestants and others, were a measure of the gravity of what was at stake and not simply a manifestation of rudeness. It also helps to give students examples of other Renaissance writers, to show them that the period had made an art of negative and otherwise very colorful language. Schütz Zell was not unusual. In fact, modern "political correctness" would have seemed like abdication of serious faith to practically everyone in her day. Sixteenth-century religious polemic must be put in the context of the theological, historical, and literary situation that produced it, as the reverse side of the passionate faith that compelled women and men to speak out.

Katharina Schütz Zell's extensive writings present one of the liveliest voices of the Protestant Reformation, a singularly stimulating addition to almost any course on early modern Europe.

IV

Holy Women in the Age of the Inquisition

FRANCISCA DE LOS APÓSTOLES:
A VISIONARY SPEAKS

Gillian T. W. Ahlgren

Francisca de los Apóstoles (b. 1539) has a great deal to teach us about sixteenth-century life. A *beata*[1] who dedicated herself to the cause of ecclesiastical reform primarily by attempting to found, with her sister, a new religious house for women, Francisca came to the attention of the Inquisitional tribunal of Toledo when she was thirty-six years old. Her trial gives us an instant window into both inquisitorial procedure and the vicissitudes of Spanish urban life, particularly as they were experienced by a woman who possessed a keen social and religious conscience. In this essay, I shall suggest some of the ways that her story and voice can be incorporated into a number of classes, both graduate and undergraduate, in ways that challenge our current understanding of sixteenth-century religious life and make the past come to life in vivid and unique ways.

Little is known about Francisca other than what can be gleaned from the Inquisitional archives, which contain the record of her trial (1574–78); six letters, which she introduced into evidence; a set of vows she took after a series of religious experiences; and statements from twenty-six witnesses. She was born in the town of Novés and came to Toledo at the age of sixteen, when she lived as a *beata* at the convent of Santa María la Blanca. Francisca

---

1. The term *beata* encompasses many forms of religious life in Spain. In general, *beatas* were independent religious women who did not take formal vows but devoted themselves, nonetheless, to religious life, at times through a specific religious order and at times independently, under the supervision of a confessor. *Beatas* often wore some form of religious habit and engaged in religious responsibilities, even in religious instruction to young women. Because they did not take formal vows, however, they were allowed to change their status if, for example, they chose to marry. For more information about Spanish *beatas*, see, for example, Gillian T. W. Ahlgren, "Negotiating Sanctity: Holy Women in Sixteenth-Century Spain," in *Church History* 64 (1995): 373–88; and Mary Elizabeth Perry, *Gender and Disorder in Early Modern Seville* (Princeton, N.J.: Princeton University Press, 1990), 97–117.

stayed there for approximately eight years, until her father took her from the convent and had her move in with her younger sister, Isabel Bautista, in about 1563. The two women achieved a certain notoriety when they attempted to found a convent for women without dowries in the city of Toledo. Although the city already had a significant religious infrastructure, it had eroded somewhat in the absence of the city's archbishop, Bartolomé de Carranza. Ironically, Carranza had been considered orthodox enough to represent the church at the Council of Trent, but after the publication of his catechism in 1558 and his appointment to the prestigious see of Toledo, Carranza had been accused, by some of his own Dominican brothers, of heterodoxy and denounced to the Spanish Inquisition. Carranza argued successfully that, because he was such a public figure, he would not receive a fair trial in Toledo. He was sent to Rome for investigation in 1559 and languished there until his case was resolved in 1576.[2] As one historian has noted, "it was a scandal without precedent in the history of the Spanish church."[3] As a result, many aspects of Catholic religious life, including religious training, access to convents for women, and various forms of church-based social relief, suffered during the 1560s and 1570s.[4]

Carranza's absence caused a grave situation for the Toledan church. Carranza had been a reform-minded bishop; on his first visit to the archdiocese of Toledo, in October 1558, he had overseen plans for bread distribution to the poor, and he appeared to have a commitment to intensifying poor relief. In his absence, the church was run by an administrative council that appears to have been neither efficient nor attentive to the needs of the poor. When Francisca and her sister attempted to acquire official permission to found a religious house for women, it was not forthcoming. After consulting with religious figures around the city, Isabel set out for Rome in the hope that she would be able to meet with Carranza and receive authorization to build up her religious community, for which she had drafted a formal monastic

2. Carranza's verdict reflects the church's ambivalence toward him. Not condemned of heresy, he was nonetheless declared "suspect," and his release from Roman inquisitorial confinement was not a full exoneration. Exhausted and defeated by his many years of trial, he died just two weeks after being released. For more information about his case, see José Ignacio Tellechea Idígoras, *El Arzobispo Carranza y su tiempo*, 2 vols. (Madrid: Guadarrama, 1968).

3. Sara T. Nalle, *God in La Mancha: Religious Reform and the People of Cuenca, 1500–1650* (Baltimore: Johns Hopkins University Press, 1992), 33.

4. For more detail and analysis of Toledo's socioreligious climate, see Francisca de los Apóstoles, *The Inquisition of Francisca: A Sixteenth-Century Visionary on Trial*, ed. and trans. Gillian T. W. Ahlgren, The Other Voice in Early Modern Europe (Chicago: University of Chicago Press, 2005), 8–11. See also Linda Martz, *Poverty and Welfare in Habsburg Spain* (New York: Oxford University Press, 1972).

rule. Francisca remained in Toledo, dedicated to the cause of reform, and began having extraordinary experiences of prayer, which appeared to confirm the divine ordination of the sisters' religious work. In a series of apocalyptic visions, inspired perhaps by the Last Judgment scene that dominated the Toledan cathedral where she often prayed, Francisca began to understand God's dissatisfaction with the current state of the Toledan church, particularly the imprisonment of Carranza and the corruption of the city's clerics and religious leaders. In response, she offered herself and the religious community she would found as intercessors before God on behalf of the church and of humanity at large. At the same time, women began to approach her, asking if they could live together in an informal community until the sisters' foundation was approved. Francisca had the support, in all of these endeavors, of several religious figures in the city, including a Hieronymite prior and some Franciscan friars. In addition to referring several women to Francisca, several of her male supporters offered to embark on the trip to Rome as advocates for her cause. By 1575, Francisca found herself at the very center of a charismatic circle of religious reform whose prophetic challenge to ecclesiastical governance was viewed by some with suspicion and concern.

However, the Inquisitional case against Francisca did not originate with those who might have felt threatened by the criticism of the status quo that Francisca's religious visions expressed. Instead, members of Francisca's own religious community, supported by a Jesuit priest who was their confessor, lodged the first formal complaints against Francisca with the Toledan Inquisitional tribunal, and it appears that the tribunal was not initially concerned, believing that Francisca's reform was "women's business" and under the province of the archdiocesan vicar for religious orders. Called to account for his apparent negligence in prosecuting them, Toledan Inquisitor Juan de Llano de Valdés wrote to the Supreme Council of the Inquisition on September 1, 1575, saying that "because of the weakness of the testimony against them, we did not pursue the matter."[5] Valdés proceeded to arrest Francisca, her sister Isabel (who had returned from Rome in mid-December 1574), and their confessor Miguel Ruíz on October 1, 1575.

The subsequent trial provides genuine insight into both the mind of Francisca and the challenges that reform-minded Catholics, particularly laywomen, experienced as they sought a ministerial role in the church. Asked to render an account of her religious life at the outset of her Inquisitional trial, Francisca's initial testimony is candid, forthright, and not quite but almost serene. She spends several weeks recounting her orientation to religious life,

5. Francisca, *Inquisition*, 18.

her experiences of prayer, and her consultation with religious advisors; furthermore, when peppered with questions by Inquisitor Valdés, she appears to have had a good understanding of the rules and norms for the discernment of spirits. Thus it was a great shock to her to be confronted, on January 25, 1576, with 144 accusations against her, ranging from spiritual arrogance to deception, blasphemy, and abuse of religious experience and authority. Upon hearing the charges, Francisca wept and said, "These things should not have come to this!"[6] Recovering herself, Francisca began a spirited defense, which she maintained through mid-February, when the trial reached its crescendo. For two weeks, Francisca and Valdés engaged in a long and intense debate over the nature of her visions, the evidence she could marshal for their authenticity, and her apparent pride and vanity in making public her religious experiences. By February 14, Francisca, feverish and sick, conceded that the Inquisitor was "a person with more light from God to understand those things than she is," and "she said that she will not make a determination about whether they were from God or from the devil any more than to say that whatever the Lord Inquisitor says and instructs her, that is what she will believe."[7]

Any religious authority Francisca had acquired over the course of her reform efforts was destroyed in the public *auto de fe* on April 13, 1578, when Francisca abjured her errors and received her penance as an *alumbrada*:[8] three years' exile from Toledo and one hundred lashes. Francisca's voice disappears from history at that moment. Although she states clearly in her appeal to the Inquisitor for a lighter sentence that she intends to marry a fellow prisoner ("And seeing myself in the difficulties that this affair has caused me and understanding my liberty to be in great danger, I have decided to change my estate and marry because perhaps I will save myself better in this other estate . . . "[9]), the preliminary inquiries I made in Toledo for parish records

6. Francisca, *Inquisition*, 118.

7. Francisca, *Inquisition*, 148, 147.

8. A careful definition of *alumbradismo*, particularly as it was investigated and prosecuted throughout Spain in the 1570s, continues to elude us. Indeed, Francisca's case gives us clues as to how the Inquisition determined that a person had been "falsely illumined" rather than divinely inspired, and it must be reviewed carefully in any construction of a definition of *alumbradismo*. Comparison of Francisca's testimony with much of Teresa of Avila's discussion of the discernment of spirits reveals that there are at least as many similarities between the two women as there are differences. There are also significant gender differences that would be necessary to articulate in the definition. I take up some of the critical issues that are in need of further research before we can claim to understand the phenomenon of *alumbradismo* in the introduction to the text, 32–36.

9. Francisca, *Inquisition*, 154.

that might confirm the marriage did not bear fruit. At this point, Francisca's fate after the *auto de fe* is unknown.

The drama and innate interest of an Inquisitional trial coupled with the poignancy of Francisca's story make this potent material for an exploration of sixteenth-century religious life and practice. My undergraduate students report that reading the trial serves a purpose similar to "the way that a biology experiment sheds light on a concept in the sciences."[10] Francisca's trial provides a unique window into Inquisitional practices, clarifies the characteristics, purposes, and functions of the institution, and highlights some of the effects on society and religious life. Reading an actual trial transcript makes it possible for students to assess some of the statements made about the Spanish Inquisition, in both academic and popular literature, and enables them to move beyond overviews and vague impressions.

In what is left of this essay, I would like to review some of the ways I have made use of Francisca's story in the undergraduate classroom. Before I do so, it may be helpful for me to say a few words about the academic disciplines I represent and my pedagogical context. I was trained primarily as a historian of Christianity, at the Divinity School of the University of Chicago, working in the fields of theology, church history, social history, and religion and literature. While my understanding of church history is firmly rooted in the study of primary texts, it is also broad and incorporates social history, the history of ideas, institutional history, artistic representations of religious ideas and practices, and the translation of theological ideas and spiritual practice into reform movements. In addition, I have always been particularly interested in the role and influence of women within social and religious structures; this orientation has guided and focused many of the questions I asked as a student and, now, as a scholar. My dissertation focused on the work of the sixteenth-century Spanish mystic and reformer Teresa of Avila (1515–82), as a woman writing around the strictures of Inquisitional scrutiny and censure, and over the course of my academic career I have continued to explore the transformative effects religious women have had in the various spheres of community, church, and society.

I have taught undergraduates and graduate students (candidates for our M.A. in Theology) at Xavier University for fifteen years. Within this Catholic, Jesuit context, members of the Theology Department approach theology as an ongoing interpretive and synthetic *process* as much as a product. Thus my colleagues and I view the Christian tradition as a living entity, flawed by the shortcomings of fallen humanity, but nonetheless also infused

10. Student response to survey on text from Theology 224: Saints and Heretics.

by the ongoing movements of the divine as it works its way through human history, by means of the day-to-day interactions of human persons. In keeping with the Jesuit trademark of "finding God in all things," I encourage students to "read" human history, both past and present, in terms that would not only reveal the assumptions, insights, and shortcomings of historical and cultural milieux but would also allow us to identify and explore possible manifestations and unfoldings of the divine-human partnership. Concurrently, and also in keeping with the Jesuit expression "a faith that does justice," we probe human interactions for the absence of what might be called "the values of the reign of God," exploring the effects of social, political, and religious institutions on all levels of society, with special attention to the marginalized.

It is in this context that a story like Francisca's is particularly meaningful, but, because it brings into relief any number of interpretive issues, in historical, sociopolitical, and theological realms it can be put to broad use in many curricula. With respect to Inquisitional studies, it is a ready-made case study of inquisitorial procedure. I have included the heart of the proceedings against Francisca, with enough material in the appendices to deepen or to broaden the kinds of questions explored within the classroom. Appendix A, for example, consists of a translation of the theological consultant's evaluation of witness statements. It thus gives readers a sense of what witnesses had testified, how the theologian who served as an Inquisitional consultor interpreted the testimony, and, more generally, the ways statements were assessed for theological orthodoxy. Appendix B does a cursory analysis of the 144 accusations eventually made against Francisca. Because of their sheer number, they can literally overwhelm the reader—as they did Francisca herself. The transcript records that, after hearing all of the accusations, which took nearly an entire afternoon to read aloud, Francisca was "overcome by a fainting spell and was a bit disoriented."[11] In order to save the reader from a similar fate, I sorted the accusations into categories that would convey a sense of the Inquisition's concerns and of all that Francisca had to address in her own defense. Using this appendix can help focus discussion of how the term *alumbradismo* was understood and applied in sixteenth-century Spain as a way to control religious expression and the claims to authority that religious people might make. Both of these appendices allow for a fuller discussion of religious belief and practice in sixteenth-century Spain and make the book suitable for use in Reformation courses, whether they are oriented to social history, institutional history, intellectual history, or even women's history.

11. Francisca, *Inquisition*, 118.

For those unfamiliar with an Inquisitional trial transcript, I should note that such transcripts contain verbatim testimony of witnesses and of the accused, and thus they are a precious resource for social history, as well as being an important "reality check" for intellectual historians and philosophers, who sometimes work under the assumption that religious doctrines (and the orthodoxy that emerges from them) are clearly articulated, taught, and understood, from generation to generation. Any basic study of Spanish Inquisitional records would shatter any such assumptions, as many cases centered around *practices* at least as much as *beliefs*. Thus we find that judgments of heresy often do not evolve around significant questions of doctrinal orthodoxy. For example, it was not at all uncommon for a person to be indicted as a "judaizer" for doing laundry on Friday. Clearly, determinations of "heresy" did not always involve heterodox thinking on the part of the accused or even necessarily an attitude of disrespect for the church and its teachings. Indeed, as many have noted, the popular movement toward more spiritual forms of religious self-expression drove an even greater demand for communal conformity to specific religious practices, rituals, and dogmatic formulations, leading to a particular formulation of Catholicism rooted in paradoxes: "highly personal yet strongly conformist; localized yet nationalist; dogmatic yet proudly independent."[12]

Despite efforts to "contain" and regularize religious expression, Inquisitional trial transcripts reveal that Spaniards were often frank, casual, opinionated, and highly creative in conceptualizing and practicing their faith.[13] Francisca's testimony indicates the ubiquity and familiarity of God in many people's lives: not only did Francisca describe extraordinary and intimate experiences of God, but, clearly, her contemporaries accepted their veracity. Francisca's case indicates that religious figures had a certain degree of freedom both in conceptualizing and in practicing their faith. Such autonomy and the reform movements that it generated were likely significant and were probably tolerated unless or until the dissent had significant economic or political ramifications. Exposure to these sociohistorical circumstances is usually enough to get students to question a more stereotypical presumption of the hegemonic power of the Spanish Inquisition—or "the Church," for that matter.

12. Nalle, *God in La Mancha*, 209.

13. See, for example, the many anecdotes in Henry Kamen, *The Spanish Inquisition: A Historical Revision* (New Haven, Conn.: Yale University Press, 1998); Nalle, *God in La Mancha*; and Mary Giles, ed. *Women in the Inquisition: Spain and the New World* (Baltimore: Johns Hopkins University Press, 1999).

I have used Francisca's case with success in three different courses: a scholars seminar on the Spanish Inquisition, geared to upper-level undergraduates; a course on the Catholic Reformation, geared to general undergraduates; and a more specialized undergraduate course (that consists primarily of nonmajors) exploring the theory and practice of determinations of sanctity and orthodoxy entitled "Saints and Heretics." I taught two sections of this latter class during the spring semester 2005. I was pleased to be able to use the book in its entirety during the four-week section on the Spanish Inquisition. In addition to providing students with a concrete example of Inquisitional practice, *The Inquisition of Francisca* introduced a new dynamic into our discussions. Students responded quite positively to the "you are there" perspective that the trial gave them. They prepared the readings carefully for classes, and I could tell, from the interpretive questions and responses they brought with them, that they had often read the material more than once. I found myself not needing to rely on questions to stimulate discussion and analysis; instead, students took a great deal more interpretive initiative on their own. The material was complex enough that the students themselves, in conversations with one another, reflected a range of interpretive possibilities, whether they were addressing the criteria for assessing the authenticity of religious experience, the "inevitability" of the trial's outcome, the autonomy and agency of religious women in sixteenth-century Spain, or any number of other questions the trial raises. The text also "personalized" the material in such a way that students felt not only more engaged in their study but also more invested in their understanding of sixteenth-century religiosity. For many, this study generated more questions about contemporary forms of social, religious, and political orthodoxy and helped them to see that such questions are hardly abstract but influence the lives and choices of real persons each day.

The adoption of this text requires a general introduction to the Spanish Inquisition. Because the Spanish Inquisition is such a controversial subject, permeated by various manifestations of the "black legend" (*leyenda negra*) and all of its stereotypes,[14] it can be interesting to ask students, prior to the first day's discussion of the actual mechanics and procedures of the Inquisition, to bring in a citation or two, illustrating their understanding of the Inquisition. I suggest that instructors allow students to draw from a very broad list of sources, thus exposing them to the wide range of ways that people characterize the Inquisition—some responsible and others verging on inflammatory.

14. For a review of historiographical issues in the study of the Spanish Inquisition, see Kamen, *Spanish Inquisition*, 305–20.

Students can then be asked, after they have read Francisca's case, to assess these very same quotes for accuracy. In and of itself, this exercise is an interesting example of historiographical review and analysis.

With respect to providing students with a balanced, historically informed introduction to the Spanish Inquisition, I ask students to read several chapters from Henry Kamen's *The Spanish Inquisition: An Historical Revision.* Chapters 4 and 5 elucidate the growing power of the Spanish Inquisition, from the 1520s through the 1550s, as it slowly became something more than a "crisis instrument"[15] formed to address perceived problems introduced by the proliferation of "new Christians" and instead began to monitor the behavior of old Christians and their attitudes toward ecclesiastical traditions and structures. Chapter 8 is a helpful introduction to the procedure of the Inquisition, a procedure that is clearly borne out in the structure of Francisca's trial and offers students something of a roadmap as the trial unfolds.

Some contextualization of the issues that Inquisitional activity raised for women is also important, and there are many good resources to draw from, depending on the amount of time one devotes to the study of Francisca and *alumbradismo.*[16] At the graduate level or in an upper-level undergraduate seminar a fascinating and more in-depth review and analysis of women's religious life in the "heart" of counter-Reformation Spain—that is, in the 1570s—could be developed, using the lives and thought of Teresa of Avila, María de San José, and Francisca de los Apóstoles, among others. Resources for such a study are ample.[17] Such study would do a great deal to refine

15. See Henry Kamen, *Inquisition and Society in Spain in the Sixteenth and Seventeenth Centuries* (Bloomington, Ind.: Indiana University Press, 1985), 46: "Because the Inquisition was a crisis instrument, it may be that Ferdinand never intended it to be permanent (no steps, for example, were taken to give it a regular income). This certainly was the feeling of the Toledo writer who commented in 1538 that 'if the Catholic kings were still alive, they would have reformed it twenty years ago, given the change in conditions.' The unprecedented activities of the Holy Office were deemed to be acceptable only as an emergency measure, until the crisis had passed."

16. See Giles, *Women in the Inquisition.* An older but perhaps still useful general introduction to the ambiguities of religious life for Spanish women is my "Negotiating Sanctity," 373–88. Discussion of the challenges faced by women reformers in sixteenth-century Spain is also covered in Jodi Bilinkoff's well-known *Avila of Saint Teresa: Religious Reform in a Sixteenth-Century City* (Ithaca: Cornell University Press, 1989). The introductory chapter of my *Teresa of Avila and the Politics of Sanctity* (Ithaca: Cornell University Press, 1996) may also prove useful, as would the introductory chapter of Alison Weber's *Teresa of Avila and the Rhetoric of Femininity* (Princeton, N.J.: Princeton University Press, 1990).

17. The bibliography on Teresa is, of course, extensive, including all that has been mentioned in the preceding note, as well as J. Mary Luti's *Teresa of Avila's Way* (Collegeville, Minn.: Liturgical Press, 1991) and my *Entering Teresa of Avila's Interior Castle: A Reader's Companion* (Mahwah, N.J.: Paulist Press, 2005). Alison Weber's study of María de San José and María's own *Book for the Hour of Recreation*, The Other Voice in Early Modern Europe (Chicago: University of Chicago Press,

our understanding of sixteenth-century religious life and the dynamics of religious reform. Additionally, of course, it serves the stated purpose of Chicago's Other Voice series: to recognize and honor "the call for justice issued as long as six centuries ago by those writing in the tradition of the other voice... as the source and origin... of the realignment of social institutions accomplished in the modern age."[18]

This last objective bears some final comment. For Francisca's story can open up a number of questions about the process of social, religious, and political reform, and, in addition to being particularly relevant in courses of women's studies, it also has much to contribute to an interdisciplinary course in Peace Studies or Human Rights Studies. As Henry Kamen also concludes, study of the Spanish Inquisition raises complex questions about tolerance, repression, power, reform, and ideology, and "it is in the nature of the inquisitional phenomenon that no answer can match the complexity of the questions." Studying the Spanish Inquisition thus enables us to reflect on the reality that "even today in the twentieth century other nations have had and continue to have their Inquisitions: the human condition is subject to frailties that are not limited to any one people or faith and that regularly reverses the gains made in previous generations by 'civilization' and 'progress.'"[19] The dynamics of Francisca's trial and what they reveal about the interplay of prophetic power, social reform, and institutional structures help ground such questions in a historical and theological way, enabling students to make connections between the past and the present, especially in the ongoing struggle to affirm human dignity, to transform institutions, and to promote social justice and equality.

2002), introduces another dynamic conversational partner into the mix of women's religious voices from this decade of intense religious reform.

18. Margaret L. King and Albert Rabil Jr., series editors' introduction, *The Inquisition of Francisca*, xxvii.

19. Kamen, *The Spanish Inquisition*, 320.

"MUTE TONGUES BEGET UNDERSTANDING": RECOVERING THE VOICE OF MARÍA DE SAN JOSÉ

Alison Weber

I first became acquainted with María de San José Salazar (1549–1603) through the letters written to her by Teresa of Ávila (1515–82), the famous Carmelite mystic and monastic reformer. The letters convey Teresa's warmth and admiration for the young nun (whom she teasingly called her "letrera" or bookworm), but also her occasional exasperation. I subsequently learned that María, raised in a ducal palace, had a notable penchant for ignoring orders from her superiors and that her defiance twice resulted in imprisonment. I was further intrigued to discover that María was a skilled writer, the author of a small corpus of poetry, several autobiographical letters, and the first dialogue written in Spanish by a woman. As I learned more about this intelligent and dangerously assertive daughter of Saint Teresa, I became convinced that her *Book for the Hour of Recreation* would be an excellent text for introducing students to an "other voice" from early modern Spain—a voice that was by turns bold and self-effacing, passionate and ironic, derisive and compassionate. In addition to its value as a splendid, if unusual, example of early modern life-writing, *Recreation* can offer students "a sense of Catholic Reform in the making" and an appreciation for the precariousness of women's roles within it.[1]

This fictional dialogue represents the interaction of a group of nuns during the time of day when they were allowed to break the rule of silence

---

1. Electa Arenal and Stacey Schlau, *Untold Sisters: Hispanic Nuns in Their Own Works*, trans. Amanda Powell (Albuquerque: University of New Mexico Press, 1989), 19. In this landmark bilingual anthology, Arenal, Schlau, and Powell introduced María de San José and other early modern women religious to the English-speaking world. On María see especially chap. 1, 19–117. Her writings were first published early in the twentieth century. For the Spanish edition, see *Escritos espirituales*, ed. Simeón de la Sagrada Familia (Rome: Postulación General O.C.D., 1979).

and entertain one another with conversation and music. Written at a time when the Discalced Carmelite general was threatening to abolish this custom, *Recreation* constitutes a defense of the practical and spiritual benefits of relaxed friendship. The dialogue begins when Gracia (María's fictional alter ego) complains to the punctilious Justa that her confessor has ordered her to write her spiritual autobiography. Abashed and apprehensive, she wonders how she can escape this mandate. Justa recommends that she write instead the story of the life of their foundress Angela (that is, Teresa of Ávila). In the subsequent conversations, other nuns join the pair to discuss a variety of topics—the history of their order, whether women are permitted to "meddle" in interpreting scripture, doubts over feelings experienced during prayer, troubles with the Inquisition, and the death of a beloved novice. These are not topics that are immediately compelling to American undergraduates, but I have nevertheless successfully introduced the *Recreations* into literature and culture courses on early modern Spain.

In my undergraduate literature course, *Book for the Hour of Recreation* follows a unit on Teresa of Ávila. Initially I ask students if they have any preconceptions about life in early modern convents. Were they like prisons or posh boarding schools for girls? Why did women join convents? What did they do all day? Did they suffer from boredom and loneliness or did they have the leisure to pursue artistic and intellectual interests? Most students admit that they have never considered these questions; others confess sheepishly that their notions have been shaped by popular culture—movies such as Whoopie Goldberg's *Sister Act*. Next, I ask students to make lists of those aspects of Teresa's *The Book of Her Life* that they find most off-putting or puzzling and, conversely, most comprehensible. Students often report that they can relate to Teresa's sense of frustration over not being believed. They are surprised by her flashes of irony and moved by her suffering but perplexed by her insistence that "suffering is good for you." Some find the descriptions of ecstatic prayer puzzling; others respond with titters. Most of all, students are intrigued by the contrast between the way Teresa asserts her spiritual certainty and yet acquiesces to male authority. After comparing these reactions, I ask students to keep these questions in mind as we read more examples of monastic women's writing: did life in an early modern convent nourish or constrain opportunities for women's self-actualization? Or is this a false dichotomy? What would "self-actualization" have meant for sixteenth-century women? My goal for this initial discussion is to overcome what a friend has called the "yucky Catholicism reaction" (the feeling that the material is too weird and irrelevant to their own experience to merit serious consideration) without denying the distance between early modern and contemporary notions of self-actualization.

At this point, I ask students to read two historical essays, my "Little Women: Counter-Reformation Misogyny" and Jodi Bilinkoff's "Woman with a Mission: Teresa of Avila and the Apostolic Model."[2] I have found that it is easier to engage students with the historical context of early modern monasticism once they have formulated specific questions. From my essay, I hope students will appreciate why Catholic ecclesiastics mistrusted female mystics and visionaries and why, in the wake of the Protestant Reformation, the Catholic Church interpreted the Pauline exhortation "Let your women keep silent in the churches" (1 Cor 14:34–36) as a wide-ranging prohibition against women's participation in most kinds of religious discourse. From Bilinkoff's essay, I want them to appreciate that the Counter-Reformation was also a Catholic Reformation and that the schism awakened in women like Teresa a sense of mission, an urgent and sometimes frustrated desire to serve their church. This is also the appropriate time to discuss post-Tridentine mandates for monastic enclosure. The best analogy for Teresa's ideal enclosed convent was suggested some years ago by a student who said, "The convent was supposed to be sort of like a think tank; only it was a prayer tank."

Following these discussions on the historical context for Teresa's *Life*, we return to the text to consider questions of genre and style. Students are now better prepared to understand that this is a peculiar kind of autobiography— a "commanded autobiography"—produced so that Teresa's confessors could examine the orthodoxy of her spiritual beliefs and experiences.[3] At the beginning of class, students work in pairs, confessing a real or imagined peccadillo to a "confessor." Each one then tries to convince a skeptical partner that some unusual experience was not a lie or delusion. After this exercise, students are more attuned to some of the unusual features of Teresa's discourse: the way she interweaves confession and self-justification; the way

2. Jodi Bilinkoff, "Woman with a Mission: Teresa of Avila and the Apostolic Model," in *Modelli di santità e modelli di comportamento*, ed. Giulia Barone et al. (Turin: Rosenberg & Sellier, 1994), 295–305; Alison Weber, "Little Women: Counter-Reformation Misogyny," in my *Teresa of Avila and the Rhetoric of Femininity* (Princeton: Princeton University Press, 1990), 17–41. For a discussion of the implications underlying the labels Counter-Reformation versus Catholic Reform, see John O'Malley, *Trent and All That* (Cambridge: Harvard University Press, 2000), esp. 1–15.

3. "Commanded autobiography" ('autobiografía por mandato') is a term coined by Sonja Herpoel in "Autobiografías por mandato: una escritura feminina en la España del Siglo de Oro," unpublished *Thèse de doctorat*, Université d'Anvers, 1987.

she couches assertions with expressions of insufficiency and deference, and the way she disguises spiritual teaching as autobiographical experience. After reviewing the paradigm of female inferiority—the view that women were weak in judgment, sensual, vain, more susceptible to demonic illusions, and more likely to fabricate supernatural gifts—we look again at Teresa's negative references to herself and women in general. Had she internalized the misogynistic attitudes of her contemporaries? Was she "working around" these views by playing upon the expectations of her male readers? My goal here is to encourage students to be alert for the "stratagems of the weak," that is, the rhetorical strategies used by the disempowered to turn weakness to their advantage.[4]

Once students are familiar with these key concepts—Counter-Reformation mistrust of female spirituality and the restrictions on women as spiritual teachers, the Discalced Carmelites' longing for an apostolate of prayer, and the nature of the "commanded autobiography"—*Recreation* is more accessible. Having read Teresa of Ávila's *Life*, students can better understand the seeming contradiction between Gracia's intellectual self-confidence and her acquiescence to male authority. Her protestations of humility and her willingness to see benefit in suffering seem less bizarre. They can appreciate how similar María is to Teresa in terms of rhetorical strategy and her sense of humor. But they can also see that *Recreation* is a *parody* of the "commanded autobiography," since the fictional Gracia ignores her confessor's command to write her own life and instead transforms the mandate into an invitation to compose, with her sisters' help, a "hodgepodge" of things that are of importance to them—the life of their mother foundress, the history of their order, and their questions about interior prayer. From my introduction to the translation, students are aware that María did not fear her confessor, Jerómino Gracián. In fact, they were close allies. The contrast between Teresa's anxious relationship with her potentially censorious addressees and María's warm friendship with Gracián is instructive. It not only helps to explain differences in style and tone, it reminds us that men and women were not always antagonists in the religious culture of early modern Europe.[5]

4. "The stratagems of the weak" is a term coined by Josefina Ludmer, "Las tretas del débil," in *La sartén por el mango: Encuentro de escritoras latinoamericanas*, ed. Patricia Elena González and Eliana Ortega (Rio Piedras: Huracán, 1984), 47–54. See also Electa Arenal and Stacey Schlau, "Stratagems of the Strong, Stratagems of the Weak: Autobiographical Prose of the Seventeenth-Century Hispanic Convent," *Tulsa Studies in Women's Literature* 9 (1990): 25–42.

5. On male/female collaboration in religious life, see Jodi Bilinkoff, *Related Lives: Confessors and Their Female Penitents, 1450–1750* (Ithaca, N.Y.: Cornell University Press, 2005).

We next turn to the question of why María cast her story as a dialogue. Students generally agree that a dialogue would have been more fun to read or listen to. I point out that the dialogue was a popular "teaching" genre in the Renaissance and that, with some exceptions, one speaker usually stands out as the voice of authority or right thinking. Is this a typical didactic dialogue? Students can appreciate that Gracia is María's mouthpiece, but they also note that other characters make good points and sometimes challenge or tease Gracia. Women students in particular find the way Gracia and Justa "get on each other's case" understandable, and they are quick to point out that there are some "stressors in the sisterhood." One student remarked that the dialogue was better suited than a first-person narrative for a situation in which "showing off" would not be appreciated; as María remarks in her prologue, "mute tongues beget understanding" (34). Another student suggested that since the nuns are not mute, but quite talkative, this remark might better be understood as "Actions speak louder than words." In pondering the meaning of "mute tongues," students can begin to discern the pedagogical ideal María was putting forth in this dialogue.

Comparing María's style with Teresa's requires students to revisit some of their previous characterizations of a "colloquial" or "feminine" style. They can see that although María's style is clearly conversational, it is more regular in syntax, less digressive, and less repetitive than Teresa's. The contrast between María and Teresa's styles is even more evident when we compare, side by side, passages from *The Book of Her Life* and María's "edited" version in *Recreations*. In terms of rhetorical strategy, both nuns frequently deploy *concessio* and *reticencia* and resort to the *topio* of humility, incompetence, bashfulness, and insignificance. But students can grasp that there is a difference—María's rhetoric of femininity is self-conscious and witty; indeed, it represents a gentle parody of Teresa's rhetoric.

At this point, I introduce the concepts of "anxiety of influence" and "anxiety of authorship" and explain how they have been used to describe the psychological barriers faced by nineteenth-century women writers. Are these appropriate terms for a sixteenth-century woman writer? Why is it important to have a literary forebear? Who was the more important forebear for María—Teresa or her well-educated and beloved confessor Gracián? María imitates Gracián by writing a humanist dialogue, but she also closely imitates Teresa. In fact, her voice almost merges with Teresa's as she incorporates passages from the *Life* into the dialogue. But in the final chapter, Angela/Teresa disappears and Gracia/María emerges as the heroic protagonist of a particularly difficult foundation. Whose "self" dominates this dialogue—María's "I," Teresa's "she," or the nuns' "we"? These questions can lead students to think more deeply about how women constructed a sense of self in early modern culture.[6]

A question that unfailingly elicits a lively debate is whether María can be considered a feminist. Students recognize that Gracia cites scripture, excoriates ignorant priests, and defends women's intellectual and spiritual capacities, but they also see that her critique of male arrogance is not directed toward achieving political rights or social equality for women. She appeals to the women of the New Testament to authorize her conviction that "we [women] should speak and know of [Christ's] teachings" (102), but she also concedes "it is not ours to pry into mysteries" (102). Should we call this feminism, protofeminism, or something else? My aim here is not to pin the proper label on the nun but to encourage students to reflect on the varieties of feminist consciousness.[7]

Now that *For the Hour of Recreations* is available in English, I look forward to teaching it in a transnational context. The following describes a planned course on women and religion in early modern Catholic Europe, divided into units on nuns, married women, "failed saints," and "women on the margins." To give students an idea of the variety of conditions in early modern convents, I would ask students to compare *Recreations* with examples of convent theater, such as those included in Elissa Weaver's *Convent Theatre in Early Modern Italy*.[8] The writings of Jacqueline Pascal, who defied the wishes of her famous brother Blaise to pursue her religious vocation, can be read against Arcangela Tarabotti's *Paternal Tyranny*, an impassioned protest against forced vocations.[9] The letters of Teresa of Ávila to her brother Lorenzo and those of Suor Maria Celeste Galilei (1600–1634) to her father,

6. Instructors may wish to have students read two theoretical studies that have shaped these debates: Sandra M. Gilbert and Susan Gubar, "Infection in the Sentence: The Woman Writer and the Anxiety of Authorship," in *Feminisms: An Anthology of Literary Theory and Criticism*, ed. Robyn R. Worhol and Diane Price Herndl (New Brunswick: Rutgers University Press, 1997), 21–32; Sidonie Smith, *A Poetics of Women's Autobiography: Marginality and the Fictions of Self-Representation* (Bloomington, Ind.: Indiana University Press, 1987). See also my analysis of María's problematic relationship with her powerful foremother, "On the Margins of Ecstasy: María de San José as (Auto)biographer," *Journal of the Institute of Romance Studies* 4 (1996): 251–68.

7. In thinking through this issue, I have benefited from Gerda Lerner, *The Creation of Feminist Consciousness from the Middle Ages to Eighteen-Seventy* (New York: Oxford University Press, 1993).

8. Elissa B. Weaver, *Convent Theatre in Early Modern Italy: Spiritual Fun and Learning for Women* (Cambridge: Cambridge University Press, 2002). For examples of convent plays from Spain, see chapter 2 of Arenal and Schlau, *Untold Sisters*, and Stacey Schlau, ed., *Viva al Siglo, muerta al mundo: Selected Works by María de San Alberto (1568–1640)* (New Orleans: University Press of the South, 1998).

9. Jacqueline Pascal, *A Rule for Children and Other Writings*, ed. and trans. John J. Conley, SJ (Chicago: University of Chicago Press, 2003); Arcangela Tarabotti, *Paternal Tyranny*, ed. and

Galileo Galilei, illustrate how some nuns maintained intimate ties to their earthly families.[10] The life of Marie de l'Incarnation, who abandoned her young son to join the Ursulines, presents a very different story, one of family ties severed by spiritual longing.[11] The selections are designed to illustrate that if the convent was a *hortus conclusus* for some women and a prison for others, for still others it was a world of complex relationships, with occasions for joy and sorrow.

Early modern Catholicism offered laywomen a variety of paths to manifest their piety, and I would try to give students an idea of how social status and wealth determined the range of these options. Possible readings include Carolyn Valone's richly illustrated study of the women who patronized the early Jesuits;[12] selections from the poetry of Gabrielle de Coignard, a merchant's widow who expressed her loneliness and mystical longings in spiritual sonnets; and Allyson Poska's essay on the peasant women of northern Spain who proved indifferent to inquisitorial efforts to reform their sexual mores.[13] The essays in *Widowhood in Medieval and Early Modern Europe* provide further examples of how laywomen negotiated their secular and spiritual needs.[14]

For the unit entitled "Failed Saints," I would assign readings from the inquisitorial trials of Francisca de los Apóstoles (1539–after 1578) and Cecilia Ferrazzi (1609–1684).[15] Both were laywomen who attempted to organize communities for women at risk—women like themselves who, lacking

---

trans. Letizia Panizza, The Other Voice in Early Modern Europe (Chicago: University of Chicago Press, 2004).

10. Celeste Galilei, *Letters to Father. Suor Maria Celeste to Galileo, 1623–1633*, trans. Dava Sobel (New York: Penguin, 2001); Teresa de Jesús, *The Collected Letters of St. Teresa of Avila. Volume One: 1546–1577*, trans. Kieran Kavanaugh (Washington, D.C.: Institute of Carmelite Studies, 2001). Volume 2 is forthcoming.

11. See chapter 2 of Natalie Zemon Davis, *Women on the Margins: Three Seventeenth-Century Lives* (Cambridge: Harvard University Press, 1995). "Failed saint" is a term first coined by Anne Jacobson Schutte, "Per Speculum in Enigmate: Failed Saints, Artists, and Self-Construction of the Female Body," in *Creative Women in Medieval and Early Modern Italy: A Religious and Artistic Renaissance*, ed. E. Ann Matter and John Coakley (Philadelphia: University of Pennsylvania Press, 1994), 185–200. She has also suggested "aspiring saint" to refer to individuals whom ecclesiastical courts investigated for suspicion of "pretense of sanctity"; Anne Jacobson Schutte, *Aspiring Saints* (Baltimore: Johns Hopkins University Press, 2001).

12. Carolyn Valone, "Piety and Patronage: Women and the Early Jesuits," in *Creative Women in Medieval and Early Modern Italy*, 157–84.

13. Allyson Poska, "When Bigamy Is the Charge," in *Women in the Inquisition: Spain and the New World*, ed. Mary E. Giles (Baltimore: Johns Hopkins University Press, 1999), 189–205.

14. Sandra Cavallo and Lyndan Warner, eds., *Widowhood in Medieval and Early Modern Europe* (New York: Longman, 1999).

15. *The Inquisition of Francisca: A Sixteenth-Century Visionary on Trial*, ed. and trans. Gillian T. W. Ahlgren, The Other Voice in Early Modern Europe (Chicago: University of Chicago Press,

dowries, were unable to marry or enter convents. Both were eventually denounced for pretense of sanctity. Their inquisitorial confessions encourage reflection on how some women attempted to fashion careers as religious reformers and "holy women" and the dangers this path entailed. How did religious authorities distinguish between legitimate living saints and frauds? What opportunities did these women have to defend their actions and beliefs before their interrogators? What criteria can we, at the beginning of the twenty-first century, use to determine whether they were cynical pretenders or earnest reformers? To conclude this unit, students can be asked to speculate on how close Teresa of Ávila and María de San José came to being "failed saints."

In the final weeks of the semester, I would have the class consider the lives of women who, in open defiance or in secret, rejected their status as daughters of the Catholic Church. Marie Dentière's *Epistle to Marguerite de Navarre* offers students a window into the life of a nun who left the convent, married a former priest, and became active in the Reformation in Geneva. Her vigorous defense of women's right to teach the word of God in public can serve as a point of comparison to the accommodations other Catholic women made to restrictions on their apostolic role. Essays by Gretchen Starr-LeBeau, Renée Levine Melammed, and Mary Elizabeth Perry in *Women in the Inquisition* address the situation of Spain's Jewish and Moorish minorities, who were forced to convert to Christianity at the end of the fifteenth and the beginning of the sixteenth centuries.[16] Were the *conversas* who lit candles on Friday night and removed the sciatic vein from the lamb before cooking it secret Jews or sincere Christians who had retained some Jewish customs? How did *moriscas*, baptized Moorish women, transmit secret knowledge of Islamic law and custom to their children? This final unit is designed to encourage students to reflect on the fluidity of religious identities and the possibilities for resistance at a time when the church's monopoly over religious expression was less complete than generally imagined.

Whether included in a course with a literary or historical focus, *For the Hour of Recreation* can engage students in a productive debate over the extent

2005); *Autobiography of an Aspiring Saint*, ed. and trans. Anne Jacobson Schutte, The Other Voice in Early Modern Europe (Chicago: University of Chicago Press, 1996).

16. Marie Dentière, *Epistle to Marguerite de Navarre*, ed. and trans. Mary B. McKinley, The Other Voice in Early Modern Europe (Chicago: University of Chicago Press, 2004); Gretchen Starr-Lebeau, "Mari Sánchez and Inés González: Conflict and Cooperation among Crypto-Jews," (19–41); "María López, a Convicted Judaizer from Castile," 53–72; "Contested Identities: The Morisca Visionary, Beatriz de Robles," 171–88, in Mary E. Giles, ed., *Women in the Inquisition: Spain and the New World* (Baltimore: Johns Hopkins University Press, 1999).

to which women were able to contest the cultural and political constraints of early modern patriarchy. That the voice of this brilliant and creative woman, who probably understood the complexity of Teresa's thought better than any of her contemporaries, was muted for centuries is instructive in itself.

CECILIA FERRAZZI AND THE PURSUIT OF
SANCTITY IN THE EARLY MODERN WORLD

Elizabeth Horodowich

While the savvy historian acknowledges that archival documents are also literary constructions, the seventeenth-century trial of Cecilia Ferrazzi (1609–84) represents a unique opportunity to explore the relationship between history and literature. Tried by the Roman Inquisition for feigning holy behavior, Ferrazzi requested the right to dictate her autobiography to a court-appointed scribe in the hopes of defeating such accusations. The first four interrogations and autobiography have been translated and introduced in Anne Jacobson Schutte's volume, *Cecilia Ferrazzi: Autobiography of an Aspiring Saint.*[1] Faced with the challenge of exploring early modern religious culture with twenty-first-century undergraduates—who in the modern, secular world often find it difficult to relate to the spiritual motivations of historical actors—Ferrazzi's story provides an ideal text through which to engage students, as it is brief (fifty-three pages), easy to read, and compelling. Her combined trial and autobiography offers an unusual opportunity for students to investigate the links among gender, spirituality, and individual self-fashioning in the early modern world. This essay will briefly outline several of the many possible ways to present this text to an undergraduate class by tying Ferrazzi's dramatic account both to the historical setting in which she lived and to the lives and perceptions of modern students themselves.

A fruitful way to open a discussion of Ferrazzi's tale is by asking students to summarize briefly the events of her life and trial. What is the general story, why did this trial take place, and why does this trial include an autobiography? Such a line of questioning assures that students unfamiliar with the office of the Inquisition or the process of sanctification will be pulled up to

1. Cecilia Ferrazzi, *Autobiography of an Aspiring Saint*, ed. Anne Jacobson Schutte, The Other Voice in Early Modern Europe (Chicago: University of Chicago Press, 1996).

speed and will be equally prepared for a discussion of this text. In addition, it is useful to ask a student to read out loud from Ferrazzi's testimony where she lists all of the possible reasons she can imagine for why she was imprisoned (28). For instance, she says that some people claimed she wore "gold overskirts, and pearls around [her] neck." Why would this have been problematic? Others claimed that she forced young girls to confess to her. What would have been wrong with this? Reviewing the myriad reasons that Ferrazzi imagined could have brought her to prison reveals quite a bit about day-to-day life and social structure in early modern Venice: that only nobles could wear noble clothing and only priests could hear confession. This was a world socially stratified and culturally organized according to class, gender, profession, status, and rank.

A discussion of the nature of this text as a historical source is key to getting students to engage with questions of how we know about history. Ideally, students should come to see how the craft of history is not a search for truth, but rather the construction of an interpretive narrative derived from imperfect and incomplete evidence. There is no better document for exploring such issues than courtroom testimony. After a general discussion has established what we know about Ferrazzi's life from trial records, discussion can move to another level by asking, What are some of the problems associated with learning about history from such a source? What are some of the pitfalls inherent in studying history from the records of crime, and what types of information are left out of this record? By contrast, what types of evidence does courtroom testimony offer that we could not find, for instance, in other sources like wills or chronicles? As Schutte has discussed in her introduction to the text (3–4), many historians have debated the relative merits and problems of trials as historical documents. Courtroom testimony is a highly circumscribed source: Ferrazzi responds to questions formulaically and under duress, surely hoping to tell the inquisitor what he wishes to hear. At the same time, in courtroom testimony, like in no other source, when speakers in the courtroom articulate unusual ideas or break out of rote patterns of questioning, we can be reasonably sure we are reading the close transcription of a voice from the past, making such testimony an invaluable historical record. Raising this issue allows students to be critical of the text's structure and content throughout their discussion.

Another fruitful line of questioning involves focusing students' attention on the strategic goals driving Ferrazzi's autobiography. What is the point of her recounting her life story, and why did she compose this text? How does she structure her narrative, and what is she trying to achieve by dictating it to a court scribe? Once the class has established that Ferrazzi employs her narrative to construct herself as a saint, discussion can turn to a consideration of what sainthood means. What makes someone a saint, and what does sanctity entail? With these questions in mind, students should cite specific examples from the text of potential evidence of Ferrazzi's sanctity: her numerous visions (25, 39, 49, 54, 57), possible signs that she received the stigmata (29), trances (44–45, 53, 66), and miracles and miraculous cures (44, 48). At the same time, students should question when it is that a potential saint becomes a heretic, what is the dividing line between saintly and demonic behavior? In trying to assert her sanctity, how and when did Ferrazzi overstep the boundaries of piety to become labeled a heretic? Questions such as these lead students to an understanding of the repressive character of the Counter-Reformation: an age that consistently sought to classify and categorize unorthodox behaviors in an attempt to tighten the screws on all types of deviance.

Although at first it may appear to be a presentist question, in order to understand the spiritual and cultural motivations of mystics like Ferrazzi, it is sometimes provocative to ask female students why they think a woman might not want to marry, and then more specifically, why remaining unmarried might interest a woman in Ferrazzi's time. Ferrazzi mentions, for instance, that her mother had twenty-two children (42)—a fate any woman might choose to avoid. In soliciting responses to this question, the instructor may wish to point out that Ferrazzi belonged to a long tradition of Christian martyrs, mystics, and saints who rebelled against their families of origin in order to become brides of Christ and a part of the larger spiritual family of the church. Women such as Vibia Perpetua, Joan of Arc, Margery Kempe, and Saint Catherine of Siena offer similar examples of female sanctity.[2] In addition, linked to questions of marriage is the issue of chastity. Although Schutte discusses sexual purity in her introduction to the text (9–10), the subject of chastity merits further discussion. Why was chastity so important in this world? Why was it particularly important to Ferrazzi, enough so that her personal responsibilities eventually came to include the protection of over three hundred virgins? It is important to emphasize the significance of chastity on the multiple levels of the individual, the family, and the state; the loss of chastity could lead a girl into prostitution, interfere with a family's honor and inheritance strategies, and symbolically undermine the stability

2. For those interested in integrating a PowerPoint presentation into discussion, there exist numerous images that demonstrate visually the beliefs and actions of these women. For instance, the frescoes of Saint Catherine of Siena by Giovanni de Vecchi from the church of Santa Maria Sopra Minerva in Rome and Bernini's statue of the Ecstasy of Saint Teresa from the church of Santa Maria della Vittoria in Rome provide other useful visual examples of female sanctity.

of the state at large inasmuch as the orderly family underlay and exemplified the orderly state.

Beyond these more general questions, there are several additional lines of discussion that instructors may choose to pursue. For instance, while students might conceive of figures such as kings, princes, elites, or military men as those wielding power in the early modern world, Ferrazzi's trial illuminates the great authority possessed by the confessor in the more localized arenas of neighborhood and community. As we can see in her autobiography, confessors were like spiders at the center of all the gossip, news, and information of premodern communities. They possessed a type of local power that everyday people were often much more responsible to and aware of than the power exercised by political elites. Instructors can elicit such discussion by asking questions such as, what did confessors do? How often did people see them, and what did they tell them? As one of the accusations leveled against Ferrazzi was that of hearing the confessions of the girls under her protection, one might ask, why was this a crime? Why would churchmen seek to limit the number of people who could legitimately hear a confession? Answers to such questions shed much light on instances of threatened male power. Religious authorities sought to limit those in possession of the "magical" powers of saying a Mass or hearing a confession to the ranks of ordained males.

Perhaps most intriguingly, how did Ferrazzi appear to feel about her confessors, such as Polacco? This question is particularly useful in getting students to place Ferrazzi's account into the broader trends of the Reformation and Counter-Reformation and in getting students to see that Ferrazzi and her case were very much products of their time. Instructors should remind students that in the background of this trial, Catholics and Protestants were slaughtering one another in epic numbers during the Thirty Years' War, in part over issues pertaining specifically to religious culture. Martin Luther argued that many aspects of traditional Christian practice such as confession or prayer through saints were the shackles of a tyrannical church that free Christians needed to throw off. Ferrazzi's story at times betrays this perspective, as she usually describes her confessors' orders and her corresponding obedience. However, Ferrazzi is also clear in expressing the comfort and consolation she received from both receiving confession and praying to various saints.[3] Female saints offered her relief from her various torments (52), and at times she goes so far as to beg for her confession (53). Pointing out the

3. See Thomas N. Tentler, *Sin and Confession on the Eve of the Reformation* (Princeton, N.J.: Princeton University Press, 1977).

often conflicting ways that Ferrazzi relates to Catholic practice allows for a broader discussion of questions such as did Martin Luther misinterpret or misunderstand the role of the sacraments and saints in the lives of everyday Christians? Did the sacraments appear to give Christians more of a sense of oppression or consolation? And how are such questions further complicated with issues of gender? That is, can we argue that perhaps confession or female saints were more important in the minds of women?

Considering the ways in which religious culture is inflected with gender leads to another potentially fruitful line of discussion: the body. Leaning on Carolyn Walker Bynum's by now classic study, *Holy Feast and Holy Fast*, instructors can apply some of the questions Bynum poses about female saints in the Middle Ages to the case of Cecilia Ferrazzi.[4] For instance, what types of physical trials and tribulations did Ferrazzi endure? Ferrazzi suffered physically through excessive vomiting (23–24), flagellation (25), the pain of receiving the stigmata (29), and sleeping on bare boards (55). While students may argue that Ferrazzi mentions many of her pains as a result of lasting physical ailments like bladder stones or epilepsy, it is important to note how Ferrazzi emphasizes and reemphasizes such suffering as part of her rhetorical, narrative strategy of asserting her sainthood. As Bynum has argued, students should be encouraged to understand her physical suffering not as a manifestation of a concept of dualism—she did not draw a dichotomy between flesh and spirit. Rather, she sought to imitate the suffering of Christ, as she states, "I turned in anguish from the pain to implore that crucified Christ to clothe me in the love of His Passion and allow me to feel some of His pain" (29).

Instructors should then question, based on students' knowledge, if male and female saints appeared to undertake the same types of challenges or if they pursued sanctity in different ways. While students may not have a broad understanding of a variety of saints' lives, a brief discussion of or nod to Saint Francis's emphasis on poverty points to the often striking differences between male and female saints: men tended to renounce property and possessions, and women, by contrast, tended either to renounce (or fixate upon) food. We can see that both feasting and fasting were clear metaphors for Ferrazzi's piety; she claimed to live on the Eucharist alone (23), to go for long periods eating very little (40, 65), and to slake her thirst from a wound in Christ's side (58). Perhaps one of the most provocative and intriguing questions that can be asked of this evidence is, Why might male

4. Caroline Walker Bynum, *Holy Feast and Holy Fast: The Religious Significance of Food to Medieval Women* (Berkeley: University of California Press, 1987).

saints have focused more on poverty and female saints on food and fasting? Bynum's argument posits that people could only renounce that over which they wielded control. Women, as the traditional caretakers of home and hearth, including food gathering and preparation, considered food a spiritual metaphor, as it was a resource that they controlled, unlike property.[5] Students can debate this point and see if they agree or disagree with this argument. Another point worth discussing is whether mystical women like Ferrazzi used the power of their suffering bodies and Eucharistic visions to assert an alternative to, and therefore a critique of and substitute for, male religious authorities like priests and confessors. This question is especially pertinent to Ferrazzi since she was accused of confessing the girls under her protection.

A final question that always resonates powerfully with students is that of whether or not we could consider Ferrazzi's behavior to be an example of anorexia or bulimia. It works well to pose this question as a vote to the entire class, asking students (especially those who are often less participatory) why they would or would not classify her actions this way. While again this question risks projecting a presentist vision onto Ferrazzi's case, it is nevertheless useful in engaging students since it relates their own perception of the physical body to ideas about the body in history. One could argue that Ferrazzi's was not a case of anorexia or bulimia in that thinness was not valued in the early modern world as it is today. However, students often successfully argue that her behavior in fact does suggest this disorder in the way that Ferrazzi punishes her body in an attempt to gain a level of control over her world and her surroundings.[6]

For a more interactive discussion exercise that encourages students to enter into the worldview of early modern thinkers, Ferrazzi's trial lends itself well to a reenactment in the classroom. Ferrazzi herself states that "some proclaimed that I was a saint and others that I was possessed" (71), a pertinent quote to introduce this role-play. The instructor can ask, Which side would you take? Students can respond to the question by undertaking a debate or trial in several different ways, for instance, by dividing the class in half and asking each half to argue that Ferrazzi was or was not a saint. Alternatively, the instructor can appoint two lawyers, one to represent Ferrazzi and the other to act as a prosecutor. After consulting with groups of "advisors," a mock trial can cross-examine a student appointed as Ferrazzi, decided on by

5. Bynum, *Holy Feast and Holy Fast*, 189–91.

6. For more discussion on this topic, see Rudolph M. Bell, *Holy Anorexia* (Chicago: University of Chicago Press, 1987), and Bynum, *Holy Feast and Holy Fast*, 201–7.

another student appointed as the inquisitor. The instructor can also choose to take on any of these roles as well. In any case, no matter how this debate or trial is organized, most crucial is to allow students time to build their arguments based on textual citations, which they must be required to cite as evidence in their trial or debate. While students may initially resist the role-play approach to understanding and critiquing a text, discussions oriented around performance and reenactment such as these always yield the result of forcing students to enter a historical mentality in a more personal way.

While examples of saints and would-be saints like Ferrazzi's abound throughout the Middle Ages, Ferrazzi's trial and autobiography are exceptional for their detail, clarity, and completeness. Her tale offers students a window into questions of sanctity, women, and gender, and the broader issues of religious culture driving the European Reformations and Counter-Reformations. Her story allows students to question traditional periodization inasmuch as it is one of an aspiring saint in the seventeenth century, occurring much later than many other more studied examples of female sanctity. It encourages students to question when the Middle Ages end and the modern world begins. Her narrative offers an excellent addition to general courses on the Renaissance and Reformation, religious studies and the history of religion, and the history of women and gender.

V

Post-Reformation Currents

CONVENT AND DOCTRINE: TEACHING JACQUELINE PASCAL

John J. Conley, SJ

Teaching the works of Jacqueline Pascal presents a particular challenge not only because of their religious nature, but also because they reflect a doctrinal dispute (the Counter-Reformation quarrel over grace) and a religious way of life (a cloistered Cisterican convent) that even the most devout student finds difficult to grasp. In my translation of the works of Jacqueline Pascal (1625–61),[1] I presented a critical edition of the treatises, poetry, and letters of the sister of Blaise Pascal who became a nun at the Port-Royal convent in the Parisian region. All of her mature works are influenced by the radical Augustinianism championed by the Jansenist movement in Catholicism. When I first had the occasion to teach the works of Jacqueline Pascal to undergraduates, I knew that I would need to explain the rudiments of the Jansenist controversy: the biography of Cornelius Jansenius (1585–1638), the theological tenets of the Jansenist disciples, the conflict with the Jesuits, the struggle with king and pope, the role of Port-Royal as the physical and moral center of the movement. I soon discovered, however, that to make these monastic works intelligible, I needed to provide a much broader theological background.

My first occasion to teach Jacqueline Pascal was in two sections of an honors seminar for sophomores at Fordham University. The topic of the seminar was modern philosophy and theology. This seminar was given in the same semester in which the honors students took seminars in modern English literature and modern European history. To provide thematic unity for the seminar, I focused on the religious thought of the period, specifically the

---

1. See Jacqueline Pascal, *A Rule for Children and Other Writings*, ed. and trans. John J. Conley, SJ, The Other Voice in Early Modern Europe (Chicago: University of Chicago Press, 2003). Hereafter cited as *RCOW*.

challenge of skepticism and various religious responses from the Counter-Reformation. We started with Saint Francis de Sales's *Introduction to the Devout Life* in order to study one of the most influential spiritualities of the Counter-Reformation, one that found particular resonance with educated women.[2] We then examined the more skeptical of Montaigne's *Essays* to understand how cultural and ethical relativism challenged Christian allegiances.[3] Next we analyzed Descartes' arguments for God's existence, noting the controversy over the religious sincerity of these arguments.[4] At the end of the semester we studied the works of Blaise and Jacqueline Pascal. As we progressed through the *Pensées*,[5] I had the occasion to discuss the severe version of Augustinian theology championed by the Jansenists and by Blaise Pascal himself. When we ended the seminar with the writings of Jacqueline Pascal, we focused on her educational theories and practices, as sketched in her treatise, *A Rule for Children*. We also discussed the spiritual empowerment of women represented by her order's abolition of the dowry requirement and by her epistolary defense of the right of women to engage in theological disputes.

The religious focus of the entire seminar clearly helped the students to grasp several of the salient traits of Jacqueline Pascal's writings. They easily linked her emphasis on the obscurity of God to the "hidden God" of her brother and the religious ambiguity of both Montaigne and Descartes. Similarly, they saw how distinctively modern was Jacqueline Pascal's appeal to the rights of conscience and how it was tied to the defense of subjective experience present in the texts of the previous authors. It soon became apparent, however, that the students were experiencing serious difficulties in understanding the texts of Jacqueline Pascal because they had little knowledge of the convent culture that had nurtured them and only the vaguest notion of the theological doctrine of grace, which formed the background for the persecution of the nuns at Port-Royal.

Interpreting Jacqueline Pascal's major work, *A Rule for Children* (1657),[6] required extensive background on convent life in general and the particular

2. See Saint Francis de Sales, *Introduction to the Devout Life* (New York: Vintage Spiritual Classics, 2002).

3. See Michel de Montaigne, *The Complete Essays*, ed. M.A. Screech (London and New York: Penguin Classics, 1993), esp. "On Cannibals," "On Presumption," "On Imagination."

4. See René Descartes, *Discourse on Method and Related Writings*, ed. Desmond M. Clarke (London and New York: Penguin Classics, 2000), esp. *Meditations*, bks 3 and 5.

5. See Blaise Pascal, *Pensées*, ed. A. J. Krailsheimer (London and New York: Penguin Classics, 1995), esp. *Meditation*, bks 3 and 5.

6. See Jacqueline Pascal, *A Rule for Children*, in RCOW, 69–120.

vocation of cloistered nuns devoted to contemplation.[7] A lengthy treatise explaining the spirit and methods of the convent school at Port-Royal, the *Rule* presents a thoroughly monastic model of education in which young laywomen participate in many of the practices associated with monastic life. It is impossible to understand the daily order of the school without understanding the hours of the divine office, which the nuns chanted in the convent church throughout the day and night. Terms such as matins, lauds, sext, terce, none, vespers, and compline required explanation. Other monastic practices used at the school required clarification. Port-Royal pupils participated in the chapter of faults, small-group sessions in which individual pupils accused themselves of minor faults, asked their peers for pardon, and received admonition and penance from the nun-schoolmistress who presided over the session. Pupils were also required to follow the monastic grand silence, which prohibited all speaking from the beginning of the night office until after the conclusion of breakfast the next day.

Seminar students quickly noticed and appreciated the more modern dimensions of the education championed by Jacqueline Pascal. The most striking was the tutorial system used in the convent school. Each schoolmistress was to have a weekly personal conference with each pupil assigned to her care. During these interviews the teacher would assess the intellectual, moral, and religious progress of the pupil; at its conclusion, the schoolmistress would give the pupil personalized counsel on how she could make further progress in the future. My students found it more difficult, however, to perceive the paramount value accorded a pupil's persevering in a state of grace and maintaining her hope of salvation, although these religious goals structured the content of the tutorial interview and permeated the school's ascetical practices.

Careful attention to the monastic culture of the Port-Royal school helped the seminar students to perceive how this apparently anachronistic approach to education represented a spiritual empowerment for women. Access to Scripture, patristic authors, and theological texts was no longer limited to the clergy; both laywomen and nuns were to build their piety on these sources. Active participation in the liturgy was no longer limited to clergy and members of religious orders; from an early age at the Port-Royal school, laywomen were to assist in chanting the Divine Office and to

7. A synthetic presentation of the state of Catholic women's orders in France during the early modern period can be found in Elizabeth Rapley, *The Dévotes: Women and Church in Seventeenth-Century France* (Kingston, Ontario: McGill-Queen's University Press, 1989). A comprehensive history of Catholic women's orders can be found in Jo Ann Kay McNamara, *Sisters in Arms: Catholic Nuns through Two Millenia* (Cambridge, MA: Harvard University Press, 1996).

participate in the Mass through hymns and an active knowledge of the basic Latin texts. The nuns who taught in the convent school assumed a ministerial status in their counsels for spiritual development during the chapter of faults and a theological status when they taught catechism not through rote memorization but through lectures on religious problems and regular question-and-answer sessions for their pupils. To grasp how Jacqueline Pascal's philosophy of education represented an "other voice" advocating on behalf of the rights of women, it was crucial to recognize the distinctively monastic way in which this enhancement of women's spiritual authority occurs.

Another work requiring detailed contextualizing was the *Report of Soeur Jacqueline de Sainte Euphémie to the Mother Prioress of Port-Royal des Champs* (1653),[8] Jacqueline Pascal's autobiographical account of the "crisis of the dowry." When Jacqueline Pascal entered the Port-Royal convent in 1652, she expected that a third of the inheritance left by her father Étienne, who had died in 1651, would be used as her dowry when she professed her vows as a nun at the end of her novitiate. A bitter dispute arose when her sister Gilberte and especially her brother Blaise announced their opposition to the dowry and their intention to keep the inheritance within the family. Threats of litigation followed. Since the dowry had long been customary for a choir nun in a Benedictine or Cistercian convent and since the prominent Pascal family clearly possessed the funds to support it, the question of the dowry deteriorated into a bitter feud between Jacqueline and Blaise. The *Report* recounts how Mère Angélique Arnauld (1591–1661), the abbess of Port-Royal, counseled the embittered Jacqueline to profess her vows undowered; the abbey was perfectly happy to accept such an obviously sincere vocation and the lack of a dowry would amplify the vow of poverty Soeur Jacqueline would be taking. But the aristocratic Jacqueline, who had known the adulation of the court as an adolescent poet prodigy, could not easily accept such a social humiliation imposed by her brother's pique at her vocation. The *Report* vividly describes her struggle to accept an undowered vocation and the climactic decision of Blaise to concede a substantial financial gift to the convent at the moment of Jacqueline's profession as a nun.

To understand the crisis of the dowry, it was necessary for the seminar students to grasp the role of the dowry in convents, especially those that were strictly cloistered. For many students at the beginning of the course, the dowry was simply a marital anachronism that survived in obscure parts of Africa and Asia. They were surprised to learn that the possession of a dowry

8. See Jacqueline Pascal, *Report of Soeur Jacqueline de Sainte Euphémie to the Mother Prioress of Port-Royal des Champs*, in RCOW, 41–68.

was a requirement to place a daughter in a Benedictine or Cistercian convent in France. Many of these convents were designed primarily to accommodate aristocratic widows or spinsters who desired (or more commonly had fathers who desired for them) to live a pious but comfortable life of retirement. For the Pascal family, a prominent member of the *noblesse de robe*, to deny a dowry to Jacqueline was to insult her and, in most contemplative convents of the period, to destroy her chance to pursue a vocation she had desired for years. One of the liberating innovations introduced by Mère Angélique Arnauld in her reform of Port-Royal was to abolish the dowry requirement. This abolition meant that the convent would accept impoverished candidates with authentic vocations to the monastic life and conversely that it would refuse to accept candidates who were being coerced into the convent by their parents or who clearly lacked the capacity to live the rigorous ascetical life of the reformed Port-Royal. Students began to see that the issue of the dowry was more than an economic one; it concerned the vocational freedom of an individual woman to choose her state in life and the associational freedom of a religious community to choose its members on the basis of religious and moral rather than economic criteria.

As students recognized the spiritual empowerment of women represented by the abolition of the dowry requirement, they developed a deeper understanding of how the reformed governance structure of Port-Royal enhanced the spiritual authority of women.[9] Rather than being appointed by the monarch for a lifetime term, the abbess of the reformed Port-Royal was elected by the chapter of the convent's choir nuns. Although subject to ratification by the archbishop of Paris, the constitutions and statutes of the convent were written, debated, and approved by the nuns themselves assembled in chapter. The abbess nominated the male clerics, notably the chaplain and confessors, necessary for the spiritual life of the convent. These varied reforms represent distinctively monastic ways of expanding the prerogatives for self-governance by women.

Another problematic religious arena for the interpretation of Jacqueline Pascal concerned the doctrinal disputes that embroiled the convent in the middle of the seventeenth century. In 1661, the French throne ordered the nuns to sign a formulary that accepted the Catholic Church's judgment that five theological propositions concerning grace and freedom were

9. The Constitutions of Port-Royal are the written, legal embodiment of the major innovations, including the abolition of the dowry requirement, introduced by the Angelican reform of the convent. See Mère Agnès Arnauld, *Les constitutions du monastère de Port-Royal du S.-Sacrement* (Mons: G. Migeot, 1665).

heretical and that Cornelius Jansenius had defended these propositions in his posthumously published work *Augustinus* (1640). Antoine Arnauld, the leading theologian of the Jansenist movement, had devised the ingenious *droit / fait* distinction to place limits on church authority. According to this distinction, the church could bind the conscience of its members on matters of *droit* (law), namely, matters of faith and morals, since the church enjoyed the inspiration of the Holy Spirit to guide its members toward salvation. On matters of *fait* (empirical fact), however, the church did not enjoy such divine assistance. It could certainly make such judgments about a particular theologian or book, but this judgment remained fallible, open to revision or even reversal. The application to the controversial formulary was clear. The Jansenists should give a reserved signature, indicating their assent to the condemnation of the five propositions (which they agreed were heretical), but refusing to assent to what they considered an erroneous judgment of fact concerning Jansenius.

Like most Port-Royal nuns, Jacqueline Pascal contested this subtle distinction. Although she ultimately gave a reserved signature to the formulary under pressure from the convent confessors, she underscored the dangers of using such a subterfuge. For her, the "crisis of the signature" touched the very integrity of the Christian faith. In her perspective, Jansenius had correctly interpreted the doctrine of Saint Augustine concerning grace, a position repeatedly affirmed by popes and church councils, and Augustine had correctly interpreted Saint Paul's inspired biblical teaching on grace. To sign a statement that clearly condemned Jansenius, whatever casuistic reservation one tried to place on it, was to deny the very grace of Christ and to imperil one's salvation.

Seminar students admired the courage Jacqueline Pascal displayed in a series of letters opposing compromise on the signature and denouncing the political and ecclesiastical abuses of authority that had brought Port-Royal to the brink of excommunication and destruction. In a letter of June 23, 1661, to Soeur Angélique de Saint-Jean, she develops a stirring defense of the rights of conscience: "I know very well that it's not up to girls to argue the cause of truth. Still, we can see in the present sad circumstances that since the bishops are showing the courage of girls, the girls should be showing the courage of bishops. Nonetheless, if it's not up to us to defend the truth, it's up to us to die for the truth and to suffer everything rather than abandon it."[10] Students struggled, however, with understanding the object of

10. Soeur Jacqueline de Sainte-Euphémie Pascal to Soeur Angélique de Saint-Jean Arnauld d'Andilly, 23 June 1661, in *RCOW*, 150.

Soeur Jacqueline's courageous defense: the doctrine of Christ's grace. It was necessary to explore the long-simmering *querelle de la grâce*, in which various parties within early modern Catholicism contested the relationship between human freedom and divine grace in the act of salvation.[11] For the Jesuits, God's grace must be received freely by each human person, and each Christian must freely cooperate with God's grace to produce the works of justice and charity. For the neo-Augustinian party, including the Jansenists, such an exaltation of human free will undercuts God's grace and turns humanity into the architect of its own salvation. According to the Jansenist doctrine of efficacious grace, God saves an elect group of human beings through a sovereign act of the divine will, and the moral actions of the redeemed flow from a grace freely bestowed by God without consideration of human merit.

To understand Jacqueline Pascal's resistance during the crisis of the signature, it is insufficient to portray her as a champion of the rights of conscience against an overbearing church and state. Her conscientious refusal to bow to the religious demands of the throne is based on specific theological truth-claims: that we are radically dependent on God's grace for salvation and for the performance of good works, that the Jesuit exaltation of human freedom is a counterfeit of the gospel, and that even mitigated assent to the ecclesiastical condemnation of Jansenius is a tacit denial of the grace of Christ. An adequate grasp of Jacqueline Pascal's crisis of conscience during the controversy over the signature requires a careful study of the underlying doctrinal issues concerning grace, freedom, and necessity in the theological wars of the Counter-Reformation.

My experience of teaching the works of Jacqueline Pascal to undergraduate honors students has taught me that effective reading, discussion, and analysis of such theological texts requires two specific kinds of religious illumination. The first is background instruction on the conventual culture in which the texts emerged. Students are often sensitive to the mystical experience and the personal biography of the nun who is a writer. But it is often the instructor who must encourage them to examine the communitarian culture of the convent that has nurtured these works. The monastic vows, the liturgical office, the ascetical practices, the biblical and patristic

11. For an excellent overview of the quarrel over grace in early modern Catholicism, see Louis Cognet, *Le Jansénisme*, 7th ed. (Paris: Presses universitaires de France, 1995). For a more focused discussion of the Pascalian theology of grace and its effort to maintain a coherent theory of human freedom, see Michael Moriarity, "Grace and Religious Freedom in Pascal," in *The Cambridge Companion to Pascal*, ed. Nicholas Hammond (Cambridge: Cambridge University Press, 2003), 144–61.

reading, and the exercise of authority by the abbess and other convent officers must be explored for such conventual texts to acquire intelligibility for the contemporary American student. Similarly, the complex doctrinal controversies of early modern Christianity require clarification if Jacqueline Pascal's struggle against abuses of authority and moral compromise is to be understood. These questions of doctrine and monastic ethos are not foreign to the central questions of gender posed by Jacqueline Pascal and the other authors studied in the Other Voice series. Soeur Jacqueline's robust defense of the spiritual rights of women simply cannot be perceived apart from the elected abbesses, the psalm-chanting laywomen, and the quarrels over grace that march through her writings.

JOHANNA ELEONORA PETERSEN (1644–1724): PIETISM AND WOMEN'S AUTOBIOGRAPHY IN SEVENTEENTH-CENTURY GERMANY

Barbara Becker-Cantarino

Those of us who teach in the early modern period outside of English literature, history, and culture know how difficult it is to find suitable texts by women that engage today's student reader. Here is a personal narrative written by a Pietist German woman who insisted on speaking out and publishing on religious issues at a time when women were supposed to be silent in matters of the church. Johanna Eleonora Petersen, nee von und zu Merlau (1644–1724), wrote and published her autobiography as an explanation and defense of her turn to a religious life. It is the first autobiography written *and* published by a woman in German.[1] Petersen's autobiography goes beyond a presentation of and reflection on the religious life, which was customary among Pietists and usually composed when facing death. Petersen *defends* her "other path," her choice of joining the Pietists, a marriage outside her class, and the publication of her religious thoughts. She describes in relatively great detail her secular life: her rather desolate childhood in the wake of the Thirty Years' War, her service at court, her life as a Pietist in Frankfurt, and her marriage. Her religious visions conclude the volume as a climax of her inner biography, her destiny since childhood. At the same time she defends herself against accusations and lies of (unidentified) enemies and others, of whose worldly lifestyle she disapproves. Petersen ends her autobiography with mystic images of calling, reminiscent of the mystic Jacob Boehme and the English visionary Jane Lead.[2]

1. Johanna Eleonora Petersen von Merlau, *The Life of Lady Johanna Eleonora Petersen as Told by Herself*, ed. and trans. Barbara Becker-Cantarino, The Other Voice in Early Modern Europe (Chicago: University of Chicago Press, 2005).

2. See below, note 22 and related text.

Recent shifts in interest and teaching methodology and their effect on teaching the early modern period can be summarized and put to good use for new course designs as follows:

1. The shift to cultural studies provides an opportunity for teaching the early modern period as no longer tied to canonical texts of "high" literary, aesthetic value nor to predominantly philological considerations. The work within its cultural and historical context is now more important than the artistic merit within what German literary historians have held sacrosanct as "Höhenkammliteratur" (highbrow literature).

2. We now often strive to include multidisciplinary material: from literature, history, music, art, philosophy, or religion, depending on the topic or theme rather than staying within one genre or national (literary) tradition. For many themes of the early modern period, a comparative approach, that is to say, not limited to German (or English, or French, or Spanish) material alone, can be illuminating.

3. There is now a need for good, readable, authentic translations into English to make up for not only the increasing lack of language proficiency in German, but also in Latin, French, and Spanish of the early modern period.

4. The importance of the early modern period in understanding our cultural roots needs to be stressed in our teaching. And in our teaching of it we need to recognize the distinction between that period and our own.

The Life of Lady Johanna Eleonora Petersen, Written by Herself is an excellent text for teaching within these parameters. The text is an easy read (and short), but it is sophisticated in its structure, subtle in content, and can be taught in multidisciplinary ways at both the undergraduate and graduate levels in history, women's studies, literature, and religion. It can and should, of course, also be taught in a German program and can be used at the graduate level as a starting point for research. I shall treat these areas separately, although it goes without saying that issues and suggestions overlap and complement each other. Petersen's *Life* is best taught together with a series of other, similar texts from the same period, including texts by men that facilitate a focus on gender differences and contemporary texts that reveal historical differences.

AS "EGO" DOCUMENT IN A HISTORY CLASS

The recent trend toward interdisciplinary teaching in history courses and the emphasis on, if not shift to, the social and everyday means greater attention to individuals, as opposed to a focus on great statesmen, wars, empires, and institutions. Letters, speeches, diaries, and autobiographies provide insight into a deeper truth about what individuals were thinking and what they believed. An autobiography is as authentic a document as we can rescue from the past; it documents "ego," a persona, as presented, viewed, and judged by its author. Pederson's *Life* gives marginalized women a voice.

Her *Life* requires historical contextualization, which includes the Protestant Reformation and the Thirty Years' War; the class system and the role of women; and courts, absolutist rulers, and principalities in a decentralized German (Holy Roman) Empire.[3] The first half of the narrative lends itself to discussion of the effects of war, the role of the family, court and city life, the emerging Pietist movement, the role and authority of the clergy, and the functions of the (city) government. Focusing on the individual life, we might ask about the nature of Petersen's socialization, the importance of religion, "reputation" (for a woman) and "rumor," engagement and marriage, reading and the role of the Bible, and issues of tolerance and religious dissent. The second half of the text is spiritual and visionary. Why did the year 1685 (the year of the revocation of the Edict of Nantes) leave such an impression on her mind and visions? What kind of utopia is the "New Jerusalem"?

The text can also be used as a basis for a seventeenth-century biography assignment, for an in-class presentation or a short (response) paper on one woman's life.[4] It can be paired with and contrasted to another woman's life story during the Thirty Year's War, the fictional, satirical *Runagate Courage* (1670) by the eminent German author Hans Jacob Christoph von Grimmelshausen.[5] The spirited female protagonist Courage dresses as a soldier,

3. In addition to the bibliography in *Life*, see http://www.germanhistorydocs.ghi-dc.org/, "From the Reformation to the Thirty Years' War (1500–1648)," introduction, documents, images, and maps, all in English.

4. See Carole Levin, "Illuminating the Margins of the Early Modern Period: Using Women's Voices in the History Class," in *Teaching Tudor and Stuart Women Writers*, ed. Susanne Woods and Margaret P. Hannay (New York: Modern Language Association, 2000), 261–76, at 262–63. The essay discusses the inclusion of women's experiences in early modern history courses.

5. *Landstörtzerin Courasche* has been translated several times: by Robert L. Hiller and John C. Osborne as *Runagate Courage* (Lincoln: University of Nebraska Press, 1965), by Hans Speer as *Courage: The Adventuress and the False Messiah* (Princeton, N.J.: Princeton University Press, 1964), and by Mike Mitchel as *The Life of Courage* (Sawtry, Cambs, UK: Dedalus, 2001). It is part of

goes through several marriages and rapes, and ends up as a gipsy captain's wife; she falls morally and socially from a gentleman's illegitimate daughter to an outcast who makes a living by stealing, whoring, and cursing God, a warning to all men.

AS AN AUTHENTIC, SELF-EMPOWERING TEXT IN A WOMEN'S STUDIES OR GENDER STUDIES CLASS

A women's studies course on early modern European women ought to provide for its twenty-first-century students a broad sense of the women's lives, activities, and achievements, especially their literary output. The latter can include poems, prose works, plays, pamphlets, letters, diaries, or autobiographical texts. These have proved scarce, either in seventeenth-century translations or modern editions, although the Other Voice series is doing the most to fill this gap for texts by women written in languages other than English.

When teaching Pedersen's *Life*, we can first reflect on the cultural space allowed to women and the expectations of a Christian woman's role. Martin Luther in his sermons on marriage, such as *On Married Life*, clearly outlined woman's role as wife (her husband's "helpmeet") and mother (bearing children in "labor" [pain]). The husband was to be the provider by means of his work and his wife's steward, who was allowed to punish her, even physically, if need be. The husband was the head of the household (*Hausvater*), just as the prince was the head of the state (*Landesvater*) and God the head of the community of believers (*Gottvater*); the wife was the "weaker vessel,"[6] whose sexuality was to be channeled into procreation, not pleasure. Luther also emphasized that since both man and woman were created by God, women should receive a religious education. Thus educational tracts in seventeenth-century Germany usually refer to woman's education with the advice, "Two things belong in a woman's hand: a prayerbook and a spindle."[7] Religion and housework (the spindle standing in for production of essential goods within

---

the novel cycle *Simplicissimus*, in which the hero finds solace from the world of war as a hermit serving God. The female figure Courage is the moral and fictional antagonist of Simplicissimus. See Barbara Becker-Cantarino, "Dr. Faustus and Runagate Courage: Theorizing Gender in Early Modern Germany," in *The Graph of Sex and the German Text: Gendered Culture in Early Modern Germany 1500–1700*, ed. Lynne Tatlock and Christiane Bohnert (Amsterdam and Atlanta: Rodophi, 1994), 27–44.

6. See Antonia Fraser, *The Weaker Vessel: Woman's Lot in Seventeenth-Century England* (New York: Knopf, 1984). This is an excellent historical overview of women's lives based on individual biographies and archival work.

7. Hans Michhael Moscherosch, *Insomnis cura parentum: Christliches Vermächtnuß oder schuldige Vorsorg eines Trewen Vatters* (1643; repr. Halle: Niemeyer, 1893).

the household) were the cornerstones of a woman's life. With this in mind, Petersen's attitude toward and decision for marriage appear in a different light. She turned her "arranged" marriage into one of an activist couple (*Streiterehe*) based on their religious calling (not on her personal emancipation).

One may want to initiate classroom discussion of Petersen's personality by looking at her portrait (1) and observing her features, gaze, posture, and clothing: her headdress as a matron, her carefully arranged locks, her straight look, her dark dress, her finger pointing at the biblical book of Revelation. In the text we can explore a woman's strength and self-determination—her fight against lies (83–84), the boat in the storm scene (79–80), and her decision to turn to God away from a respectable and enjoyable life at court (75–76) are signs of self-empowerment. However, this self-empowerment does not serve Petersen's own end but arises out of an inner, religious calling. Petersen finds identity in her role as "doer of the word,"[8] as messenger or prophetess of God. Her calling is expressed in the image of a nightingale,[9] a symbol of faithful and lasting prophecy, and in late medieval paintings of Mary, a sign of the soul's heavenly desire or of an indefatigable reader of the Bible. Petersen also makes a case for her authorship, not as a modern author would for writing literary, fictional texts for her own "honor," but as a vessel of God's word, "a weak and low instrument" (27). It is with this argument that she defies the traditional interpretation of the Pauline dictum that women be silent in matters of the church.

Our students as modern readers might question such a stance and apply a critical, psychological approach to this woman's religious turn of mind and life: was she only "bored" with the strict order at court, with the courtiers' fascination with hunting, gaming, and the military? Did she not get a husband of her class? Was she ambitious but too poor to play a role within the nobility? Was religion, prophecy, and missionary work a substitute for "success" in the world? What about her overbearing deference to men: to her father, the Pietist ministers, God? Indeed, some modern historians have suggested such reasons to explain the widespread fascination with Pietism by women from the (often impoverished) lower nobility, the gentry, and patrician families; later in the eighteenth century, Pietists were criticized as narrow-minded hypocrites, as in Karl Philipp Moritz's (1756–93) novel *Anton Reiser* (1785–90).[10] Already in 1736 an anonymously published comedy, *Die Pietisterey im*

---

8. Täterin des Wortes, *Life*, 78 n. 38.

9. "To raise my voice like a nightingale," *Life*, 98.

10. Karl Philipp Moritz, *Anton Reiser: A Psychological Novel*, trans. Ritchie Robertson (New York: Penguin, 1997). The novel is based on Moritz's childhood and youth when his pious father

Fischbeinrocke, had ridiculed all too credulous women and bourgeois ministers who were after the well-to-do women for their attention, money, and social status. The popular comedy, an adaptation of a French play, was penned by the learned Louise Adelgunde Victoria Gottsched (1713–52),[11] the eminent German Enlightenment author and tireless, unacknowledged collaborator of her husband Johann Christoph Gottsched (1700–66), Leipzig professor and reformer of the German language, theater, and literature. Such criticism of the later movement as well as doubts from a modern perspective should be carefully weighed against the spiritual testimony in the text of Peterson's *Life*.

AS A SPIRITUAL CONFESSION IN A RELIGION CLASS

With regard to teaching (comparative) religion, we would carefully embed Petersen's text first into church history and then examine some of its religious tenets. Martin Luther's overwhelming influence on German Protestantism needs to be remembered.[12] We should describe the impact of the religious wars and the rise of Protestant orthodoxy in seventeenth-century Germany in order to convey the growing impact of reform-minded clergy like Johann Arndt and Jacob Spener and their works.[13] The influential educational work of August Hermann Francke, founder of the pedagogical institution Franckesche Stiftungen,[14] and that of Count Zinzendorf and the Moravian Brethren need to be sketched. Francke and other Pietists' ideas were influential in the organization and education of the fast-rising state of Prussia.[15] Both groups, Francke's and Zinzendorf's followers, were instrumental in the

especially, a follower of the Quietist Madame Guyon, had tyrannized the son to suppress his willpower and senses.

11. Luise Gottsched, *Pietism in Petticoats and Other Comedies*, trans. and introduced by Thomas Kerth and John R. Russell (Columbia, S.C.: Camden House, 1994).

12. See the very professional Web site http://www.MartinLuther.de/ for historical material and texts. This is a bilingual Web site of the Lutheran Church, Germany, providing accurate historical and theological information about Luther, his texts, his contemporaries, the Reformation in Germany, and key texts by Luther and pictures. Most are also provided in English translation.

13. See their most popular works: Johann Arndt, *True Christianity*, trans. and ed. Peter Erb (New York: Paulist Press, 1979), and Jacob Spener, *Pia Desideria, or Heartfelt Desire for a God-Pleasing Reform of the True Evangelical Church, Together with Several Simple Proposals Looking toward This End* [1675–76], ed. and trans. Theodore Trappert (Philadelphia: Fortress Press, 1964).

14. Located in Halle and reconstructed after the end of the communist regime in East Germany, the large-scale social and educational institution can be viewed at http://www.francke-halle.de/ (Franckesche Stiftungen, historical and cultural survey of Pietist institutions, in German only).

15. See F. Ernest Stoeffler, *German Pietism during the Eighteenth Century*, Studies in the History of Religions 24 (Leiden: Brill, 1965). This is the best concise presentation of the religious movement, its leaders, and its cultural and social effects.

settlement of Pennsylvania, founded German Town in (what is now) Philadelphia as well as New Bethlehem, and carried their missionary and colonizing work from these centers along the east coast and after 1800 into the Midwest.

Petersen tells of her (chance?) meeting with a progressive minister identified as Jacob Spener, the "father of German Pietism."[16] She herself is the foremost female lay protagonist of that reform movement within the German Protestant church. Her conventicles in Frankfurt gave Protestant women for the first time a forum for speaking out on religious matters; her teaching of girls and young women helped her to develop devotional texts based on the Bible suitable for her audience. Petersen's first publication, *A Heart's Conversation with God* (1689),[17] is a devotional text with prayer samples, but her later ones take up theological issues and argue dogmatic questions like understanding Revelation, the return of all creatures, or the "secret of the first born." Like Luther, Petersen reads the Bible closely as the only true source; her amazing range of quotes needs to be discussed in relation to contemporary biblical piety and the practice of biblical reading, as does her millenarianism, in view of the coming centennial (1700), which was widely believed to signal the end of the world.

A number of aspects are noteworthy for seventeenth-century religious life: Petersen's networking with like-minded believers; her contacts in England and specifically with the visionary Jane Lead;[18] her correspondence with the Dutch learned woman Anna Maria van Schurman[19] who became a follower of Labadie; the practice of "thumbing"—still followed today in some American sectarian churches (85), a gesture at an incipient religious tolerance and what is later called ecumenism.[20]

A class discussion might center on Petersen's faith and the ways in which her path to God mirrors and reflects Christ's passion. Further religious tenets can be found in the second half of her autobiography (86–98): "essential

16. James K. Stein, *Philipp Jakob Spener: Pietist Patriarch* (Chicago: University of Chicago Press, 1986), an insightful biography of Spener based on much recent scholarship.

17. See the annotated bibliography of Petersen's works in *Life*, 45–51.

18. See below, note 22 and related text.

19. See Anna Maria van Schurman (1607–78), *Whether a Christian Woman Should be Educated and Other Writings from Her Intellectual Circle*, ed. and trans. Joyce L. Irwin, The Other Voice in Early Modern Europe (Chicago: University of Chicago Press, 1998). For additional excerpts from her writings, see Katharina Wilson and Frank J. Warnke, eds., *Women Writers of the Seventeenth Century* (Athens, Ga.: University of Georgia Press, 1989).

20. Petersen, *Life*, 88. In her theological works she expressed more strongly her conviction that all believers, including Jews and heathens, would be united in God's kingdom to come.

love," the "return of all things," the future "conversion of heathens and Jews," the "article of justification," the notion of "the divine God-man," and the "heavenly Jerusalem."[21] Petersen's farewell letter to her sisters (105–19) deserves notice for the path to a new life, a "new creature," described there. Her at times mystic language and often colorful pictures and dreams can be compared with passages from the visionary Jane Lead's spiritual diary, *A Fountain of Gardens, Watered by the Rivers of Divine Pleasure and Springing Up in All the Variety of Spiritual Plants* (1696–1701).[22]

AS AUTOBIOGRAPHY IN A LITERATURE CLASS

In my undergraduate class "Autobiography, Gender, and Identity (and the Discovery of the Self)," I set as objectives,

1.   To study autobiographies as "ego documents"—individual expressions of a life history as discovery of a self, an identity;

2.   To study the cultural and historical context of early modern life with reference to gender, class and society, and religion;

3.   To critically appreciate the text, its language and "message."

The structure/classroom activities comprise three units:

1.   Historical and cultural introduction to life and religion in early modern Germany (1500–1800, from the Reformation to the French Revolution/German classicism). Topics include Saint Augustine, the medieval church, the Reformation (Luther, Zwingli, Calvin), the Thirty Years' War, Pietism (Spener, Francke, Zinzendorf, the Moravian Brethren), Pietism in England and the United States, the social class system and the feudal system in early modern Germany, the Enlightenment and secularization,

21. See Klaus Garber, *Imperiled Heritage: Tradition, History, and Utopia in Early Modern German Literature*, ed. and introduced by Max Reinhart, Studies in European Cultural Transition 5 (Aldershot, UK: Ashgate, 2000), 1–18 (on visions of peace from Isaiah to Kant) and 19–40 (on questions of tolerance, liberty, and nature in the literature and deeds of humanism).

22. The three published volumes were put together from notes made since 1670 by Dr. Francis Lee who assisted the (later) blind Lead. The complete, authentic, digitized text is available at the Web site "Jane Lead. On-line Manuscripts," http://www.eebo.chadwyck.com/. "Early English Books Online" contains photographic reproductions of Jane Lead's *A Fountain of Gardens* and many other works. See also http://www.passtheword.org/Jane-Lead/, "Jane Lead. Seventeenth-Century Prophetess of God 1624–1704. On-line Manuscripts"; digitized, authentic versions of all of Jane Lead's writings, this site (established by Shofar Ministries) also contains unabridged, digitized texts by Jacob Böhme and other seventeenth-century esoteric and dissident religious writers, all in English translations.

the French Revolution as received in Germany, women in early
modern Germany, women in the church.

2.   Reading and discussion of four autobiographies: Saint Augustine,
Petersen, and Goethe, "Confessions of a Beautiful Soul" and *Truth
and Fiction*. The reading of the autobiographies gives occasion for
comparison. Petersen's different point of conversion is noted.
Hers is not a sin of the flesh, not a male desire for a woman, but
the disgust with the pleasures of an empty courtly life and God's
grace (78–79). Petersen retells the popular legend of Saint
Augustine's quest for understanding the Holy Trinity (97), but her
position is rather that of a female believer trying to overcome
gender barriers. Her *Life* can be instructively compared with the
"Confessions of a Beautiful Soul," the centerpiece of Goethe's
novel *Wilhelm Meister's Apprenticeship* (1796–97), a (fictionalized) first
person narrative of a Pietist woman who is so involved with her
own salvation that she misses her female calling in life:
motherhood. Goethe's interpretation of Susanne von Klettenberg
(a prominent Pietist and friend of his mother's in Frankfurt)
reshaped religious biography. Klettenberg refused to marry and
refused to join a Pietist settlement near Frankfurt in order to retain
her independence. Goethe reshapes this story into the tale of a
woman neglecting her female destiny.[23] In 1797 such an
interpretation was very much in keeping with the ideology of
sexual difference and woman's destiny as wife and mother.
Goethe's own expansive autobiography, the famous *Truth and
Fiction* (1812–14),[24] set a standard for the secular autobiography,
for male authorship and dominance in the literary marketplace.
Nevertheless, *The Life of Lady Johanna Eleonora Petersen* continues to
serve as an example for a carefully crafted spiritual autobiography
of a woman.

3.   Student projects—oral presentations in a miniconference—during
the last week of classes.

23. Johann Wolfgang von Goethe's "Confessions of a Beautiful Soul," in *Wilhelm Meister's Ap-*
prenticeship, trans. Eric A. Blackall in cooperation with Victor Lange (New York: Suhrkamp,
1989).

24. Goethe, *The Autobiography of Goethe: Truth and Fiction Relating to My Life*, trans. John Oxenford
(Honolulu: University Press of the Pacific, 2003).

APPENDIX
APPROACHES TO TEACHING PRESENTED
IN THE VOLUME

All of the authors of the essays in this volume suggest a number of different ways of organizing and approaching the teaching of the texts they discuss. For convenience, their suggestions are summarized below. The essays in each case may be consulted for more detailed information.

1. *Women's Devotional Writing in Late Medieval and Early Modern Italy: An Anthology*, ed. Lance Lazar

   a) The approach is understanding the texts as religious texts; there are other possibilities listed but not explored in the essay: historical surveys, comparative literature, Italian literature, art history, and music history, owing to the important role women played in convents and pious associations as patrons and also as producers of literature, art, and music.

   b) Religious experiences and practices that were at the core of women's identities in premodern Europe. These are approached in two ways: questions to be asked (5) and issues to be explored (4) that give specific guidance in teaching these texts as religious texts.

2. Sister Bartolomea Riccoboni, *Life and Death in a Venetian Convent*, ed. Daniel Bornstein

   a) Bornstein himself, in a course on women and religion in medieval Europe, uses the Riccoboni text to open students' minds to the strangeness of the world of medieval convent life and religious practice, and at the end of the course to measure intellectual growth by seeing how perceptions have changed as a result of a semester's exposure to other worlds that are strange to them (do they remain so strange?).

   b) Other colleagues (whose comments he solicited) have used it in history rather than religion courses:

      1) Alison Frazier has used it to explore the range of religious institutions and practices in Renaissance Italy: convent life vs. religious life in other contexts, the writing itself and its relation to other kinds of writing

during the same period (e.g., Petrarch and Boccaccio), and questioning the nature of canon formation.

2) Lu Ann Homza uses it as a context for the Reformation, focusing on the Great Schism and pairing it with *The Imitation of Christ* to explore late medieval spiritual ideals.

3) Sharon Strocchia uses the necrology in a freshman seminar on medicine in the age of plague: how illness and death were approached.

c) Other possible uses (suggested by Bornstein):

1) History of monasticism.

2) Operations of memory and the writing of history.

3) Compared with the urban chronicles of Dino Compagni or Giovanni Villani as examples of medieval historiography.

4) Compared with Arcangela Tarabotti's *Paternal Tyranny* or *Monastic Hell* to reveal sharply different experiences of female monasticism.

5) Read alongside Thomas of Siena's "Life of Maria of Venice" to point out the intersections of household and convent, religion and society.

3. Lucrezia Tornabuoni, *Sacred Narratives*, ed. Jane Tylus

a) Tornabuoni was an important member of Florence's most powerful family. Her very writing of sacred narratives raised the question of how one could best practice an authentic Christian life within the Renaissance city or of how the active and contemplative lives can be lived together. The point of contact with the biblical narratives is that all the characters about whom she writes (Judith, Susanna, Esther, Tobias, and John the Baptist) were in conflict with their communities. They were all marginal—as were women in Florence (see Alberti's *On the Family*).

b) The point of contact between Tornabuoni and the biblical narratives she writes about is the iconographical tradition in Florence, which has many representations of these biblical figures. Tylus discusses these representations in relation to Tornabuoni's narrative, which at once confronts the biblical narrative with contemporary Florence (both Tornabuoni's representations of the stories and the artistic works depicting the persons and events in which they were involved). These juxtapositions (discussed in detail by Tylus) raise many questions that are interesting to pursue with students and generate a richly contextualized historical discussion.

4. Antonia Tanini Pulci, *Saints' Lives and Biblical Stories for the Stage, 1483–92,* ed. Elissa Weaver

a) Weaver has taught these plays in courses on the *sacre rappresentazioni*, Italian Renaissance theater, Italian women's literature, and the writing of women in Europe and New Spain in the early modern period.

b) Italian theater

1) *Sacre rappresentazioni*, a Florentine form, ca. 1450–1500, based on the history of redemption (Creation, Fall, Resurrection, Ascension, Pentecost) and on morality plays and saints' lives.

2) As part of background, include late fifteenth-century English morality plays, e.g., *Abraham and Isaac,* as well as, of course, Pulci's five plays and Lorenzo de' Medici's *Play of Saints John and Paul* (available in a bilingual edition).

3) If reading aloud is part of the strategy of teaching, the *Saint Guglielma Play* would be a good one to use. Pulci's plays are discussed here in enough detail to aid the teacher.

c) Italian Renaissance theater

1) Includes plays by Feo Belcari, Antonia Pulci, and Castellano Castellani, as well as Lorenzo de' Medici if time permits.

2) Performances of Plautus and Terence in humanist schools and signorial courts.

3) Angelo Poliziano's *Orfeo,* which introduced ancient pastoral themes to modern theater.

4) Aspects of the stage and set.

5) *Commedia dell'arte* and religious theater in post-Tridentine Italy.

d) Early modern women writers: Europe and New Spain

1) Begin with two classics of the *querelle des femmes*: Christine de Pizan, *Book of the City of Ladies,* and Sor Juana Inés de la Cruz, *Response to Sor Filotea de la Cruz.*

2) Between these two classics (1405–1691) there are a number of possibilities from texts written in English, French, Italian, and Spanish in different literary genres:

a) Letters: Alessandra Macinghi Strozzi and/or Maria Celeste Galilei.

b) Plays: Pulci, *Saint Francis Play, Saint Domitilla Play, Death of Saul and Tears of David;* Elizabeth Cary.

c) Treatises: Laura Cereta, Cassandra Fedele, Isotta Nogarola.

d) Autobiography: Saint Teresa of Avila.

e) History of women's literature in Italy, thirteenth–seventeenth centuries (central focus on how women in early modern Italy assumed the authority to write and publish, that is, found an entry into male literary society and built a literary tradition of their own).

1) The question of Compiuta Donzella, possibly the first known Italian woman writer.

2) Selections from the letters of Saint Catherine of Siena and from the humanists on women's role in family and society and the education deemed appropriate for them.

3) Pulci's plays paired with Tornabuoni's *The Story of Judith*.

4) Vittoria Colonna's poetry.

5) From the seventeenth century there are many texts of lyric poetry, prose romance, pastoral theater, spiritual comedies and tragedies, and treatises.

6) Conclude with Arcangela Tarabotti's *Paternal Tyranny*.

5. Vittoria Colonna, *Sonnets for Michelangelo*, ed. Abigail Brundin

a) Begin with a study of the aims and ideas governing the practice of the Petrarchan genre in the sixteenth century:

1) Its role and status in the emerging canon of vernacular literature.

2) The role of *imitatio*. Cf. Bembo. Begin with the genre of *centones*.

3) The Protestant Reformation, especially the idea of *sola fide*, and its relation to Colonna's poetry and thus the link between Petrarchan poetry and reformed spirituality in Italy.

b) Proceed with a close reading of Colonna's sonnets.

1) Sonnets 1, 21, and 22 reveal her assertiveness (cf. *Orlando furioso*, canto 37, where she is represented by Ariosto as self-effacing).

2) Sensuality of her sonnets in relation to the sensuality of religious poetry during this period generally.

6. Rouben Cholakian, "Marguerite de Navarre, Religious Reformist"

a) There is first the question of whether she is a divided writer, composing both religious and secular works. There really is no division: she was a humanist who became deeply interested in religious reform (as did a number of male humanists).

b) Give attention to the ideas of religious reform that emerged during Marguerite's lifetime (see the opening pages of McKinley's essay on Marie Dentière). Read *Mirror of the Sinful Soul* in which she defends her reformist religious views.

c) The *Heptameron*, ostensibly a secular work, is at the same time a religious reformist text: the bible reading (Oisille), the "true" character of the stories, sexual abuse involving clerics or monks, the discussions after the tales in which religious views are often expressed (sometimes true also in the tales themselves, e.g., 33, 22, and the discussion following 56).

7. Marie Dentière, *Epistle to Marguerite de Navarre and Preface to a Sermon by John Calvin*, ed. Mary McKinley. McKinley's essay outlines and offers strategies and resources for teaching each of Dentière's texts. Her discussion focuses on the *Epistle*, which is divided into three sections:

a) In the first she develops rhetorical strategies for defending women (see 1–21 of the introduction and 51–56 of the *Epistle*).

1) Addressing Marguerite and speaking of "we women," thus identifying with Marguerite or Marguerite with her.

2) Asking Marguerite to intervene and suggesting that she has political power. There are a number of limitations here: examples of women silenced in the *Heptameron*, limitations imposed on women's speaking in public by the New Testament.

b) In the second she praises women, beginning with those in the New Testament.

c) In the third (and longest) she discusses the doctrinal issues raised by the Protestant Reformation: the authority of Christ alone, salvation by faith alone, the sole authority of the Bible, denial of the need for a human intermediary between the believer and God (and so rejection of the sacrament of Penance). The Catholic Church is attacked for the appropriation of power by priests, refusal of the church to allow priests to marry, dietary restrictions, and false doctrines leading to idolatry (pilgrimages, indulgences, veneration of saints, devotion to objects such as the crucifix). The greatest of the false doctrines is the Catholic Mass, to which Dentière gives much attention.

8. Jeanne de Jussie, *The Short Chronicle*, ed. Carrie F. Klaus. Interdisciplinary seminar for first-year students on early modern women's writing.

a) Before reading Jussie, students had read Arcangela Tarabotti's *Paternal Tyranny*. Although a century apart, the texts worked well together because both women came from relatively affluent families that would have had difficulty providing inheritances for all their children, and both were destined early in life for the convent. The different positions taken by the two writers on monachization make students more sensitive to the complexity of the decision to take or not take monastic vows.

b) Each class begins with questions to get students talking (see the end of Klaus's essay for questions on incidents within the text on which she focused).

1) First day: students were interested in the character of the vicaress and appalled by the trickery used by Reformers to gain access to the convent (it was necessary to remind students of Jussie's bias as a narrator).

2) Second day: discussion of a handful of Genevan women who spoke out for or against the Reformation, all of whom appear in Jussie's text. Among these was Marie Dentière (who exhorted the women to leave the convent and marry—as she had done). Dentière's text is used as a counterfoil to Jussie's; very good for class discussion, especially the issue of women's right to engage in theological debates. (Role-playing makes for an even livelier class.)

9. Katharina Schütz Zell, *Church Mother: The Writings of a Protestant Reformer in Sixteenth-Century Germany*, ed. Elsie McKee

a) In the first of two parts of her essay, McKee provides a good deal of social historical information about the roles of women in early modern

Europe: housewife, daughter, wife, mother, citizen, woman. This would be good background reading for both instructors and students.

b) The second part provides useful information about women within a Christian community: the religious worldview and its language and the biblical student and Protestant reformer. Here as well there is much useful background information.

c) At the end of the second part McKee offers some comments on her own teaching of the texts of Schütz Zell.

1) It is almost always in the context of a number of other texts related to women's spirituality.

2) Her theology is that of a layperson and gives us a good idea of how some basic Protestant doctrines got to many people in the pew.

a) Her exposition of the Lord's Prayer can be read in relation to Luther's in his catechism (for a fuller picture of what "priesthood of all believers" meant).

b) Her polemic against clerical celibacy and for biblical authority reveals what both laity and clergy believed was essential in the new church order, where the laity disagreed, and why.

c) Her correspondence with Caspar Schwenckfeld demonstrates how ordinary people felt freed to make up their minds about religious matters, even things over which the learned disagreed.

d) Her letter to the women of Kentzingen opens a feminine window on the issue of suffering for "the gospel."

e) She provides not only a female voice, but one from the "middling class," an urban phenomenon.

f) Her "nasty name calling" calls for some explanation (and suggestions are made in the final paragraph for dealing with it).

10. Francisca de los Apóstoles, *The Inquisition of Francisca: A Sixteenth-Century Visionary on Trial*, ed. Gillian T. W. Ahlgren. In the second half of her essay for this volume, Ahlgren discusses how she has made use of this text in the classroom.

a) Her interests are theology and women, and she teaches at a Catholic university; her students are undergraduates and candidates for graduate degrees in theology. Francisca has been taught in three different courses: a scholars seminar on the Spanish Inquisition (upper-level undergraduates), a general course on the Catholic Reformation (general undergraduate audience), and a more specialized undergraduate course (primarily nonmajors) exploring the theory and practice of determinations of sanctity and orthodoxy. In the latter course the book was used in its entirety.

b) Adoption of the text requires an introduction to the Spanish Inquisition. Several resources are suggested for this and for each of the courses in which Francisca is used.

c) Despite the goal of the Inquisition, which was to regularize religious expression, the trials reveal that Spaniards were often frank, opinionated, and highly creative in conceptualizing and practicing their faith. Students responded to the "you are there" perspective the trial gave them. Questions were not needed; students took interpretive initiative and engaged in conversations with one another. This invested them in sixteenth-century religiosity.

11. María de San José Salazar, *Book for the Hour of Recreation,* ed. Alison Weber

a) Weber teaches *Book for the Hour of Recreation* in an undergraduate literature course.

1) It follows Teresa's *Book of Her Life.* Some initial questions put to the class that students admit they had never even considered:

a) Were early modern convents like prisons or posh boarding schools for girls?

b) Why did women join convents?

c) What did they do all day? Did they suffer from boredom and loneliness or did they have the leisure to pursue artistic and intellectual interests?

2) Students are then asked to make a list of aspects of Teresa's *Life* that they find off-putting and, conversely, most comprehensible. Students are asked to keep their questions in mind as they read other examples of monastic women's writing. Other questions are then posed:

a) Did life in an early modern convent nourish or constrain opportunities for women's self-actualization? Or is this a false dichotomy?

b) What would self-actualization have meant for sixteenth-century women?

3) Two historical essays are then assigned: Weber's "Little Women: Counter-Reformation Misogyny" and Jodi Bilinkoff's "Woman with a Mission: Teresa of Avila and the Apostolic Model." These historically contextualize Teresa (e.g., her sense of mission resulting from the Protestant Reformation).

4) We then turn to Teresa's text to consider questions of genre and style. Students can now appreciate a "commanded autobiography."

a) We role-play a confessor and a nun, one trying to convince a skeptical partner of the authenticity of some unusual experience. This attunes students to the unusual nature of some of Teresa's discourse.

b) We review the paradigm of female inferiority and look again at Teresa's negative references to herself and women in general. Was she "working around" these views by playing upon the expectations of her male readers? The goal is to make students sensitive to the "stratagems of the weak."

5) We are now prepared to look at *Recreation*:

a) First the contrast between Teresa's relationship to her confessors and that of María (which is much warmer).

b) Why María cast her story as a dialogue. Is this a typical didactic dialogue?

c) How does María's style differ from Teresa's? E.g., syntax is more regular, less digressive, less repetitive. Both use the rhetorical topoi of humility, incompetence, bashfulness, and insignificance. But María's style is more self-conscious and witty, a gentle parody of Teresa's.

d) Now the concept of "anxiety of influence" is introduced (a concept earlier applied to psychological barriers faced by nineteenth-century women). Is this an appropriate term to describe sixteenth-century women? Why is it important to have a literary forebear? Such questions can lead students to think more deeply about how women constructed a sense of self in early modern culture.

e) Can María be considered a feminist? This unfailingly elicits a lively debate among students.

b) A course in a transnational context for teaching *Recreation* divided into four parts:

1) Nuns: students would be asked to compare *Recreations* with other kinds of texts:

a) Examples of convent theater. See Elissa Weaver's *Convent Theatre in Early Modern Italy*.

b) The writings of Jacqueline Pascal read against Arcangela Tarabotti's *Paternal Tyranny* (attachment to the monastic life and critique of forced monachization).

c) The letters of Teresa of Avila to her brother Lorenzo; those of Suor Maria Celeste Galilei to her father, Galileo Galilei; and the life of Marie de l'Incarnation who abandoned her young son to join the Ursulines (different kinds of relationships of nuns to their families).

2) Laywomen: the range of options provided by Catholicism for laywomen in various social classes:

a) Read Carolyn Valone's study of women who patronized the early Jesuits.

b) Gabrielle de Coignard's poetry expressing her loneliness and mystical longings in spiritual sonnets.

c) Allyson Poska's essay on peasant women in northern Spain indifferent to Inquisitorial efforts to reform their sexual mores.

3) "Failed saints": inquisitorial trials of Francisca de los Apóstoles and Cecilia Ferrazzi:

a) How did religious authorities distinguish between legitimate living saints and frauds?

b) What opportunities did these women have to defend their actions and beliefs before their interrogators?

c) What criteria can we, at the beginning of the twenty-first century, use to determine whether they were cynical pretenders or earnest reformers?

d) How close did Teresa of Avila and María de San José come to being "failed saints"?

4) "Women on the margins": women who rejected their status as daughters of the Catholic Church:

a) Marie Dentière's *Epistle to Marguerite de Navarre* is by a nun who left the convent, married a former priest, and became active in the Reformation.

b) Essays in *Women in the Inquisition* by Gretchen Starr-LeBeau, Renée Levine Melammed, and Mary Elizabeth Perry address the situation of Spain's Jewish and Moorish minorities (the fluidity of religious identities):

1) Were the *conversas* who lit candles on Friday night secret Jews or sincere Christians who retained some Jewish customs?

2) How did *moriscas*, baptized Moorish women, transmit secret knowledge of Islamic law and custom to their children?

12. Cecilia Ferrazzi, *Autobiography of an Aspiring Saint*, ed. Anne Jacobson Schutte

a) Ferrazzi's story is an ideal text with which to engage students: it is brief, easy to read, and compelling. It facilitates investigation among gender, spirituality, and individual self-fashioning in the early modern world.

b) Teaching the book:

1) Have students briefly summarize the events of her life and trial. The following questions will assure that students will learn of the office of the Inquisition and the process of sanctification:

a) Why did this trial take place?

b) Why does the trial include an autobiography?

2) Have a student read aloud from Ferrazzi's testimony all the possible reasons she could have imagined for being imprisoned (28). Reviewing the reasons she gives tells a lot about Venice at the time.

3) Discussion of the nature of this text as a historical source raises questions about the nature of trial documents as evidence in studying history: what kinds of evidence does courtroom testimony offer that we would not find in wills or chronicles? Raising such questions allows students to be critical of the text's structure and content.

4) Another line of questioning focuses on the goals of her autobiography:

a) What is the point of her recounting her life story, and why did she compose this text? How does she structure her narrative, and what is she trying to achieve by dictating it to a court scribe? What does sainthood (which Ferrazzi is trying to achieve) mean and what does sanctity entail? Relevant here are her visions (25, 39, 49, 54, 57), stigmata (44–45, 53, 66), and miracles and miraculous cures (44, 48).

b) Other questions elicit an understanding of the repressive character of the Counter-Reformation: When is it that a potential saint becomes a heretic? When did Ferrazzi overstep the boundaries of piety and become labeled a heretic?

5) It is provocative to ask female students why they think a woman might not want to marry, and more specifically, why remaining unmarried might interest a woman in Ferrazzi's time.

6) Questions about confessors ("like spiders at the center of all the gossip, news, and information . . .") can elicit discussion:

a) What do confessors do? How often did people see them and what did they tell them?

b) Ferrazzi heard the confessions of girls in her schools. Why was this a crime? Why would churchmen seek to limit the number of people who could legitimately hear confession? Such questions throw light on male power and issues of threatened male power.

c) How did Ferrazzi appear to feel about her confessors? This question points to the conflicting ways Ferrazzi relates to Catholic practice and generates further questions: Did the sacraments appear to give Christians more a sense of oppression or consolation? How are such questions further complicated with issues of gender, e.g., can we argue that confession or female saints were more important in the minds of women?

7) The body is also a useful line of questioning (cf. Carolyn Walker Bynum, *Holy Feast and Holy Fast*): What kinds of physical trials and tribulations did Ferrazzi endure? Did male and female saints appear to undertake the same types of challenges or did they pursue sanctity in different ways? Why might male saints have focused more on poverty and female saints on food and fasting?

8) A final question that always resonates with students: could we consider Ferrazzi's behavior an example of anorexia or bulimia?

9) Ferrazzi's trial lends itself to reenactment in the classroom. The class could be divided in half, some arguing for and others against Ferrazzi's claims for sainthood. Or two lawyers could be appointed, one representing Ferrazzi and other serving as prosecutor. A mock trial can cross-examine another student, chosen as Ferrazzi, and a decision can be made by another student appointed as inquisitor. (The instructor can take on any of these roles as well.)

13. Jacqueline Pascal, *A Rule for Children and Other Writings*, ed. John J. Conley, S.J.

a) This was taught to an honors seminar for sophomores at Fordham University, the topic of the seminar being modern philosophy and theology.

The focus of this seminar was on the challenge of skepticism and various religious responses from the Counter-Reformation.

1) We began with Saint Francis de Sales's *Introduction to the Devout Life*, which found particular resonance with educated women.

2) Montaigne's *Essays*, to examine his skepticism.

3) Descartes's arguments for the existence of God in *Discourse on Method and Related Writings*.

4) Blaise Pascal, *Pensées*.

5) Jacqueline Pascal, *A Rule for Children*.

b) Students were able to relate Jacqueline Pascal to earlier writers we discussed: the emphasis on the obscurity of God to the "hidden God" of her brother and the religious ambiguity of both Montaigne and Descartes. And they saw the distinctiveness of her appeal to the rights of conscience.

c) But students had serious difficulty in understanding the text. To facilitate that required knowledge of convent culture, the crisis of the dowry, and the theological doctrine of grace that informed the nuns of Port-Royal. Explanations of these matters (and other sources to consult) are provided in this essay, a great help to instructors who wish to teach this text. Here are the dilemmas discussed:

1) Convent culture: the daily order of the school followed the hours of the divine office (matins, lauds, sext, terce, none, vespers, compline); the pupils participated in the chapter of faults, small-group discussions in which individual pupils accused themselves of minor faults and asked pardon; pupils also were required to follow the monastic grand silence, which prohibited all speaking from the beginning of the night Office until after the conclusion of breakfast the next day.

2) Her "Report of Soeur Jacqueline de Sainte Euphémie to the Mother Prioress of Port-Royal des Champs" requires understanding the "crisis of the dowry," the refusal of her brother to come forth with her dowry after her father's death and its outcome. This crisis related to the larger role of the dowry in convents.

3) The doctrine of grace: the Catholic Church judged five theological propositions of Cornelius Jansenius concerning grace and freedom to be heretical. Understanding the distinction between *droit* and *fait*, devised by Antoine Arnauld to enable Jansenists to approve the church's teaching without abandoning Jansenius, is necessary to understand the dilemma in which Jacqueline Pascal found herself.

14. Johanna Eleonora Petersen, *The Life of Lady Johanna Eleonora Petersen, Written by Herself*, ed. Barbara Becker-Cantarino

a) Becker-Cantarino points out that teaching methodology has changed in recent years, facilitating new course designs as follows:

1) Historical context is now more important than artistic merit.

2) We now include multidisciplinary material: literature, history, music, art, philosophy, and religion, rather than staying within one discipline; also we cross national boundaries (German, Spanish, French, English, etc.).

3) These changes have produced a need for readable and authentic translations of texts from other languages into English.

4) The early modern period is important for understanding our cultural roots.

5) *The Life of Lady Johanna Eleonora Petersen* is an excellent text for teaching within these parameters. The text is short but sophisticated in structure and content. It can be taught at the undergraduate or graduate level in history, women's studies, literature, or religion.

b) Teaching *The Life of Lady Johanna Eleonora Petersen*:

1) Teaching the text as an "Ego" document in a history class:

a) Contextualization is required (as it would be for any kind of course): the Protestant Reformation and the Thirty Years' War, the class system and the role of women, the court and city life, the emerging Pietist movement, role of the family, authority of the clergy, functions of city government (see the book's introduction for discussion and sources).

b) The text is in two parts:

1) Petersen's own life: socialization, importance of religion, reputation (for a woman), reading and the role of the Bible.

2) Spiritual and visionary: why did the revocation of the Edict of Nantes make such an impression on her? What kind of utopia is the "New Jerusalem"?

c) The text can be paired with *Runagate Courage* by Hans Jacob Christoph von Grimmelshausen, whose protagonist, Courage, is a woman who dresses as a soldier and ends as a warning example to all men.

2) Teaching the text as an authentic, self-empowering text in a Women's Studies or Gender Studies class.

a) The cultural space allowed women. See Luther's sermons on marriage such as "On the Married Life."

b) Study her portrait and explore in the text her fight against lies (83–84), the boat in the storm scene (79–80), and her decision to turn to God away from a respectable and enjoyable life at court (75–76). All are related to self-empowerment. But in her case this arises out of an inner religious calling. She finds her identity in her role as "doer of the word." And she justifies her authorship in terms of being a vessel of God's word.

c) Students may raise critical questions (as scholars have) as to why she took this turn: Did she not get a husband of her class? Was she ambitious but too poor to play a role within the nobility? Were religion, prophecy, and missionary work a substitute for "success" in the world? What of her overbearing deference to men: her father, the Pietist ministers, God?

3) As spiritual confession in a religion class.

a) The background here is the overwhelming influence of Martin Luther on German Protestantism, the impact of religious wars, and the rise of Protestant orthodoxy in seventeenth-century Germany. These set the stage for the pietism of Johann Arndt, Jacob Spener, August Hermann Francke, and Count Zinzendorf (and the Moravians).

b) Petersen uses an amazing range of quotations from the Bible, the only true source for her. These need to be discussed in relation to contemporary biblical piety and the practice of biblical reading, as does her millenarianism.

c) Her networking, especially her contacts with England (Jane Lead) and her correspondence with Anna Maria van Schurman (who became a follower of Jean de Labadie), need to be discussed.

d) Discussion should focus on her faith and the ways in which her path to God mirrors and reflects Christ's passion. Other religious tenets are also in the second half of her *Life* (86–98): essential love, return of all things, future conversion of heathens and Jews, justification, the divine God-man, the heavenly Jerusalem.

4) As autobiography in a literature class. A class on "Autobiography, Gender, and Identity (and the Discovery of the Self)" has three units:

a) Historical and cultural introduction to life and religion in early modern Germany (1500–1800), from the Reformation to the French Revolution/German classicism.

b) Reading and discussion of four autobiographies: Saint Augustine, Petersen, and Goethe's "Confessions of a Beautiful Soul" in *Wilhelm Meister's Apprenticeship* and *Truth and Fiction*.

c) Student oral presentations during the final week of classes.

BIBLIOGRAPHY

PRIMARY SOURCES

Agrippa, Henricus Cornelius. *Declamation on the Nobility and Preeminence of the Female Sex*. Edited and translated by Albert Rabil, Jr. The Other Voice in Early Modern Europe. Chicago: University of Chicago Press, 1996.

Alberti, Leon Battista. *The Family in Renaissance Florence*. Introduction and translated by Renée Neu Watkins. Columbia, S.C.: University of South Carolina Press, 1969.

Alberto, Maria de San. *Viva al Siglo, muerta al mundo: Selected Works by María de San Alberto (1568–1640)*. Edited and translated by Stacey Schlau. New Orleans: University Press of the South, 1998.

D'Ancona, Alessandro, ed. *Sacre rappresentazioni dei secoli XIV, XV e XVI*. 3 vols. Firenze: Successori Le Monnier, 1872.

Andreini, Isabella. *Mirtilla*. Edited by Maria Luisa Doglio. Lucca: Pacini Fazzi, 1995.

Arenal, Electa, and Stacey Schlau, eds. *Untold Sisters: Hispanic Nuns in Their Own Works*. Translated by Amanda Powell. Albuquerque: University of New Mexico Press, 1989.

Arlotto, Piovano. *Motti e Facezie*. Edited by Gianfranco Folena. Milan and Naples, 1953.

Arndt, Johann. *True Christianity*. Edited and translated by Peter Erb. New York: Paulist Press, 1979.

Battista da Varano, Camilla. *Le opere spirituali: Nuova ed. del V centenario della nascita secondo i più antichi codici e stampa con aggiunta di alcuni inediti*. Edited by Giacomo Boccanera. Prefazione di Piero Bargellini. Iesi: Scuola Tip. Francescana, 1958.

———. *My Spiritual Autobiography*. Edited and translated by Joseph R Berrigan. Saskatoon: Peregrina Publishing Co., 1986.

Bigolina, Giulia. *Urania*. Edited by Valeria Finucci. Rome: Bulzoni, 2002. *Urania: A Romance*. Edited and translated by Valeria Finucci. The Other Voice in Early Modern Europe. Chicago: University of Chicago Press, 2005.

Birgitta of Sweden, [Bridget of Sweden]. *Birgitta of Sweden: Life and Selected Revelations*. Edited by M. T. Harris. New York: Paulist, 1990.

Briefwechsel der Brüder Ambrosius und Thomas Blaurer. 3 vols. Edited by Traugott Schiess. Freiburg, i.B.: Friedrich E. Fehsenfeld, 1908–12.

Buoninsegni, Francesco/Arcangela Tarabotti. *Satira Antisatira*. Edited by Elissa Weaver. Rome: Salerno Editrice, 1998.

Cary, Elizabeth. *The Tragedy of Mariam the Fair Queen of Jewry*. Edited by Barry Weller and Margaret Ferguson. Berkeley: University of California Press, 1994.

Castiglione, Baldassare. *The Book of the Courtier*. Translated by George Bull. New York: Penguin, 1967.

Catherine, of Bologna, [Caterina Vegri]. *Le sette armi spirituali*. Edited by Cecilia Foletti. Padua: Antenore, 1985.

————. *The Seven Spiritual Weapons*. Translated and with notes by Hugh Feiss and Daniela Re. Toronto: Peregrina Publishing Co., 1998.

Catherine of Genoa. *Libro de la vita mirabile et dottrina santa de la beata Caterinetta da Genoa, Nel quale si contiene una utile et catholica dimostratione et dechiaratine del purgatorio* (Stampata in Genoua, per Antonio Bellono, MDLI [1551]). Edited by Valeriano da Finalmarina, OFM Cap. Genoa, 1957.

————. Marabotto, Cattaneo. *Vita della serafica s. Caterina da Genova, colla mirabile sua dottrina contenuta nell'insigne Trattato del Purgatorio, e nel Dialogo tra il corpo, l'anima, l'umanità, lo spirito, ed il Signor Iddio, composti dalla medesima santa. In questa nuova impressione, o sia ristampa esattamente corretta, e colla giunta di nuove postille in margine migliorata, ed accresciuta di notizie del concetto, stima, e culto di detta santa fino alla di lei canonizzazione*. Genova: Nella stamperia del Franchelli, 1737.

————. *Life and Doctrine of St. Catherine of Genoa*. Edited by L. T. Hecker. New York, 1874.

————. *Purgation and Purgatory: The Spiritual Dialogue*. Translated by Serge Hughes. New York: Paulist, 1979.

Catherine of Siena. *The Dialogue*. Translated by Suzanne Noffke, OP. New York: Paulist, 1980.

————. *Le Lettere di S. Caterina da Siena*. 6 vols. Edited by Piero Misciatelli. Florence: Marzocco, 1947.

Cereta, Laura. *Letters of a Renaissance Feminist*. Edited and translated by Diana Robin. The Other Voice in Early Modern Europe. Chicago: University of Chicago Press, 1997.

Cherubino da Siena, frate (OFM). *Regole della vita spirituale e matrimoniale* [Florence, 1490]). *Regole della vita matrimoniale di frate Cherubino da Siena*. Edited by F. Zambrini and C. Negroni. Bologna: Commissione per i testi di lingua, 1969.

Colonna, Vittoria. *Rime*. Edited by Alan Bullock. Rome: Laterza, 1982, 223–462.

————. *Sonnets for Michelangelo*. Edited and translated by Abigail Brundin. The Other Voice in Early Modern Europe. Chicago: University of Chicago Press, 2005.

Dante Aligheri. *The Divine Comedy*. Translated by Allen Mandelbaum. New York: Bantam, 1994.

Dentière, Marie. *Epistle to Marguerite de Navarre and Preface to a Sermon by John Calvin*. Edited and translated by Mary B. McKinley. The Other Voice in Early Modern Europe. Chicago: University of Chicago Press, 2004.

Descartes, René. *Discourse on Method and Related Writings*. Edited by Desmond M. Clarke. London and New York: Penguin Classics, 2000.

Dominici, Giovanni, OP. *Regola del buon governo di cura familiare compilata dal beato Giovanni Dominici, Fiorentino, dell'Ordine de' frati predicatori*. Testo in lingua dato in luce e illustrato con note dal prof. Donato Salvi . . . Florence: A. Garinei, 1860.

————. *On the Education of Children, Parte quarta della regola del governo di cura familiare.* Translated by A. B. Cote. Dissertation, Catholic University, 1927.

The Early French Novella: An Anthology of Fifteenth and Sixteenth Century French Tales. Translated and with an introduction by Patricia F. Cholakian and Rouben C. Cholakian. Albany, N.Y.: State University Press, 1972.

Farel, Guillaume. *Le Pater Noster et le Credo en françoys.* Edited by F. Higman. Geneva: Droz, 1982.

Ferrazzi, Cecilia. *Autobiography of an Aspiring Saint.* Edited and translated by Anne Jacobson Schutte. Chicago: University of Chicago Press, 1996.

Francis de Sales, Saint. *Introduction to the Devout Life.* New York: Vintage Spiritual Classics, 2002.

Francisca de los Apóstoles. *The Inquisition of Francisca: A Sixteenth-Century Visionary on Trial.* Edited and translated by Gillian T. W. Ahlgren. The Other Voice in Early Modern Europe. Chicago: University of Chicago Press, 2005.

Galilei, Celeste. *Letters to Father: Suor Maria Celeste to Galileo, 1623–1633.* Translated by Dava Sobel. New York: Penguin, 2001.

Lehmijoli-Gardner, Maihu, ed. *Dominican Penitent Women.* Introduced and translated by Maiju Lehmijoli-Gardner, with contributions by Daniel Bornstein and E. Ann Matter. Preface by Gabriella Zarri. Mahwah, N.J.: Paulist Press, 2005.

The Geneva Bible: A Facsimile of the 1560 Edition. Madison: University of Wisconsin Press, 1969.

Von Goethe, Johann Wolfgang. "Confessions of a Beautiful Soul." In *Wilhelm Meister's Apprenticeship,* translated by Eric A. Blackall in cooperation with Victor Lange. New York: Suhrkamp, 1989.

————. *The Autobiography of Goethe: Truth and Fiction Relating to My Life.* Translated by John Oxenford. Honolulu: University Press of the Pacific, 2003.

Goldsmith, Elizabeth, and Colette Winn, eds. *Lettres des femmes, texts, inédits et oubliés du XVe au XVIIIe siècles.* Paris: Champion, 2004.

Gottsched, Luise. *Pietism in Petticoats and Other Comedies.* Translated and with an introduction by Thomas Kerth and John R. Russell. Columbia, S.C.: Camden House, 1994.

Von Grimmelshausen, Hans Jacob. *Runagate Courage.* Translated by Robert L. Hiller and John C. Osborne. Lincoln, Neb.: University of Nebraska Press, 1965.

————. *Courage: The Adventuress and the False Messiah.* Translated by Hans Speer. Princeton, N.J.: Princeton University Press, 1964.

————. *The Life of Courage.* Translated by Mike Mitchel. Sawtry, Cambs, UK: Dedalus, 2001.

Von Grumbach, Argula. *Argula von Grumbach: A Woman's Voice in the Reformation.* Edited by Peter Matheson. Edinburgh: T & T Clark, 1995.

Guillaume Briçonnet/Marguerite d'Angoulême: Correspondance. Edited by Christine Martineua, Michel Veissiére, and Henry Heller. 2 vols. Paris: L'Imprimerie Lahure, 1975–79.

Inez de la Cruz, Sor Juana. *The Answer/ La Respuesta Including a Selection of Poems.* Edited and translated by Electa Arenal and Amanda Powell. New York: Feminist Press of the City University of New York, 1994.

De Jussie, Jeanne. *Short Chronicle.* Edited and translated by Carrie Klaus, The Other Voice in Early Modern Europe. Chicago: University of Chicago Press, 2006.

Thomas à Kempis. *The Imitation of Christ*. Translated and with an introduction by Leo Sherley-Price. New York: Penguin Books, 1952.

Lazar, Lance, ed. *Women's Devotional Writing in Late Medieval and Early Modern Religion: An Anthology*. Translated by Lance Lazar. The Other Voice in Early Modern Europe. Chicago: University of Chicago Press, forthcoming.

Lead, Jane. *A Fountain of Gardens, Watered by the Rivers of Divine Pleasure and Springing Up in All the Variety of Spiritual Plants*. 1696–1701.

Marguerite de Navarre. *Chansons spirituelles*. Edited by Georges Dottin. Geneva: Droz, 1971.

———. *Les comédies bibliques*. Edited by Barbara Marczuk. Geneva: Droz, 2000.

———. *Dialogue en forme de vision nocturne*. Edited and translated by Renja Salminen. Helsinki: Suomalainen Tiedeakatemia, 1985.

———. *Heptaméron*. Introduction and notes by Gisèle Mathieu-Castellani, Paris: Livre de Poche, 1999.

———. *Heptaméron*. Edited by Renja Salminen. Geneva: Droz, 1999.

———. *Heptameron*. Translated by Paul Chilton. New York: Penguin, 1984.

———. *Oeuvres choisies: Marguerite de Navarre*. Vol 1. Edited by H. P. Clive. New York: Appleton-Century-Crofts, 1968.

———. *Pater Noster et Petit Œuvre dévot*. Edited by Sabine Lardon. Vol. 1 of *Œuvres complètes*, edited by Nicole Cazauran. Paris: H. Champion, 2001.

———. *Marguerites de la Marguerite des princesses* and *Suite des Marguerites de la Marguerite des princesses*. 1547.

De' Medici, Lorenzo. *Lorenzo de' Medici: Selected Writings*. Edited and translated by Corinna Salvadori. Dublin: Belfield Italian Library, 1992.

Michelangelo Buonnarroti. *The Poetry of Michelangelo*. Edited and translated by James M. Saslow. New Haven: Yale University Press, 1991.

Montaigne, Michele de. *The Complete Essays*. Translated by M. A. Screech. London and New York: Penguin Classics, 1993.

Moritz, Karl Philipp. *Anton Reiser: A Psychological Novel*. Translated by Ritchie Robertson. New York: Penguin, 1997.

Nuovo corpus di sacre rappresentazioni fiorentine del Quattrocento. Edited by Nerida Newbigin. Bologna: Commissione per i testi di lingua, 1983.

Pascal, Jacqueline. *A Rule for Children and Other Writings*. Edited and translated by John J. Conley, SJ. The Other Voice in Early Modern Europe. Chicago: University of Chicago Press, 2003.

Pascal, Blaise. *Pensées*. Edited by A. J. Krailsheimer. London and New York: Penguin Classics, 1995.

Petersen, Johanna Eleonora Petersen von Merlau. *The Life of Lady Johanna Eleonora Petersen as Told by Herself*. Edited and translated by Barbara Becker-Cantarino. The Other Voice in Early Modern Europe. Chicago: University of Chicago Press, 2005.

De Pizan, Christine. *The Book of the City of Ladies*. Translated by Earl Jeffrey Richards. New York: Persea Books, 1982.

———. *The Book of the City of Ladies*. Translated by Rosalind Brown-Grant. New York: Penguin Books, 1999.

Pulci, Antonia. *Florentine Drama for Convent and Festival: Seven Sacred Plays*. Edited by James Wyatt Cook and Barbara Collier Cook. Translated and annotated by James

Wyatt Cook. The Other Voice in Early Modern Europe. Chicago: University of Chicago Press, 1997.

Pulci, Antonia Tanini. *Saints' Lives and Biblical Stories for the Stage (1483–92)*. Edited by Elissa Weaver. Translated by James Wyatt Cook. The Other Voice in Early Modern Europe. Chicago: University of Chicago Press, 2008 (a revised edition of the earlier volume listed above).

Riccoboni, Sister Bartolomea. *Life and Death in a Venetian Convent: The Chronicle and Necrology of Corpus Domini, 1395–1436*. Edited and translated by Daniel Bornstein. The Other Voice in Early Modern Europe. Chicago: University of Chicago Press, 2000.

Salazar, María de San José. *Book for the Hour of Recreation*. Edited and translated by Alison Weber. The Other Voice in Early Modern Europe. Chicago: University of Chicago Press, 2002.

———. *Escritos espirituales*. Edited by Simeón de la Sagrada Familia. Rome: Postulación General O.C.D., 1979.

Van Schurman, Anna Maria. *Whether a Christian Woman Should Be Educated and Other Writings from Her Intellectual Circle*. Edited and translated by Joyce L. Irwin. The Other Voice in Early Modern Europe. Chicago: University of Chicago Press, 1998.

Schütz Zell, Katharina. *Church Mother: The Writings of a Sixteenth-Century Reformer*. Edited and translated by Elsie Anne McKee. The Other Voice in Early Modern Europe. Chicago: University of Chicago Press, 2006.

———. *Volume Two: The Writings, A Critical Edition*. Edited by Elsie Anne McKee. Leiden: Brill, 1999.

Spener, Jacob. *Pia Desideria, or Heartfelt Desire for a God-Pleasing Reform of the True Evangelical Church, Together with Several Simple Proposals Looking toward This End* [1675–76]. Edited and translated by Theodore Tappert. Philadelphia: Fortress Press, 1964.

Stampa, Gaspara. *Rime*. Introduction by Maria Bellonci. Annotated by Rodolfo Ceriello. Milan: Rizzoli, 1994.

Tarabotti, Arcangela. *Paternal Tyranny*. Edited and translated by Letizia Panizza. The Other Voice in Early Modern Europe. Chicago: University of Chicago Press, 2004.

Teresa of Ávila. *The Book of Her Life*. In *The Collected Letters of St. Teresa of Ávila. Volume One: 1546–1577*. Translated by Kieran Kavanaugh. Washington, D.C.: Institute of Carmelite Studies, 2001, 53–365.

———. *The Life of Saint Teresa of Ávila by Herself*. Translated and with an introduction by J. M. Cohen. New York: Penguin Books, 1957.

Tornabuoni, Lucrezia. *I poemetti sacri di Lucrezia Tornabuoni*. Edited by Fulvio Pezzarossa. Florence: Olschki, 1978.

———. *Lettere*. Edited by Patrizia Salvadori. Florence: Olschki, 1993.

———. *Sacred Poems*. Edited and translated by Jane Tylus. The Other Voice in Early Modern Europe. Chicago: University of Chicago Press, 2001.

Wieck, Roger, ed. *Time Sanctified: The Book of Hours in Medieval Art and Life*. New York: George Braziller/Walters Art Gallery, 1988 (appendix).

Weyda, Ursula. *Wyder das unchristlich schreyben und Lesterbuoch des Apts Simon Zuo Pegaw.* [Augsburg], 1524.

Wilson, Katharina, and Frank J. Warnke, eds. *Women Writers of the Seventeenth Century*. Athens, Ga.: University of Georgia Press, 1989.

SECONDARY SOURCES

Ahlgren, Gillian T. W. *Entering Teresa of Avila's Interior Castle: A Reader's Companion* Mahwah, N.J.: Paulist Press, 2005.

———. "Negotiating Sanctity: Holy Women in Sixteenth-Century Spain." *Church History* 64 (1995): 373–88.

———. *Teresa of Avila and the Politics of Sanctity*. Ithaca, N.Y.: Cornell University Press, 1996.

D'Alençon, Édouard. *Frère Jacqueline, recherches historiques sur Jacopa de Settesoli, l'amie de Saint-François*. Paris: Société et Librairie Saint-François d'Assise, 1927, and Rome: Postulation Générale des f.f. m.m. Capucins, 1927.

Aquino, María Pilar, Daisy L. Machado, and Jeanette Rodríguez, eds. *A Reader in Latina Feminist Theology*. Austin, Tex.: University of Texas Press, 2002.

Arenal, Electa, and Stacey Schlau. "Stratagems of the Strong, Stratagems of the Weak: Autobiographical Prose of the Seventeenth-Century Hispanic Convent." *Tulsa Studies in Women's Literature* 9 (1990): 25–42.

Arnauld, Mère Agnés. *Les constitutions du monastère de Port-Royal du S.-Sacrement*. Mons: G. Migeot, 1665.

Ashley, Kathleen, and Pamela Sheingorn, *Writing Faith*. Chicago: University of Chicago Press, 1999.

Audin, Jean-Marie-Vincent. *Histoire de la vie, des ouvrages et des doctrines de Calvin*. Paris: L. Maison, 1856.

Backus, Irena. "Les Clarisses de la rue Verdaine / The Poor Clares of the Rue Verdaine." In *Le guide des femmes disparues / Forgotten women of Geneva*, edited by Anne-Marie Käppeli. Geneva: Metropolis, 1993, 309–25.

Bainton, Roland H. *Women of the Reformation in Germany and Italy*. Minneapolis: Augsburg, 1971.

Bassanese, Fiora A. "Vittoria Colonna, Christ and Gender." *Rivista della civiltà italiana*, 40 (1996): 53–57.

Baumgartner, Frederic J. *France in the Sixteenth Century*. New York: St. Martin's Press, 1995.

Beal, Timothy K. *The Book of Hiding: Gender, Ethnicity, Annihilation, and Esther*. London: Routledge, 1997.

Becker-Cantarino, Barbara. "Dr. Faustus and Runagate Courage: Theorizing Gender in Early Modern Germany." In *The Graph of Sex and the German Text: Gendered Culture in Early Modern Germany 1500–1700*, edited by Lynne Tatlock and Christiane Bohnert. Amsterdam and Atlanta: Rodophi, 1994, 27–44.

Bell, Rudolph. *Holy Anorexia*. Chicago: University of Chicago Press, 1985.

Benedetto da Mantova, "Nota Critica." In *Il Beneficio di Cristo con le versioni del secolo XVI, documenti e testimonianze*, edited by Salvatore Caponetto. Florence: Sansoni, 1972, 469–98.

Bennett, Judith, et al., eds. *Sisters and Workers in the Middle Ages*. Chicago: University of Chicago Press, 1989.

Benrath, Carl. *Bernardino Ochino of Siena: A Contribution towards the History of the Reformation*. London: James Nisbet, 1876.

Bilinkoff, Jodi. *The Ávila of Saint Teresa: Religious Reform in a Sixteenth-Century City*. Ithaca, N.Y.: Cornell University Press, 1989.

————. *Related Lives: Confessors and Their Female Penitents, 1450–1750*. Ithaca, N.Y.: Cornell University Press, 2005.

————. "Woman with a Mission: Teresa of Ávila and the Apostolic Model." In *Modelli di santità e modelli di comportamento*, edited by Giulia Barone et al. Turin: Rosenberg & Sellier, 1994, 295–305.

Blaisdell, Charmarie J. "Angela Merici and the Ursulines." In *Religious Orders of the Catholic Reformation: In Honor of John C. Olin on His Seventy-Fifth Birthday*, edited by Richard L. DeMolen. New York: Fordham, 1994, 99–138.

Blanc, Pierre, ed. *Dynamique d'une expansion culturelle. Pétrarque en Europe XIVᵉ–XXᵉ siècle*. Actes du XXVIᵉ congrès international du CEFI, Turin et Chambéry, 11–15 décembre 1995. Bibliothèque Franco Simone 30. Paris: Honoré Champion, 2001.

Blunt, John Henry, ed. *The Myroure of Oure Ladye*. London, 1873.

Bornstein, Daniel, and Roberto Rusconi, eds. *Women and Religion in Medieval and Renaissance Italy*. Chicago: University of Chicago Press, 1996.

Bossy, John. *Christianity in the West, 1400–1700*. Oxford: Oxford University Press, 1988.

Bozza, Tommaso. *Nuovi studi sulla Riforma in Italia I. Il Beneficio di Cristo*. Rome: Storia e letteratura, 1976.

Brady, Thomas A., Heiko A. Oberman, and James D. Tracy, eds. *Handbook of European History, 1400–1600*. Leiden: Brill, 1995.

Brenner, Athalya, ed. *A Feminist Companion to Esther, Judith, and Susanna*. Sheffield: Sheffield Academic Press, 1995.

Brown, Raymond, SS, Joseph Fitsmeyer, SJ, and Roland Murphy, O.Carm., eds. *The New Jerome Biblical Commentary*. Englewood Cliffs, N.J.: Prentice Hall, 1968, 1990.

Brucker, Gene. *Renaissance Florence*. Berkeley: University of California Press, 1983.

Bryce, Judith. "Adjusting the Canon for Later Fifteenth-Century Florence: The Case of Antonia Pulci." In *The Renaissance Theatre: Texts, Performance, Design*, edited by Christopher Cairns. Aldershot, UK: Ashgate, 1999.

Bynum, Caroline Walker. *Holy Feast and Holy Fast: The Religious Significance of Food to Medieval Women*. Berkeley: University of California Press, 1987.

Cairns, Christoper. *The Renaissance Theatre: Texts, Performance, Design*. Aldershot, UK: Ashgate, 1999.

Cameron, Euan. *The European Reformation*. Oxford: Clarendon Press, 1991.

Campi, Emidio. *Michelangelo e Vittoria Colonna.Un dialogo artistico-teologico ispirato da Bernardino Ochino, e altri saggi di storia della Riforma*. Turin: Claudiniana, 1994.

Caponetto, Salvatore. *The Protestant Reformation in Sixteenth-Century Italy*. Translated by Anne C. Tedeschi and John Tedeschi. Vol. 43. Sixteenth-Century Essays and Studies. Kirksville, Mo.: Thomas Jefferson University Press, 1999.

Caritas Pirckheimer. Exhibition catalogue. Nuremberg: Katholische Stadtkirche Nuremberg, 1982.

Carroll, Jane, and Alison Stewart, eds. *Saints, Sinners and Sisters. Women and the Pictorial Arts in Northern European Art*. Burlington, Vt.: Ashgate, 2003.

Carroll, Michael P. *The Cult of the Virgin Mary: Psychological Origins*. Princeton, N.J.: Princeton University Press, 1986.

Cast, David. "Humanism and Art." In *Renaissance Humanism*, edited by Albert Rabil (q.v.), 3: 416.

Catholic Dictionary of Theology. 3 vols. New York: Nelson, 1962.

Cavallo, Sandra, and Syndan Warner, eds. *Widowhood in Medieval and Early Modern Europe*. New York: Longman, 1999.

Caviness, Madeline. *Visioning Women in the Middle Ages: Sight, Spectacle, and Scopic Economy*. Philadelphia: University of Pennsylvania Press, 2001.

Cholakian, Patricia F. *Rape and Writing in the* Heptameron *of Marguerite de Navarre*, Carbondale, Ill.: Southern Illinois University Press, 1991.

Cholakian, Patricia F., and Rouben C. Cholakian. *Marguerite de Navarre: Mother of the Renaissance*. New York: Columbia University Press, 2006.

Chorpenning, Joseph F., OSFS. *The Divine Romance: Teresa of Ávila's Narrative Theology*. Chicago: University of Chicago Press, 1992.

Chrisman, Miriam Usher. *Conflicting Visions of Reform: German Lay Propaganda Pamphlets, 1519–1530*. Atlantic Highlands, N.J.: Humanities Press, 1996.

Clive, H. P. *Marguerite de Navarre: An Annotated Bibliography*. London: Grant and Cutler, 1983.

Cognet, Louis. *Le Jansénisme*. 7th ed. Paris: Presses Universitaires de France, 1995.

Collins, A. Jeffries. *The Birgettine Breviary of Syon Abbey*. London: Henry Bradshaw Society, 1969.

Cottrell, Robert. *The Grammar of Silence*. Washington, D.C.: Catholic University Press, 1986.

Crawford, Patricia. *Women and Religion in England, 1500–1750*. London: Routledge, 1993.

Cross, F. L., and E. A. Livingston. *The Oxford Dictionary of the Christian Church*. 3d ed. New York: Oxford University Press, 1997.

Davis, Natalie Zemon. *The Gift in Sixteenth-Century France*. Oxford: Oxford University Press, 2000.

———. *Society and Culture in Early Modern France: Eight Essays*. Stanford: Stanford University Press, 1975.

———. *Women on the Margins: Three Seventeenth-Century Lives*. Cambridge, Mass.: Harvard University Press, 1995.

Dionisotti, Carlo. "Appunti sul Bembo e su Vittoria Colonna." In *Miscellanea Augusto Campana*, edited by Rino Avesani et al. Padua: Antenore, 1981, 1, 257–86.

Ditchfield, Simon. "Martyrs Are Good to Think With: Review Essay." *Catholic Historical Review* 87, no. 3 (2001): 470–73.

Doglio, Maria Luisa. "L'occhio interiore e la scrittura nelle 'Litere' di Vittoria Colonna." In *Omaggio a Gianfranco Folena*. 3 vols. Padua: Editoriale Programma, 1993, 2: 1001–13.

Domenichi, Ludovico, ed. *Rime diverse di molti eccellentiss. auttori nuovamente raccolte. Libro primo*. Venice: Gabriel Giolito di Ferrarii, 1545.

Les dominicaines d'Unterlinden. 2 vols. Exhibition catalogue. Colmar: Musée de'Unterlinden, 2000–2001.

Dubreton, J. Lucas. *Daily Life in Florence at the Time of the Medici*. New York: Macmillan, 1961.

Ellwood, Christopher. *The Body Broken: The Calvinist Doctrine of the Eucharist and the Symbolization of Power in Sixteenth-Century France*. New York: Oxford University Press, 1999.

Elton, G. R. *Reformation Europe 1517–1559*. 2d ed. Oxford: Blackwell, 1999.

Erdmann, Axel. *My Gracious Silence: Women in the Mirror of Sixteenth-century Printing in Western Europe.* Luzern: Gilhofer and Rauschberg, 1999, 206–23.

Esposito-Aliano, Anna. "St. Francesca and the Female Religious Communities of Fifteenth-Century Rome." In *Women and Faith: Catholic Religious Life in Italy from Late Antiquity to the Present,* edited by Lucetta Scaraffia and Gabriella Zarri. Cambridge, Mass.: Harvard University Press, 1999, 83–112.

Evans, Gillian R. *Bernard of Clairvaux.* Oxford: Oxford University Press, 2000.

Fanning, Steven. *Mystics of the Christian Tradition.* London: Routledge, 2001.

Fedi, Roberto. "'L'immagine vera': Vittoria Colonna, Michelangelo, e un'idea di canzoniere." *Modern Language Notes* 107 (1992): 46–73.

Fenlon, Dermot. *Heresy and Obedience in Tridentine Italy: Cardinal Pole and the Counter Reformation.* Cambridge: Cambridge University Press, 1972.

Ferguson, Gary. *Mirroring Belief: Marguerite de Navarre's Devotional Poetry.* Edinburgh: Edinburgh University Press, 1992.

Fraser, Antonia. *The Weaker Vessel: Woman's Lot in Seventeenth-Century England.* New York: Knopf, 1984.

Freccero, Carla. "Gender Ideologues, Women Writers, and the Problem of Patronage in Early Modern England and France: Issues and Frameworks." In *Reading the Renaissance,* edited by Jonathan Hart. New York: Garland, 1996, 65–74.

Garber, Klaus. *Imperiled Heritage: Tradition, History, and Utopia in Early Modern German Literature.* Edited and with an introduction by Max Reinhart. Studies in European Cultural Transition 5. Aldershot, UK: Ashgate, 2000.

Gerrish, Brian A. "Discerning the Body: Sign and Reality in Luther's Controversy with the Swiss." *Journal of Religion* 68/3 (1988): 377–95.

———. "Eucharist." In *Oxford Encyclopedia of the Reformation,* edited by Hans Hillerbrand. New York: Oxford University Press, 1996, 76.

Gilbert, Sandra M., and Susan Gubar. "Infection in the Sentence: The Woman Writer and the Anxiety of Authorship." In *Feminisms: An Anthology of Literary Theory and Criticism,* edited by Robyn R. Worhol and Diane Price Herndl. New Brunswick, N.J.: Rutgers University Press, 1997, 21–32.

Gilchrist, Roberta. *Gender and Material Culture: The Archaeology of Religious Women.* New York: Routledge, 1993.

Giles, Mary E., ed. *Women in the Inquisition: Spain and the New World.* Baltimore: Johns Hopkins University Press, 1999.

Gill, Katherine. "Open Monasteries for Women in Late Medieval and Early Modern Italy: Two Roman Examples." In *The Crannied Wall: Women, Religion, and the Arts in Early Modern Europe,* edited by Craig Monson. Ann Arbor: University of Michigan Press, 1992, 15–47.

———. "Women and the Production of Religious Literature in the Vernacular, 1300–1500." In *Creative Women in Medieval and Early Modern Italy: A Religious and Artistic Renaissance,* edited by E. Ann Matter and John Coakley. Philadelphia: University of Pennsylvania Press, 1994, 64–104.

Ginsburg, Carlo, and Adriano Prosperi. *Giochi di Pazienza: Un seminario sul "Beneficio di Cristo."* Turin: Einaudi, 1975.

Gothic and Renaissance Art in Nuremberg 1300–1550. Exhibition catalogue. New York: Metropolitan Museum of Art, and Nuremberg: Germanisches Nationalmuseum Nuremberg, 1986.

Graesslé, Isabelle. "Vie et légendes de Marie Dentière," *Bulletin du Centre Protestant d'Etudes*, 55, no. 1 (March 2003): 1–31.

Greene, Thomas M. *The Light in Troy: Imitation and Discovery in Renaissance Poetry*. New Haven: Yale University Press, 1982.

Greenblatt, Stephen. *Renaissance Self-Fashioning from More to Shakespeare*. Chicago: University of Chicago Press, 1983.

Greenfield, Kent Roberts. *Sumptuary Law in Nuremberg: A Study in Paternal Government*. Baltimore: Johns Hopkins Press, 1918.

Greengrass, Mark. *The French Reformation*. London: Blackwell, 1987.

Greer, Germaine. *Slip-Shod Sibyls: Recognition, Rejection and the Woman Poet*. 2d ed. London: Penguin, 1996.

Guernsey, Jane Howard. *The Lady Cornaro: Pride and Prodigy of Venice*. Clinton Corners, N.Y.: College Avenue Press, 1999.

Hamburger, Jeffrey. *Nuns as Artists: The Visual Culture of a Medieval Convent*. Berkeley: University of California Press, 1997.

Harline, Craig. *The Burdens of Sister Margaret: Private Lives in a Seventeenth-Century Convent*. New York: Doubleday, 1994.

Head, Thomas. "The Religion of the *Femmelettes*: Ideals and Experience among Women in Fifteenth- and Sixteenth-Century France." In *That Gentle Strength: Historical Perspectives on Women in Christianity*, edited by Lynda Coon, Katherine Haldane, and Elisabeth Sommer. Charlottesville: University Press of Virginia, 1991, 149–75.

Hempfer, Klaus W. "Per una definizione del Petrarchismo." In *Dynamique d'une expansion culturelle. Pétrarque en Europe XIVe–XXe siècle. Actes du XXVIe congrès international du CEFI, Turin et Chambéry, 11–15 décembre 1995*. Edited by Pierre Blanc. Bibliothèque Franco Simone 30. Paris: Honoré Champion, 2001, 23–52.

Herpoel, Sonia. "Autobiografías por mandato: una escritura feminina en la España del Siglo de Oro." Unpublished dissertation. Université d'Anvers, 1987.

Higman, Francis. *La Diffusion de la Réforme en France 1520–1565*. Publications de la Faculté de Théologie de l'Université de Genève, No. 17. Geneva: Editions Labor et Fides, 1992.

Hillerbrand, Hans, ed., *The Oxford Encyclopedia of the Reformation*. 4 vols. New York: Oxford University Press, 1995.

Holmes, George. *Renaissance*. New York: St. Martin's, 1996.

Howard, Peter Francis. *Beyond the Written Word: Preaching and Theology in the Florence of Archbishop Antoninus: 1427–59*. Florence: Olschki, 1995.

Hutchison, Jane Campbell. *Albrecht Dürer: A Biography*. Princeton, N.J.: Princeton University Press, 1992.

Idigoras, José Ignacio Tellechea. *El Arzobispo Carranza y su tiempo*. 2 vols. Madrid: Guadarrama, 1968.

Jones, Ann Rosalind. *The Currency of Eros: Women's Love Lyric in Europe, 1540–1620*. Bloomington, Ind.: Indiana University Press, 1990.

Jones, Pamela. "Female Saints in Early Modern Italian Chapbooks, ca. 1570–1670: Saint Catherine of Alexandria and Saint Catherine of Siena." In *From Rome to Eternity: Catholicism and the Arts in Italy, ca. 1550–1650*, edited by Thomas Worcester, SJ, and Pamela Jones. Leiden: Brill, 2002, 89–120.

Jourda, Pierre. *Marguerite d'Angoulême, duchesse d'Alençon, reine de Navarre (1492–1549): Etude biographique et littéraire*. 2 vols. Paris: Champion, 1930.

———. *Répertoire analytique et chronologique de la correspondance de Marguerite de Navarre, duchesse d'Alençon, reine de Navarre (1492–1549)*. Geneva: Slatkine, 1973.

———. "Tableau chronologique des publications de Marguerite de Navarre." *Revue du seizième siècle* 12 (1925): 209–31.

Jung-Inglessis, Eva-Maria. "Il *Pianto della Marchesa di Pescara sopra la Passione di Christo*. Introduzione," *Archivio italiano per la storia della pietà* 10 (1997): 115–47.

Kamen, Henry. *Inquisition and Society in Spain in the Sixteenth and Seventeenth Centuries*. Bloomington, Ind.: Indiana University Press, 1985.

Kelly, Joan. "Did Women Have a Renaissance?" and "Early Feminist Theory and the *querelle des femmes*, 1400–1789." In *Women, History and Theory: The Essays*. Foreword by Catherine Stimpson. Chicago: University of Chicago Press, 1984, 19–49, 65–109.

Kemp, William, and Diane Desrosiers-Bonin. "Marie d'Ennetières et la petite grammaire hébraique de sa fille d'après la dédicace de l'*Epistre* à Marguerite de Navarre (1539)." *Bibliothèque d'Humanisme et Renaissance* 60, no. 1 (1998): 117–34.

Kendrick, Robert L. "Looking at Martyrdom in Seventeenth-Century Italian Music." In *From Rome to Eternity: Catholicism and the Arts in Italy, ca. 1550–1650*, edited by Thomas Worcester, SJ, and Pamela Jones. Leiden: Brill, 2002, 121–41.

Kennedy, William J. *Authorizing Petrarch*. Ithaca, N.Y.: Cornell University Press, 1994.

Kent, Dale. *Cosimo de' Medici and the Florentine Renaissance*. New Haven: Yale University Press, 2000.

Kent, F. William. *Lorenzo de' Medici and the Art of Magnificence*. Baltimore: Johns Hopkins University Press, 2004.

———. "Sainted Mother, Magnificent Son: Lucrezia Tornabuoni and Lorenzo de' Medici." *Italian History and Culture* 3 (1997): 3–34.

Kieckhefer, Richard. *Unquiet Souls: Fourteenth-Century Saints and Their Religious Milieu*. Chicago: University of Chicago Press, 1984.

Kienzle, Beverly Mayne, and Pamela Walker, eds. *Women Preachers and Prophets through Two Millennia of Christianity*. Berkeley: University of California Press, 1998.

King, Margaret L. *The Renaissance in Europe*. New York: McGraw-Hill, 2005.

———. *Women of the Renaissance*. Chicago: University of Chicago Press, 1991.

Kirk, Pamela. *Sor Juana Inés de la Cruz: Religion, Art, and Feminism*. New York: Continuum, 1998.

Klapisch-Zuber, Christiane. *Women, Family, and Ritual in Renaissance Italy*. Chicago: University of Chicago Press, 1985.

Knecht, Robert J. *Renaissance Warrior and Patron: The Reign of Francis I*. Cambridge: Cambridge University Press, 1994.

———. *The Rise and Fall of Renaissance France: 1483–1610*. 2d ed. London: Blackwell, 2001.

Krone und Schleier: Kunst aus mittelalterlichen Frauenklöstern. Exhibition catalogue. Bonn: Ruhrlandmuseum, Essen and Kunst- und Ausstellungshalle der Bundesrepublik Deutschland, 2005.

Lazard, Madeleine. "Deux soeurs ennemies, Marie Dentière et Jeanne de Jussie: Nonnes et réformées à Genève." In *Les réformes: Enracinements socio-culturels*, edited by B. Chevalier and C. Sauzat. Paris: La Maisnie, 1985, 233–49.

Lehmijoki-Gardner, Maiju. *Worldly Saints: Social Interaction of Dominican Penitent Women in Italy, 1200–1500*. Helsinki: Suomen Historiallinen Seura, 1999.

Leonard, Amy. *Nails in the Wall: Catholic Nuns in Reformation Germany*. Chicago: University of Chicago Press, 2005.

Lerner, Gerda. *The Creation of Feminist Consciousness from the Middle Ages to Eighteen-Seventy*. New York: Oxford University Press, 1993.

———. *The Creation of Patriarchy*. New York: Oxford University Press, 1986.

Levin, Carole. "Illuminating the Margins of the Early Modern Period: Using Women's Voices in the History Class." In *Teaching Tudor and Stuart Women Writers*, edited by Susanne Woods and Margaret P. Hannay. New York: Modern Language Association, 2000, 261–76.

Levine, Amy-Jill. "'Hemmed in on Every Side': Jews and Women in the Book of Susanna." In *Feminist Companion to Esther, Judith, and Susanna*, edited by Athalya Brenner. Sheffield: Sheffield Academic Press, 1995.

———. "Sacrifice and Salvation: Otherness and Domestication in the Book of Judith." In *Feminist Companion to Esther, Judith, and Susanna*, edited by Athalya Brenner. Sheffield: Sheffield Academic Press, 1995.

Lewis, Gertrud Jaron. *By Women for Women about Women: The Sister-Books of Fourteenth-Century Germany*. Toronto: University of Toronto Press, 1996.

Lightbown, Ronald. *Sandro Botticelli, Life and Work*. New York: Abbeville Press, 1989.

Lowe, Kate. *Nuns' Chronicles and Convent Culture in Renaissance and Counter-Reformation Italy*. Cambridge: Cambridge University Press, 2003.

Ludmer, Josefina. "Las tretas del débil." In *La sartén por el mango: Encuentro de escritoras latinoamericanas*, edited by Patricia Elena González and Eliana Ortega. Rio Piedras: Huracán, 1984, 47–54.

Luti, J. Mary. *Teresa of Avila's Way*. Collegeville, Minn.: Liturgical Press, 1991.

Lyons, John, and Mary B. McKinley, eds. *Critical Tales: New Studies of the 'Heptameron' and Early Modern Culture*. Philadelphia: University of Pennsylvania Press, 1993.

Mack, Phyllis. *Visionary Women: Ecstatic Prophecy in Seventeenth-Century England*. Berkeley: University of California Press, 1992.

Maguire, Yvonne. *Women of the Medici*. London: Routledge, 1927.

Marshall, Sherrin. *Women in Reformation and Counter-Reformation Europe: Public and Private Worlds*. Bloomington, Ind.: Indiana University Press, 1989.

Martinelli, Maurizio. *Al tempo di Lorenzo*. Florence: FMG, 1992.

Martines, Lauro. *Power and Imagination: City-States in Renaissance Italy*. London: Pimlico, 2002.

Martz, Linda. *Poverty and Welfare in Habsburg Spain*. New York: Oxford University Press, 1972.

Matter, E. Ann, and John Coakley, eds. *Creative Women in Medieval and Early Modern Italy: A Religious and Artistic Renaissance*. Philadelphia: University of Pennsylvania Press, 1994.

Matthews Grieco, Sara F. "Models of Female Sanctity in Renaissance and Counter-Reformation Italy." In *Women and Faith: Catholic Religious Life in Italy from Late Antiquity to the Present*, edited by Lucetta Scaraffia and Gabriella Zarri. Cambridge, Mass.: Harvard University Press, 1999, 159–75.

Mauss, Marcel. *Sacrifice: Its Nature and Function*. Chicago: University of Chicago Press, 1968.

MacCullough, Diarmaid. *The Reformation: A History*. Harmondsworth, England: Penguin, 2004.

McGinn, Bernard. *The Presence of God: A History of Western Christian Mysticism.* New York: Crossroad, 1991–.

McKee, Elsie Anne. *Katharina Schütz Zell. Volume 1: The Life and Thought of a Sixteenth-Century Reformer.* Leiden: Brill, 1999.

McLaughlin, Martin L. *Literary Imitation in the Italian Renaissance: The Theory and Practice of Literary Imitation in Italy from Dante to Bembo.* Oxford: Oxford University Press, 1996.

McNamara, Jo Ann. *Sisters in Arms: Catholic Nuns through Two Millennia.* Cambridge, Mass.: Harvard University Press, 1996.

Merback, Mitchell. *The Thief, the Cross and the Wheel.* Chicago: University of Chicago Press, 1998.

Monson, Craig, ed. *The Crannied Wall: Women, Religion, and the Arts in Early Modern Europe.* Ann Arbor: University of Michigan Press, 1992.

Monter, E. William. *Calvin's Geneva.* New York: Wiley and Sons, 1967.

Moore, W. G. *La réforme allemande et la littérature française.* Strasbourg: La Faculté des lettres à l'Université, 1930.

Moriarity, Michael. "Grace and Religious Freedom in Pascal." In *The Cambridge Companion to Pascal,* edited by Nicholas Hammond. Cambridge: Cambridge University Press, 2003, 144–61.

Moscherosch, Hans Michhael. *Insomnis cura parentum: Christliches Vermächtnuß oder schuldige Vorsorg eines Trewen Vatters.* 1643.

Mullett, Michael A. *The Catholic Reformation.* London: Routledge, 1999.

Nalle, Sara T. *God in La Mancha: Religious Reform and the People of Cuenca, 1500–1650.* Baltimore: Johns Hopkins University Press, 1992.

Newbigin, Nerida. "Agata, Apollonia, and Other Martyred Virgins: Did Florentines Really See These Plays Performed?" In *European Medieval Drama 1997.* Papers from the Second International Conference on "Aspects of European Medieval Drama," Camerino, 4–6 July 1997, edited by Sydney Higgins. Camerino: Centro Audiovisivi e Stampa Università di Camerino, 1998, 175–97.

Newman, Barbara. *From Virile Woman to WomanChrist.* Philadelphia: University of Pennsylvania Press, 1995.

Noffke, Suzanne. "Caterina da Siena." In *Italian Women Writers. A Bio-Bibliographical Sourcebook,* edited by Rinaldina Russell. Westport, Conn.: Greenwood Press, 1994, 58–66.

Oberman, Heiko, and Charles Trinkaus, eds. *The Pursuit of Holiness in Late Medieval and Renaissance Religion.* Leiden: Brill, 1974.

O'Malley, John W. *Praise and Blame in Renaissance Rome: Rhetoric, Doctrine and Reform in the Sacred Orators of the Papal Court, c. 1450–1521.* Durham, N.C.: Duke University Press, 1979.

———. *Trent and All That.* Cambridge: Harvard University Press, 2000.

Panizza, Letizia, ed. *Women in Italian Renaissance Culture and Society.* Oxford: European Humanities Research Centre, 2000.

Panizza, Letizia, and Sharon Wood, eds. *A History of Women's Writing in Italy.* Cambridge: Cambridge University Press, 2000.

Parsons, Susan Frank, ed. *The Cambridge Companion to Feminist Theology.* Cambridge: Cambridge University Press, 2002.

Perry, Mary Elizabeth. *Gender and Disorder in Early Modern Seville.* Princeton, N.J.: Princeton University Press, 1990.

————. *The Handless Maiden: Moriscos and the Politics of Religion in Early Modern Spain.* Princeton, N.J.: Princeton University Press, 2005.

Plebani, Eleonora. *I Tornabuoni: una famiglia fiorentina alla fine del medioevo.* Milan: Franco Angeli, 2002.

Poska, Allyson. "When Bigamy Is the Charge." In *Women in the Inquisition: Spain and the New World,* edited by Mary E. Giles. Baltimore: Johns Hopkins University Press, 1999, 189–205.

Quondam, Amedeo. *Il naso di Laura. Lingua e poesia lirica nella tradizione del Classicismo.* Ferrara: Panini, 1991.

————. *Petrarchismo mediato: per una critica della forma "antologia": livelli d'uso del sistema linguistico del petrarchismo.* Rome: Bulzoni, 1974.

Rabil, Albert Jr., ed. *Renaissance Humanism: Foundations, Forms, and Legacy.* 3 vols. Philadelphia: University of Pennsylvania Press, 1988, corrected paperback edition 1991.

Radke, Gary M. "Masaccio's City: Urbanism, Architecture, and Sculpture in Early Fifteenth-Century Florence." In *The Cambridge Companion to Masaccio,* edited by Diane Cole Ahl. Cambridge: Cambridge University Press, 2002, 40–63.

Rapley, Elizabeth. *The Dévotes: Women and Church in Seventeenth-Century France.* Kingston, Ontario: McGill-Queen's University Press, 1989.

Raymond of Capua. *The Life of Catherine of Siena.* Translated by C. Kearns. Wilmington, Del.: Michael Glazier, 1980.

Rentiis, Dina de. "Sul ruolo di Petrarca nella storia dell'*Imitatio auctorum.*" In *Dynamique d'une expansion culturelle. Pétrarque en Europe XIVe–XXe siècle.* Actes du XXVIe congrès international du CEFI, Turin et Chambéry, 11–15 décembre 1995. Edited by Pierre Blanc. Bibliothèque Franco Simone 30. Paris: Honoré Champion, 2001, 63–74.

Roelker, Nancy Lyman. "The Appeal of Calvinism to French Noblewomen in the Sixteenth Century." *Journal of Interdisciplinary History* 2 (1971–72): 391–418.

Roper, Lyndal. *The Holy Household: Women and Morals in Reformation Augsburg.* New York: Oxford University Press, 1989.

Roper, Lyndal, ed. *Religion and Culture in Germany (1400–1800).* Leiden: Brill, 2001.

Rubin, Miri. *Corpus Christi: The Eucharist in Late Medieval Culture.* Cambridge: Cambridge University Press, 1991.

Rubin, Patricia Lee, and Alison Wright. *Renaissance Florence: The Art of the 1470's.* New Haven: Yale University Press, 1999.

Rusconi, Roberto. "Women's Sermons at the End of the Middle Ages: Texts from the Blessed and Images of the Saints." In *Women Preachers and Prophets through Two Millennia of Christianity,* edited by Beverly Mayne Kienzle and Pamela Walker. Berkeley: University of California Press, 1998, 173–95.

Russell, Rinaldina, ed. *Italian Women Writers: A Bio-Bibliographical Sourcebook.* Westport, Conn.: Greenwood Press, 1994.

Safley, Thomas Max. "Family." In *The Oxford Encyclopedia of the Reformation,* edited by Hans Hillerbrand. 4 vols. New York: Oxford University Press, 1995, 2:93–98.

Scaraffia, Lucetta, and Gabriella Zarri. *Women and Faith: Catholic Religious Life in Italy from Late Antiquity to the Present.* Cambridge, Mass.: Harvard University Press, 1999.

Scarry, Elaine. *The Body in Pain.* New York: Oxford University Press, 1985.

Schein, Sylvia. "Bridget of Sweden, Margery Kempe, and Women's Jerusalem Pilgrimages in the Middle Ages." *Mediterranean Historical Review* 14, no. 1 (June 1999): 44–58.

Schutte, Anne Jacobson. *Aspiring Saints: Pretense of Holiness, Inquisition, and Gender in the Republic of Venice, 1618–1750.* Baltimore: Johns Hopkins University Press, 2001.

———. "Inquisition and Female Autobiography: The Case of Cecilia Ferrazzi." In *The Crannied Wall: Women, Religion, and the Arts in Early Modern Europe*, edited by Craig Monson. Ann Arbor: University of Michigan Press, 1992.

———. "The *Lettere Volgari* and the Crisis of Evangelism in Italy." *Renaissance Quarterly* 28 (1975): 639–88.

———. "Little Women, Great Heroines: Simulated and Genuine Female Holiness in Early Modern Italy." In *Women and Faith: Catholic Religious Life in Italy from Late Antiquity to the Present*, edited by Lucetta Scaraffia and Gabriella Zarri. Cambridge, Mass.: Harvard University Press, 1999, 144–58.

———. "Per Speculum in Enigmate: Failed Saints, Artists, and Self-Construction of the Female Body." In *Creative Women in Medieval and Early Modern Italy: A Religious and Artistic Renaissance*, edited by E. Ann Matter and John Coakley. Philadelphia: University of Pennsylvania Press, 1994, 185–200.

Scott, Joan W. *Gender and the Politics of History.* New York: Columbia University Press, 1988.

Scott, Karen. "Candied Oranges, Vinegar, and Dawn: The Imagery of Conversion in the Letters of Caterina of Siena." *Annali d'italianistica* 13 (1995): 91–108.

Scribner, Robert. "Heterodoxy, Literacy, and Print." In *Religion and Culture in Germany (1400–1800)*, edited by Lyndal Roper. Leiden: Brill, 2001, 235–58.

Scribner, Bob, Roy Porter, and Mikulas Teich, eds. *The Reformation in National Context.* Cambridge: Cambridge University Press, 1994.

Shank, Michael H. "A Female University Student in Late Medieval Kraków." In *Sisters and Workers in the Middle Ages*, edited by Judith Bennett, et al. Chicago: University of Chicago Press, 1989.

Sheingorn, Pamela. *The Book of Sainte Foy.* Philadelphia: University of Pennsylvania Press, 1995.

Smith, Jeffrey Chipps. *Nuremberg a Renaissance City, 1500–1618.* Exhibition catalogue. Austin: University of Texas Art Museum, 1983.

Smith, Sidonie. *A Poetics of Women's Autobiography: Marginality and the Fictions of Self-Representation.* Bloomington, Ind.: Indiana University Press, 1987.

Solum, Stefanie. "Women, Art, and Evidence: The Case of Lucrezia Tornabouni de' Medici." Paper given at the Annual Conference of the College Art Association, 2005.

Soskice, Janet Martin, and Diane Lipton. *Feminism and Theology.* New York: Oxford University Press, 2003.

Sparr, Laurie. "Swiss Reformation Monument Gets New Additions—One a Woman." *Ecumenical News International*, October 31, 2002.

Sperling, Jutta Gisela. *Convents and the Body Politic in Late Renaissance Venice.* Chicago: University of Chicago Press, 1999.

Spiller, Michael R. G. *The Development of the Sonnet: An Introduction.* London: Routledge, 1992.

Stayer, James M. "The Radical Reformation." In *Handbook of European History*, edited by Thomas A. Brady, Heiko A. Oberman, and James D. Tracy. Leiden: Brill, 1995, 2:349–82.

Stein, James K. *Philipp Jakob Spener: Pietist Patriarch*. Chicago: University of Chicago Press, 1986.

Steinberg, Leo. *The Sexuality of Christ in Renaissance Art and in Modern Oblivion*. 2d ed. Chicago: University of Chicago Press, 1996.

Stocker, Margarita. *Judith: Sexual Warrior, Women and Power in Western Culture*. New Haven: Yale University Press, 1998.

Stoeffler, F. Ernest. *German Pietism during the Eighteenth Century*. Studies in the History of Religions 24. Leiden: Brill, 1965.

Telle, Emile. *L'Oeuvre de Marguerite d'Angoulême, reine de Navarre et la Querelle des Femmes*. Geneva: Slatkin Reprint, 1969.

Tentler, Thomas. *Sin and Confession on the Eve of the Reformation*. Princeton, N.J.: Princeton University Press, 1977.

Thysell, Carol. *The Pleasure of Discernment: Marguerite de Navarre as Theologian*. Oxford: University Press, 2000.

Tinagli, Paola. *Women in Italian Renaissance Art*. Manchester: Manchester University Press, 1997.

Tomas, Natalie. *The Medici Women: Gender and Power in Renaissance Florence*. Hampshire: Ashgate, 2003.

Tracy, James D. *Europe's Reformations, 1450–1650*. Totowa: Rowman & Littlefield, 1999.

Trexler, Richard. *Public Life in Renaissance Florence*. Ithaca: Cornell University Press, 1991.

Tylus, Jane. "Charitable Women: Hans Baron's Civic Renaissance Revisited." *Rinascimento* 43 (2004): 287–307.

Valone, Carolyn. "Piety and Patronage: Women and the Early Jesuits." In *Creative Women in Medieval and Early Modern Italy: A Religious and Artistic Renaissance*, edited by E. Ann Matter and John Coakley. Philadelphia: University of Pennsylvania Press, 1994, 157–84.

Vasta, Marilena Modica. "Mystical Writing." In *Women and Faith: Catholic Religious Life in Italy from Late Antiquity to the Present*, edited by Lucetta Scaraffia and Gabriella Zarri. Cambridge, Mass.: Harvard University Press, 1999, 205–18.

Vecce, Carlo. "Petrarca, Vittoria, Michelangelo: Note di commento a testi e varianti di Vittoria Colonna e di Michelangelo." *Studi e problemi di critica testuale* 44 (1992): 101–25.

Vittoria Colonna. Dichterin und Muse Michelangelos. Catalogue to the exhibition at the Kunsthistorisches Museum, Vienna. Curated by Silvia Ferino-Pagden, February 25–May 25, 1997. Vienna: Skira, 1997.

Voaden, Rosalynn. *God's Words, Women's Voices: The Discernment of Spirits in the Writing of Late-medieval Women Visionaries*. Rochester, N.Y.: York Medieval Press, 1999.

Weaver, Elissa B. *Convent Theatre in Early Modern Italy: Spiritual Fun and Learning for Women*. Cambridge: Cambridge University Press, 2002.

Weber, Alison. "Little Women: Counter-Reformation Misogyny." In *Teresa of Avila and the Rhetoric of Femininity*, 17–41. Princeton: Princeton University Press, 1990.

———. "On the Margins of Ecstasy: María de San José as (Auto)biographer." *Journal of the Institute of Romance Studies* 4 (1996): 251–68.

————. *Teresa of Avila and the Rhetoric of Femininity*. Princeton, N.J.: Princeton University Press, 1990.

Wieck, Roger S. *Time Sanctified: the Book of Hours in Medieval Art and Life*. New York: George Braziller, 1998.

Wiesner, Merry E. "Beyond Women and the Family: Towards a Gender Analysis of the Reformation." *Sixteenth-Century Journal* 18 (1987): 311–21.

————. "Family, Household, and Community." In *Handbook of European History*, edited by Thomas A. Brady, Heiko A. Oberman, and James D. Tracy. Leiden: Brill, 1995, 1:51–78.

————. *Women and Gender in Early Modern Europe*. Cambridge: Cambridge University Press, 1993.

Winn, Collette. "La Loi du non-parler dans l'*Heptameron* de Marguerite de Navarre." *Romance Quarterly* 33 (1988): 157–88.

Winston-Allen, Anne. *Convent Chronicles: Women Writing about Women and Reform in the Late Middle Ages*. University Park, Penn.: Pennsylvania State University Press, 2004.

Wood, Jeryldene M. *Women, Art, and Spirituality*. Cambridge: Cambridge University Press, 1996.

Woodford, Charlotte. *Nuns as Historians in Early Modern Germany*. Oxford: Clarendon Press, 2002.

Woods, Susanne, and Margaret P. Hannay, eds. *Teaching Tudor and Stuart Women Writers*. New York: Modern Language Association, 2000.

Worcester, Thomas, SJ, and Pamela Jones, eds. *From Rome to Eternity: Catholicism and the Arts in Italy, ca. 1550–1650*. Leiden: Brill, 2002.

www.eebo.chadwyck.com/. (Early English Books Online-for works of Jane Lead)

www.francke-halle.de/. (Franckesche Stiftungen zu Halle; German pietism—Web site in German)

www.MartinLuther.de/. (Luther Memorials Foundation of Saxony-Anhalt—Web site in German and English)

www.passtheword.org/Jane-Lead/ (Jane Lead: Online Manuscripts)

Zarri, Gabriella. "From Prophecy to Discipline, 1450–1650." In *Women and Faith: Catholic Religious Life in Italy from Late Antiquity to the Present*, edited by Lucetta Scaraffia and Gabriella Zarri. Cambridge, Mass.: Harvard University Press, 1999, 83–112.

————. "Living Saints: A Typology of Female Sanctity in the Early Sixteenth Century." In *Women and Religion in Medieval and Renaissance Italy*, edited by Daniel Bornstein and Roberto Rusconi. Chicago: University of Chicago Press, 1996, 219–303.

————. "Religious and Devotional Writing, 1400–1600." In *A History of Women's Writing in Italy*, edited by Letizia Panizza and Sharon Wood. Cambridge: Cambridge University Press, 2000, 79–93.

————. "Ursula and Catherine: The Marriage of Virgins in the Sixteenth Century." In *Creative Women in Medieval and Early Modern Italy: A Religious and Artistic Renaissance*, edited by E. Ann Matter and John Coakley. Philadelphia: University of Pennsylvania Press, 1994, 237–78.

Zeit und Ewigkeit: 128 Tage in St. Marienstern. Exhibition catalog. Marienstern, 1998.

CONTRIBUTORS

Gillian T. W. Ahlgren is professor of theology at Xavier University. She is the author of four books, most recently of *Entering Teresa of Avila's "Interior Castle": A Reader's Companion* (2005), and the editor and translator of Francisca de los Apóstoles's *The Inquisition of Francisca: A Sixteenth-Century Visionary on Trial*, published in 2005 in the Other Voice in Early Modern Europe series by the University of Chicago Press.

Barbara Becker-Cantarino is research professor in German at the Ohio State University. She is the author, editor, or translator of more than twenty books, most recently the editor of *The Eighteenth Century: Enlightenment and Sensibility* (Camden House History of German Literature, volume 5, 2005) and the editor and translator of Johanna Eleonora Petersen's *The Life of Johanna Eleonora Petersen, Written by Herself,* published in 2005 in the Other Voice in Early Modern Europe series by the University of Chicago Press.

Daniel Bornstein is professor of history at Texas A&M University. He is the editor or coeditor of three books, most recently of *Women and Religion in Medieval and Renaissance Italy* (1996), the author of *The Bianchi of 1399: Popular Devotion in Late Medieval Italy* (1993), and the editor and translator of Bartolomea Riccoboni's *Life and Death in a Venetian Convent: The Chronicle and Necrology of Corpus Domini,* published in 2000 in the Other Voice in Early Modern Europe series by the University of Chicago Press.

Abigail Brundin is university lecturer in Italian at the University of Cambridge. She is the author of *Vittoria Colonna and the Spiritual Poetics of the Italian Reformation* (forthcoming) and the editor and translator of Vittoria Colonna's

Sonnets for Michelangelo, published in 2005 in the Other Voice in Early Modern Europe series by the University of Chicago Press.

Rouben Cholakian is the Burgess Professor of Romance Languages, emeritus, at Hamilton College, Clinton, New York. He is the author or coauthor of eight books, most recently of *Marguerite de Navarre: Mother of the Renaissance* (2006). He is coediting an anthology of the works of Marguerite de Navarre for the Other Voice in Early Modern Europe series.

John J. Conley, SJ, is professor of philosophy at Fordham University. He is the author of *The Suspicion of Virtue: Women Philosophers in Neoclassical France* (2002) and *Creed and Culture: Jesuit Studies on John Paul II* (2004) and coeditor of *Prophecy and Diplomacy: The Moral Teaching of John Paul II* (1999). He is editor and translator of Jacqueline Pascal's *A Rule for Children and Other Writings* and Madame de Maintenon's *Dialogues and Addresses*, published in 2003 and 2004, respectively, in the Other Voice in Early Modern Europe series by the University of Chicago Press.

Elizabeth Horodowich is assistant professor of history at New Mexico State University. She has published articles in the journals *Past and Present, Sixteenth-Century Journal*, and *Renaissance Studies*, and is currently preparing her first book, *Loose Tongues: Language and Statecraft in Early Modern Venice*, as well as her second book, *A Brief History of Venice*.

Margaret L. King is professor of history at Brooklyn College and the Graduate Center, City University of New York. She is the author of eight books, most recently of *Humanism, Venice, and Women: Essays on the Italian Renaissance* (2005) and *The Renaissance in Europe* (2004). She is the coeditor and cotranslator of Isotta Nogarola's *Complete Writings: Letterbook, Dialogue on Adam and Eve, Orations*, published in 2004 by the University of Chicago Press in the Other Voice in Early Modern Europe series, which she coedits with Albert Rabil. With Rabil, King is the coeditor and cotranslator of *Her Immaculate Hand: Selected Works by and about the Women Humanists of Quattrocento Italy* (1992).

Carrie F. Klaus is associate professor of modern languages (French) at DePauw University. She is the editor and translator of Jeanne de Jussie's *The Short Chronicle: A Poor Clare's Account of the Reformation of Geneva*, published in 2006 in the Other Voice in Early Modern Europe series by the University of Chicago Press.

Lance Lazar is assistant professor of history at Assumption College. He is an associate editor of *Human Sacrifice in Jewish and Christian Tradition* (2006) and the author of *Working in the Vineyard of the Lord: Jesuit Confraternities in Early Modern Italy* (2005). He is preparing an anthology, *Women's Devotion in Medieval and Early Modern Italy*, for the Other Voice in Early Modern Europe series.

Elsie McKee is professor of Reformation studies and the history of worship at the Princeton Theological Seminary. She is the author of five books, most recently of *Katharina Schütz Zell. Volume One: The Life and Thought of a Sixteenth Century Reformer*, the coeditor of *Probing the Reformed Tradition* (1989), the editor and translator of *John Calvin: Writings on Pastoral Piety* (2001), and the author and editor of the critical edition of the collected works of Katharina Schütz Zell. She is also the editor and translator of Katharina Schütz Zell's *Church Mother: The Writings of a Protestant Reformer in Sixteenth-Century Germany*, published in 2006 in the Other Voice in Early Modern Europe series by the University of Chicago Press.

Mary B. McKinley is the Douglas Huntly Gordon Professor of French at the University of Virginia. She is the author of two books, most recently of *Les terrains vagues des "Essais": Itinéraires et intertextes* (1995), and the coeditor of three books, most recently of *Critical Tales: New Studies of Marguerite de Navarre's Heptameron and Early Modern Culture* (1993). She is the editor and translator of Marie Dentière's *Epistle to Marguerite de Navarre and Preface to a Sermon by John Calvin*, published in 2004 in the Other Voice in Early Modern Europe series by the University of Chicago Press.

Albert Rabil Jr. is Distinguished Teaching Professor of Humanities emeritus of the State University of New York, College at Old Westbury. He is the author of three books, most recently of *Laura Cereta: Quattrocento Humanist* (1981), the editor of *Renaissance Humanism: Foundations, Forms, and Legacy* (1988), and the coeditor and cotranslator of four books, most recently of *Erasmus's Annotations on Romans* (1994). He is also the editor and translator of Henricus Cornelius Agrippa's *On the Nobility and Preeminence of the Female Sex*, published in 1996 by the University of Chicago Press as the inaugural volume in the Other Voice in Early Modern Europe series, which he coedits with Margaret L. King.

Jane Tylus is professor of Italian studies and vice provost of academic affairs at New York University. She is the author of *Writing and Vulnerability in the Late Renaissance* (1993), and translator of *Sacred Narratives of Lucrezia Tornabuoni*

(2002) for the Other Voice in Early Modern Europe series. She has also edited the early modern volume for the Longman Anthology of World Literature (2004). She is completing a book on the writings of Catherine of Siena for the University of Chicago Press and is translating the poetry of Gaspara Stampa, also for Chicago's Other Voice series.

Elissa Weaver is professor of Italian at the University of Chicago. She is the author of *Convent Theatre in Early Modern Italy: Spiritual Fun and Learning for Woman* (2002); editor of the collections *The Decameron First Day* (2004) and *Arcangela Tarabotti, A Literary Nun in Baroque Venice* (2006), and of critical editions of Francesco Buoninsegni and Arcangela Tarabotti's *Satira ed Antisatira* (1998) and Beatrice del Sera's *Amor di virtù;* and coeditor of *A Well-Fashioned Image: Clothing and Costume in European Art, 1500-1850* (2002). She is editor of a revised edition of the plays of Antonia Pulci for the Other Voice in Early Modern Europe, forthcoming.

Alison Weber is professor of Spanish at the University of Virginia. She is the author of *Teresa de Avila and the Rhetoric of Femininity* (1990), the editor of *Feminist Topics* (1989), and the editor of María de San José's *Book for the Hour of Recreation*, published in 2002 in the Other Voice in Early Modern Europe series by the University of Chicago Press.

INDEX